Autism – From Research
to Individualized Practice

of related interest

Asperger's Syndrome
A Guide for Parents and Professionals
Tony Attwood
ISBN 1 85302 577 1

Autism – The Search for Coherence
Edited by John Richer and Sheila Coates
ISBN 1 85302 888 6

Understanding and Working with the Spectrum of Autism
An Insider's View
Wendy Lawson
ISBN 1 85302 971 8

Pretending to be Normal
Living with Asperger's Syndrome
Liane Holliday Willey
ISBN 1 85302 749 9

Caring for a Child with Autism
A Practical Guide for Parents
Martine Ives and Nell Munro
ISBN 1 85302 996 3

Autism – From Research to Individualized Practice

*Edited by Robin L. Gabriels, Psy.D.
and Dina E. Hill, Ph.D.*

Foreword by Dr Gary B. Mesibov

Jessica Kingsley Publishers
London and New York

First published in the United Kingdom in 2002
by Jessica Kingsley Publishers Ltd
116 Pentonville Road
London N1 9JB, England
and
29 West 35th Street, 10th fl.
New York, NY 10001-2299, USA
www.jkp.com

Copyright © Jessica Kingsley Publishers 2002
Second impression 2003

Library of Congress Cataloging-in-Publication Data

Autism: from research to individualized practiced/edited by Robin L. Gabriels and Dina E. Hill
    p. cm.
Includes bibliographical references and index.
ISBN 1-84310-701-5 (alk. paper)
    1. Autism in children. 2. Autism in children–Research. 3. Autism–Research. I. Gabriels, Robin L., 1962- II. Hill, Dina E., 1965-

RJ506.A9 A9222 2002
618.92'8982–dc21   2002021876

British Library Cataloguing in Publication Data
A CIP catalogue record for this book is available from the British Library

ISBN 1 84310 701 5

Printed and Bound in Great Britain by
Athenaeum Press, Gateshead, Tyne and Wear

Contents

Part III Family And Community Interventions

Acknowledgments

This book came about from the encouragement, support, and editorial suggestions of many people to whom we are indebted. Specifically, we would like to acknowledge Cathy Malchiodi, Teneke Warren, Lisa Boyum, Becky Pierce, Elizabeth Penland, Amanda Bryant, and Jessica Kingsley and her staff. A special thank you to the authors for their commitment to the vision of this project and willingness to share their expertise. We also want to acknowledge the families who provided us with both insight and fuel to put together a book to help make the process of parent and professional intervention collaboration more productive. Finally, we would like to thank our husbands, Mark and Bob, along with our families for their steadfast support.

This book is dedicated to our husbands
Mark Gabriels and Robert Thoma

Foreword

I am pleased to introduce this important volume focusing on the interchange between research and clinical practice in the field of autism. The critical nature of this interchange has been emphasized for many years by leading clinicians and investigators in our field. Unfortunately, it is easier to describe the many ways in which research can inform clinical practice and that clinical practice can stimulate research, than to actively pursue a dynamic collaboration or describe precisely how it might occur.

I hope that the situation will begin to change with the publication of this book. From the outset the major goal is to close the 'research to practice gap' and the editors have collected a marvelous range of examples that accomplish just that. Starting with the areas of diagnosis and assessment, where clinical work and research have overlapped most substantially and interacted most effectively, the chapters describe the collaborative possibilities that are being implemented and the rich possibilities that might still be developed. Other sections include child-centered interventions and family-community interventions where research/clinical practice interactions have not been as evident, but where excellent opportunities are abundant. The chapters in these sections are very stimulating in pointing out how and where these collaborative possibilities could be expanded.

I have no doubt that you will find this book to be as thought provoking, stimulating, and most important, motivating as I have. Through the examples and recommendations, it reminds all of us of the many rich possibilities for improving our clinical and research programs in the field if we more seriously and intensively pursue the many collaborative opportunities that are available. I thank the editors and authors for highlighting so many important opportunities and for showing us the way to make better use of them in the years ahead.

Gary B. Mesibov, Ph.D.
University of North Carolina at Chapel Hill, February 2002

CHAPTER 1

Introduction to Autism

From Research to Individualized Practice

Robin L. Gabriels and Dina E. Hill

...it would be a mistake to portray the picture as a one-way traffic from research to clinical practice. The reality is [a] more complex interplay, with each feeding into the other and each serving to correct the other's mistakes. (Rutter 1999, p.169)

Michael Rutter (1999) offered this positive insight in his review of the history of the two-way interchange between research and clinical work in the field of autism. However, historically, the communication interchange between researchers and practitioners has been difficult and often unsuccessful. The National Advisory Mental Health Council Workgroup on Child and Adolescent Mental Health Intervention Development and Deployment (2001) released a report reviewing the problems involved in disseminating research information to effect changes in clinical practice. The report acknowledged that the 'scientific model used to drive the development, refinement, and testing of...treatments does not mesh well with the exigencies of clinical community-based care' (p.74), and that this has created delays of between 10 and 20 years in the understanding of the practical implications of research. Schopler (2001) described another level of communication gap and disruptions. He noted that parents could play a role in the research to practice communication gap by their urgency to find effective treatments for their child. Parents may become involved in 'a new, experimental technique on the basis of personal testimony or anecdotal accounts of remarkable improvement' (Schopler 2001, p.9). At times, this has led to 'skepticism from professional consultants if scientific verification for this technique does not exist' (p.9). Clearly, efficient communication interchange regarding autism has been hindered on a number of levels.

It is the intent of this book to assist in the process of closing the 'research to practice gap' in the field of autism by providing a synthesis of information from research, theory, and clinical practice outcomes. This book provides examples of how this process is translated into best clinical practice through a discussion of strategies, techniques, and clinical case examples, including vivid client artwork. The chapters in this book target critical aspects of assessment, diagnosis, and treatment, as well as offering ideas on the integration of research findings and clinical application to aid the professional in addressing the individual child and family's needs. Finally, it is the goal of this book to provide a resource guide for professionals in order to work competently and creatively with children who have autism and their families from initial diagnosis through treatment.

Overview of autism

Since the mid 1980s, the general public awareness of autism has increased as indicated by the number of television and radio press releases, published literature, and funded research projects. Given the increased rate of population occurrence, 'every healthcare or educational agency serving young children can expect to see children with autism' (Filipek *et al.* 1999, p.440). Despite the media coverage and available literature on autism, families and professionals continue to struggle to understand causes and 'cures' for autism. Autism can be quite puzzling because children vary in extremes in the degree of symptom and associated symptom presentation.

Figure 1.1, titled 'Des Moines traffic light tries to hold back the flood', can be viewed as a metaphor for the overwhelming nature of autism and its impact on individuals, their families, and practitioners. Barbara Moran, an adult woman diagnosed with autism, created this artwork. Ms. Moran was misdiagnosed within the mental health system for 40 years of her life. She describes her lifelong interest in personifying objects as a means of connecting with the world (B. Moran, personal communication, April 3 2001).

Figure 1.1 Traffic light holds back the flood

The current conceptualization of autism is that this disorder is neuro-developmental in nature with a strong genetic component. Prevalence rates have shifted over time. Autism is now thought to be relatively common, occurring in about four in a thousand individuals (Bertrand *et al.* 2001). Current estimates represent a dramatic change from early prevalence rates, which were approximately '1 in every 2000 people' in the 1960s (Filipek *et al.*

1999). The core features of autism, including impairments in social interactions, delayed, absent, or impaired language skills, and stereotyped behaviors, have stood the test of time. Initial accounts of individuals with autism identified these same features (Kanner 1943), with the diagnostic criteria undergoing changes to increase specificity and clarify subtype distinctions. As noted by Bristol *et al.* (1996, p.123), 'the clinical diagnosis of autism remains one of the most reliable diagnoses in psychiatric or developmental research.' This suggests that the core deficits are relatively universally observed, although to varying degrees of impairment, and that they are readily identified by clinicians. Treatment approaches have drawn from behavior-learning theory and developmental theory, and integrated research findings into clinical practice. Many of the interventions practiced today incorporate behavior-learning theory, to some degree, within a developmental framework. Strategies advocated by the TEACCH (Treatment and Education of Autistic and Related Communication Handicapped Children) program (Schopler, Mesibov and Hearsey 1995) capitalize on the visual strengths of individuals with autism, strengths well defined by research. The success of treatment approaches has varied, as has the prognosis of individuals with autism. Evidence suggests that early intervention, specifically during the preschool years, leads to better prognosis, although as previously mentioned, factors such as intellectual functioning and language skills play a role in both treatment success and long-term outcome (Filipek *et al.* 1999).

Asperger syndrome is defined as a separate syndrome from autism, a distinction under considerable debate. The controversy arises from the uncertainty of how Asperger syndrome differs from higher-functioning autism (i.e. autism without mental retardation: Manjiviona and Prior 1999). Asperger syndrome was named after Hans Asperger, who in 1944, one year after Kanner, identified a similar set of behaviors in older children and adolescents (Wing 1997). The *DSM-IV* (American Psychiatric Assocation (APA) 1994) currently distinguishes Asperger syndrome from autism by the criteria of normal language development and no significant delays in cognitive development, including self-help skills. Similarities to autism include impairments in social interaction and stereotyped movements, restrictive interests, and repetitive behavior patterns. In addition, although these children do not have developmental language delays, communication and language problems may be evident in the use of pedantic speech and unusual words, along with a tendency to interpret language literally (Eisenmajer *et al.* 1996).

Historical influences of research and practice

Rutter (1999) presented a historical overview of the interplay between research and clinical work for the Emanuel Miller Memorial Lecture in 1998. His review covered four time periods: the 1950s and 1960s, the 1970s through the mid-1980s, the late 1980s and early 1990s, and the late 1990s. Below is a brief synopsis of his review article.

Kanner first introduced the syndrome of autism in 1943. Immediately following his now seminal paper, researchers began to differentiate autism from other diagnostic categories, particularly childhood psychosis. As early as the 1950s, key behavioral characteristics, including failure to develop social relationships, impaired language abilities, and stereotyped behaviors, were identified as differentiating children with autism from children with other psychiatric disorders. Research in the 1950s and 1960s focused primarily on further describing the nature of autism, including behavioral characteristics, cognitive functioning, and prognosis. Treatment initially focused on psychoanalytic intervention, with some early studies of the effectiveness of operant learning techniques. Investigation into the etiology of autism focused on its relationship to other medical disorders, such as congenital rubella.

During the second time period, the 1970s through mid-1980s, Rutter noted that the diagnostic criteria of autism were further defined and that standardized diagnostic tools became available. Researchers and clinicians alike became increasingly aware of the heterogeneity of symptom presentation in children with autism. In conjunction with this, the diagnosis of autism was differentiated from other diagnoses including Rett's syndrome, fragile X syndrome, and Asperger syndrome. During this time period, researchers delved further into possible medical etiologies of autism. Genetic studies were also underway, with the first clear evidence of the strong genetic influence in this disorder identified through sibling studies. It was also during this time period that the neuropsychological correlates of autism were investigated. Cognitive deficits, and their relationship to social deficits, were investigated and led to the development of the theory of mind hypothesis (see Chapter 3). The development of intervention programs was the most striking advancement during this time period. Educational programs, such as TEACCH (see Chapters 5 and 10), were developed and implemented, and psychoanalytic interventions were discarded.

The third time period, from the late 1980s to the early 1990s, was characterized by continued gains in our understanding of the etiology of autism. In particular, the genetic underpinnings of autism were further elucidated through sibling and twin studies. It was also during this time period that neuroimaging techniques were utilized to gain an understanding of the neuroanatomy and neurophysiology of individuals with this disorder. Diagnostic research focused on clarification of the behaviors and symptoms associated with milder forms of autism and Asperger syndrome. Additionally, researchers and clinicians attempted to characterize autism across the lifespan, including recognition of very early symptoms and behaviors. Neuropsychological studies continued to offer insights into the cognitive deficits associated with autism, and developed theories to explain these deficits. Intervention programs during this period shifted emphasis to include home-based programming and behavioral interventions, such as the program advocated by O. Ivar Lovaas (see Chapter 5). Although some researchers and clinicians began to evaluate interventions programs empirically, this was not the norm.

The final time period reviewed by Rutter is the late 1990s. Rutter noted the continued influence of molecular genetics in developing our understanding of the etiology of autism. After a review of genetic studies, Rutter (1999, p.181) summed up the research as follows: 'What will emerge, however, is not the gene for autism but rather several genes that, in combination, give rise to an increased vulnerability to autism.' Rutter also noted that neuroimaging, specifically functional neuroimaging, has provided useful insights into brain functioning of individuals with autism through comparisons with typical individuals (see Chapter 3). This area is very new, and the ultimate usefulness of the information to the individual with autism has yet to be determined. Rutter concluded his review of this time period by delineating the developments in the area of intervention. Specifically, he noted that treatment approaches have expanded to include the lifespan and the diagnostic spectrum of individuals with autism. For example, treatment approaches are now being implemented to aid individuals with autism in job attainment.

In conclusion, Rutter's review of the history of autism demonstrates the interplay between research and clinical practice. The gains made in our understanding of the etiology of this disorder and successful interventions are the direct result of the interaction between the two fields. However, it is still the case that many practitioners do not have easy access to the latest research developments and that many researchers are far removed from the hands-on work of clinical intervention.

Overview of the book

This book is divided into three parts based on the process of intervening with children diagnosed with autism and their families from initial early childhood assessment, diagnosis, and treatment through interventions with adolescents. For consistency of reading, children with a variety of autism spectrum disorders (ASD) are referred to as 'children with autism' throughout the text. However, it is important to note that the assessment techniques and results, as well as treatment intervention strategies discussed throughout the book, will vary depending on the individual child's developmental age, needs, and expression of autism symptoms. Of additional note, the use of the term 'mental retardation' in Part I refers to the *DSM-IV* diagnosis (APA 1994). Finally, within each chapter, the authors review and integrate issues of research, theory, and practice.

Part I: diagnosis and assessment

There is a wealth of information currently available regarding various diagnostic tools, assessment tools, and medical issues that can be overwhelming to practitioners entering the field, not to mention families. Chapter 2 presents an overview of autism and the procedures and steps necessary to diagnose a child with autism. Information on how to help families through the process of early diagnosis and making treatment choices is also presented. Current research on the neuropsychology of autism is reviewed in Chapter 3, as well as a brief overview of the neurobiology of autism and implications for treatment providers. The role of physicians as part of a multidisciplinary treatment team is discussed in Chapter 4, including addressing parent questions regarding medical intervention and other experimental treatment methods.

Part II: child-centered interventions

The heterogeneous nature of autism symptoms along with the multiple developmental needs of children with autism call for a variety of intervention specialists. The need for different service providers ultimately leads to the necessity of collaboration between diverse professional disciplines in order to help the child achieve developmental gains in overlapping areas. Chapters 5, 6, 7, and 8 provide information about different aspects of intervention with children who have autism and their families from beginning therapeutic interventions (Chapter 5), speech and language (Chapter 6) and occupational therapy interventions (Chapter 7), to adapting school curricula for children with autism (Chapter 8). The focus of the treatment-oriented chapters is on integrating what we currently know about the field of autism from research, as well as providing methods to translate this information into practical individualized treatment approaches. This is an important issue, as no one treatment model or approach has yet been researched in comparison with another, thus making it 'premature and unwise to consider any one method a treatment of choice' (Marcus, Garfinkle and Wolery 2001, p.171).

Part III: family and community interventions

The comprehensive treatment of a child with autism involves acknowledging the impact of the child's diagnosis on multiple systems (e.g. individual family members, a child's social environment, and community services). Along with this, practitioners need to 'consider both the impact of the child's handicap on the family and how the family's developmental status within the life cycle may influence their ability to cope with the child's handicap' (Harris 1988, p.208). Chapter 9 reviews the research regarding the impact of having a child with autism in the family on other siblings in the family system and provides information on psychoeducational support services to foster positive sibling relationships. Chapter 10 offers specific strategies to enhance the social development of teens with autism within an ongoing supportive group framework. Finally, Chapter 11 provides a window into parent perspectives about the impact of having a child with autism on family life cycles and defines specific aspects of professional support that are viewed as most helpful during these times.

In conclusion, the goal of this book is to provide practitioners with a synthesis of autism research, theory, and clinical practice information, while at the same time considering the individual child and family strengths and challenges in order to intervene effectively from diagnosis through treatment.

References

American Psychiatric Association (APA) (1994) *Diagnostic and Statistical Manual of Mental Disorders,* 4th edn. *(DSM-IV).* Washington, DC: APA.

Bertrand, J., Mars, A., Boyle, C., Bore, F., Yeargin-Allsopp, M. and Deconfle, P. (2001) 'Prevalence of autism in a United States population: the brick township, New Jersey investigation.' *Pediatrics 108,* 5, 1155–1161.

Bristol, M.M., Cohen, D.J., Costello, E.J., Denckla, M., Eckberg, T.J., Kallen, R., Kraemer, H.C., Lord, C., Maurer, R., McIlvane, W.J., Minshew, N., Sigman, M. and Spence, M.A.

(1996) 'State of the science in autism: report to the National Institutes of Health.' *Journal of Autism and Developmental Disorders 26*, 2, 121–154.

Eisenmajer, R., Margot, P., Leekam, S., Wing, L., Gould, J., Welham, M. and Ong, B. (1996) 'Comparison of clinical symptoms in autism and Asperger's disorder.' *Journal of the American Academy of Child and Adolescent Psychiatry 35*, 11, 1523–1531.

Filipek, P.A., Accardo, P.J., Ashwal, S., Baranek, G.T., Cook, Jr, E.H., Dawson, G., Gordon, B., Gravel, J.S., Johnson, C.O., Kallen, R.J., Levey, S.E., Minshew, N.J., Ozonoff, S., Prizant, B.M., Rapin, I., Rogers, S.J., Stone, W.L., Teplin, S.W., Tuchman, R.F. and Volkmar, F.R. (1999) 'The screening and diagnosis of autistic spectrum disorders.' *Journal of Autism and Developmental Disorders 29*, 439–484.

Harris, S. (1988) 'Family assessment in autism.' In E. Schopler and G.B. Mesibov (eds) *Diagnosis and Assessment in Autism*. New York: Plenum.

Kanner, L. (1943) 'Autistic disturbances of affective contact.' *Nervous Child 2*, 217–250.

Manjiviona, J. and Prior, M. (1999) 'Neuropsychological profiles of children with asperger syndrome and autism.' *Autism: The International Journal of Research and Practice 3*, 4, 327–356.

Marcus, L. M., Garfinkle, A. and Wolery, M. (2001) 'Issues in early diagnosis and intervention with young children with autism.' In E. Schopler, N. Yirmiya, C. Shulman and L.M. Marcus (eds) *The Research Basis for Autism Intervention*. New York: Kluwer Academic/Plenum.

National Advisory Mental Health Council Workgroup on Child and Adolescent Mental Health Intervention Development and Deployment (2001) *Blueprint for Change: Research on Child and Adolescent Mental Health*. Washington, DC: National Institute of Mental Health.

Rutter, M. (1999) 'The Emanuel Miller memorial lecture 1998. Autism: two-way interplay between research and clinical work.' *Journal of Child Psychology and Psychiatry 40*, 2, 169–188.

Schopler, E. (2001) 'Treatment for autism: from science to pseudo-science or anti-science.' In E. Schopler, N. Yirmiya, C. Shulman and L.M. Marcus (eds) *The Research Basis for Autism Intervention*. New York: Kluwer Academic/Plenum.

Schopler, E., Mesibov, G.B. and Hearsey, K. (1995) 'Structured teaching in the TEACCH system.' In E. Schopler and G.B. Mesibov (eds) *Learning and Cognition in Autism*. New York: Plenum.

Wing, L. (1997) 'The history of ideas on autism: legends, myths and reality.' *Autism: The International Journal of Research and Practice 1*, 1, 13–23.

Part I
Diagnosis and Assessment

CHAPTER 2

Bridging the Process between Diagnosis and Treatment

Cory Shulman

As we serve young, severely handicapped children, we need to examine our unspoken assumptions about both the definition of the role of the parent and the nature of the child's disability. These determine our concept of parental needs and the services we offer to these families. (Bristol 1985, p.51)

Autism, a neurodevelopmental disorder, is not easily recognizable in its early stages. The onset of autism is insidious, not usually marked by the appearance of abrupt or dramatic symptoms. Typically, families experience a gradual awareness that a problem exists, adapting to their child's difficulties without even being aware that they are changing their behavior and expectations. Parents begin to realize that they are experiencing particular difficulties in coping with their child's behavior and that their child's behavior is different than the behavior of other familiar, typically developing children. The initial symptoms of autism vary with each child and are not always identified as autism by professionals. The difficulties in diagnosing autism are manifold, as there are no clear or specific biological markers (Bristol-Power and Spinella 1999; DeLong 1999). Often the diagnosis is exclusionary, meaning that it is established by combining the presence of behaviors associated with autism with the absence of other possible diagnoses. Although early markers for autism have been identified through research (Baird *et al.* 2000; Baranek 1999; Baron-Cohen *et al.* 1996; Filipek *et al.* 1999), parents and professionals do not always accept the seriousness and the pervasive nature of the impairments inherent in autism as it expresses itself at young ages. Parents often fail to receive an accurate diagnosis from professionals and this leads to uncertainty and confusion; parents may not understand how to relate to their child, and their child may experience difficulty understanding demands placed on him or her. Moreover, professionals may have difficulty establishing effective intervention programs that meet family expectations and respond to the child's individual manifestations of autism (Prizant and Wetherby 1989). Thus, accurate diagnosis is a critical first step in treating autism.

This chapter will attempt to assist professionals in navigating through the diagnostic process and the maze of treatment options for children with autism and their families. Research findings on diagnosis will be reviewed, and a short survey of assessment tools presently used for screening and diagnosing autism will be presented. In order to assist professionals in dealing with families, this chapter will then describe parental difficulties in confronting the diagnosis of autism and the unique stresses faced by parents of children with autism. Finally, this chapter will highlight the need to establish a framework for decision-making regarding treatment programs that incorporates professional knowledge about autism and considers the unique needs of the child and the family.

Core characteristics of autism

Diagnostic criteria for autism, defined by the presence or absence of specified behaviors, have changed considerably over time (Volkmar and Lord 1998). They involve a distinct constellation of behavior symptoms, incorporating impairments in three developmental domains:

- impairment of reciprocal social interactions
- impairment in verbal and nonverbal communication, including problems in imaginative activity
- impairment in behavior, including a markedly restricted repertoire of activities and interests.

Some impairment in development must occur before the age of 3 years (APA 1994; World Health Organization (WHO) 1992).

Impairment of reciprocal social interactions

The social problems evident in autism are most keenly expressed in situations that require reciprocity. Although these children can demonstrate emotional attachments to parents and caregivers, their responses are usually qualitatively, and sometimes quantitatively, different than those of typically developing children (Capps, Sigman and Mundy 1994; Lord 1994). Children with autism seem to misinterpret or not be aware of other people's emotional behavior and feelings (Capps, Sigman and Yirmiya 1995), and thus they can behave inappropriately in social situations (Travis and Sigman 1998). Some early expressions of these difficulties reveal themselves in impaired eye contact, problems with joint attention, paucity in the use of gestures to modulate interactions, and difficulties interpreting others' gestures (Capps *et al.* 1993; Sigman 1994).

Impairment in verbal and nonverbal communication

Children with autism often fail to understand the purpose and meaning of language as a means to influence their surroundings (Watson *et al.* 1989). Since language is not consistently used as a communicative tool, it is difficult for children who develop meaningful speech to initiate and maintain a conversational topic and incorporate others' ideas and feelings into the conversation. Instead, they may provide an outpouring of details or engage in a monologue rather than a conversation. Children with autism may echo what they hear others say without taking into account whether or not the listener is following the discussion. Comprehension of language is literal, with abstract concepts being particularly difficult for them to comprehend.

Children with autism also show abnormal play and limitations in imagination. This is particularly apparent in symbolic and pretend play (Jarrold, Boucher and Smith 1993; Roeyers and van Berckelaer 1994). As a result of poor imaginative ability, children with autism lack flexible and creative use of imitation as a way to learn from the environment. Playing imaginatively and socially is particularly difficult for these children, and some of their difficulties with language may in part be due to their reduced opportunities to practice language in play situations (Howlin and Yates 1989).

Impairment in behavior

Repetitive stereotyped movements are often the most outstanding manifestation of autism. These actions often cause parents a great deal of discomfort, since they are external expressions of the 'strangeness' of their children (Shulman, Tidhar and Bukai 2001). Children with autism may exhibit a fascination with particular, often odd, objects, and they may have a temper tantrum if these objects are lost or removed. They may be preoccupied with details or information, such as bus schedules or numbers. Parents report that their children's obsessive activities cause disruption as they interfere with other family activities (Lord 1995). Routines and rituals become important to many individuals with autism, and they often cling rigidly to sameness in their daily routines. Apart from having social problems, communication impairments, and restricted play and interests, many children with autism have other behavioral issues and problems. These behavior problems are not considered diagnostically salient, although they are usually clinically important as they can cause further difficulties that require immediate attention. Some of these difficulties include sleeping and feeding problems, temper tantrums, aggression, destructiveness, hyperactivity, screaming in public, and self-injury. Many individuals with autism also experience problems in sensory integration and either are overly sensitive to sensory input or do not respond as expected.

Autism screening

The diagnostic process often begins with developmental screening during routine well-child checkups. Parents or others having interaction with the child may express concerns about behavior, lack of a social smile, or limited interaction with peers. There may be concerns about the child not responding to his or her name or not using gestures to communicate and engage the parents. Tantrums, poor imaginative play, or odd hand or body movements may alert the clinician that something is awry. Children should be evaluated immediately if they are not babbling or gesturing by 12 months of age, have no single words by 16 months, have no two-word phrases by 24 months of age, or if any loss of language or social skills is noted (Filipek *et al.* 1999). If by the age of 5 years the child is still not speaking, this is positively correlated with a diagnosis of autism (Lord and Pickles 1996). However, no one factor based on parental suspicions has been identified as necessary and sufficient to establish an autism diagnosis. Most prospective studies have failed to isolate any specific factors predictive of a later diagnosis of autism (Johnson *et al.* 1992; Lister-Brook 1992). In the Baron-Cohen and colleagues (1996) study, it was posited that deficits in pretend play and deficits in protodeclarative pointing, joint attention, and gaze monitoring at 18 months would be indicative of a higher risk for developing autism.

Screening tools include the Checklist for Autism in Toddlers (CHAT: Baron-Cohen *et al.* 1996) and the Autism Screening Questionnaire (ASQ:

Berument *et al.* 1999). The CHAT combines a parent report and the clinician's observation as a means toward identifying behaviors associated with autism spectrum disorders, and can be used with children as young as 18 months. The Autism Screening Questionnaire is used with children 4 years of age and older. Both of these instruments have been validated. Should concerns be identified through the screening process, a more thorough evaluation to establish the diagnosis is recommended.

Diagnostic process

Professionals today have a better understanding of autism and its manifestations in early years and therefore diagnosis is being ascertained earlier than ever before (Baron-Cohen, Allen and Gillberg 1992; Charman *et al.* 2001). It is possible to diagnose autism and its variants at different ages depending on the severity of the manifestations, the level of intellectual impairment, and the degree of adaptive impairment. At young ages (12–30 months), reaching a diagnosis of autism spectrum disorder is quite challenging, as the developmental level of children at these ages does not encompass skills associated with some of the behavioral manifestations of autism (e.g. empathy, language). Parental satisfaction with the diagnostic process is significantly related to the age at which their child was diagnosed. Those parents who waited longest or received a more vague diagnosis (e.g. autistic tendencies) were less satisfied than those parents who received a clear diagnosis relatively quickly (Howlin 1998). Although few practitioners deny the importance of early diagnosis, parents still report considerable frustration in their attempts to obtain a diagnosis for their child.

The diagnosis of autism is a multifaceted process and cannot be accomplished in a single assessment or within one professional discipline (Lord and Risi 2000; Rutter and Schopler 1992). As noted above, because of the tremendous heterogeneity of symptom presentation among individuals with autism, the diagnostic process must be conducted with care and needs to focus on diagnostically salient behaviors. The evaluative process must include specific activities to document the presence of such behavioral indicators associated with autism. Although there will be some variation, the evaluation will most likely involve many procedures for gathering information (Lord 1991). These may include:

- interviewing parents
- reviewing medical records for evidence of autism during early development

- observing the child in different settings and if possible on different days
- interviewing the teacher, if the child is in an educational program
- conducting a speech and language assessment and collecting a language sample if the child is verbal
- conducting a standardized psychological or developmental assessment to evaluate general intelligence
- assessing sensory motor integration skills and performing a vision and hearing test.

It is important for children of all ages to obtain a physician's statement indicating whether any of the child's learning, developmental, or behavioral issues can be attributed to physical factors (see Chapter 3).

Diagnostic tools

In order to help identify a child's specific behavioral manifestations consistent with a diagnosis of autism, several specialized diagnostic instruments have been developed. These include standardized autism rating scales, behavior checklists, and direct observation of the child. Such instruments are crucial in establishing a diagnosis. The completion of standardized scales is particularly important because autistic behavior looks different in different situations with different people. Diagnosis must be based on information collected from the people closest to the child. Evaluations must be performed by professionals who are familiar with autism and employ instruments developed for diagnosis (Lord and Risi 2000).

There are three types of autism-specific diagnostic instruments, each involving a different amount and type of participation from the parents, the child, and the examiner. Parents have a more active role when required to fill out questionnaires, while the examiner is more passive. On the other hand, interviews, some more structured than others, involve both the parents and professionals, as the professional guides the parent to the relevant examples so that they can provide the appropriate information necessary for establishing a diagnosis of autism. Finally, direct observations of interactions between the child and parents, between the child and the examiner and between the child and the environment require the most active role from the professionals.

The Autism Behavior Checklist (ABC: Krug, Arick and Almond 1980) is an example of a parent questionnaire that does not require a lot of effort to complete. There are 57 items that describe behaviors, and the person filling out the questionnaire decides if the item described is indicative of the child or not. The findings are then summarized in an algorithm in which each noted item is weighted according to its centrality to the diagnosis of autism. This instrument has proven to be particularly useful in differentiating between autism and mental retardation among children over the age of 5 years (Volkmar *et al.* 1988; Wadden, Bryson and Rodger 1991).

The Autism Diagnostic Interview – Revised (ADI-R: Lord, Rutter and LeCouteur 1994) is an example of a semi-structured interview based on the tenth edition of the International Classification of Diseases (*ICD-10*: WHO 1992) and *DSM-IV* (APA 1994) criteria for autism. The interviewer extracts information from the parents or a primary caregiver about the child's developmental history, language and communication skills, play skills, social abilities, and behaviors. Additional information is collected about behaviors that may be useful in establishing an alternative, differential diagnosis. A trained examiner then codes the examples given by the parents and the results are entered into an algorithm to establish the presence or absence of autism. This instrument has been found to be helpful at various ages and levels of development above 18 months (Lord *et al.* 1997).

Two examples of diagnostic checklists based on clinical observations are the Childhood Autism Rating Scale (CARS: Schopler *et al.* 1980) and the Autism Diagnostic Observation Schedule – Generic (ADOS-G: Lord *et al.* 2000). These two instruments are based on observing the child interact over the course of the assessment and then summarizing the existence or absence of certain predefined behaviors.

The CARS is a 15-item rating scale that assesses different aspects of behavior identified as diagnostically significant in autism. The CARS was developed in the early 1980s, and is not specifically related to a particular diagnostic criteria system such as the *ICD-10* (WHO 1992) or *DSM-IV* (APA 1994), but its reliability and validity have been proven (Eaves and Milner 1993; Sturmey, Matson and Sevin 1992). Each of the 15 items is rated from normal behavior to severely autistic behavior, with specific examples given for each rating.

The ADOS-G is a semi-structured, play-based assessment in which the examiner and the child interact and the examiner then summarizes the quality and quantity of behaviors associated with autism and assesses the overall communication and social behavior of the child. Items include construction tasks, turn-taking activities, imitation, imaginative toy play, and use of verbal and nonverbal communication. The particular situations that encourage communication are matched to the child's age and expressive language abilities. The algorithm for determining a diagnosis of autism on the ADOS is based specifically on the diagnostic criteria as defined in both the *ICD-10* and the *DSM-IV*.

Differential diagnosis

The diagnosis of autism should be made after other diagnoses that could account for the behaviors have been considered and rejected. Differential diagnosis can be difficult at times. For example, developmental language disorders (Bishop 1994) share many common features with autism, including delayed language development. However, children with expressive language disorders tend to compensate for their lack of speech by means of gesture and other forms of nonverbal communication more than would be expected from children with autism. Likewise, they also show relatively normal patterns of imaginative play, and clear reciprocity in their social interactions with adults, although peer relationships are inevitably affected to some degree. Imaginative play and social reciprocity are more impaired in children with autism. Children with more severe receptive language disorders, however, quite frequently show impairments in reciprocal social relations; imaginative play may be limited, with some evidence of ritualistic behaviors, and they may show unusual language features, such as echolalia and stereotyped speech. Generally, as children's understanding of language improves, so does their functioning in other areas, and ritualistic and obsessional behaviors are rarely as marked as in autism. Nevertheless, in early childhood in particular, it can sometimes be very difficult to differentiate between a child with a severe receptive language disorder and one with a milder form of autism.

Assessment considerations

Testing the child with autism

After establishing the diagnosis of autism, referral for further assessment to identify strengths and weaknesses and to develop treatment strategies is recommended. Specific assessment tools are described in Chapter 3. This section focuses on considerations for testing the child with autism.

Parents play an important role in describing the abilities and limitations of their child and can provide vital information about their child that will assist in the process of diagnosis. In order to maximize the value of the evaluation results, professionals should obtain information from parents and teachers (if available) about the following:

- reinforcers that are particularly enticing for the child
- the child's nature and style of learning
- potential triggers for tantrums
- particular language issues, such as whether the child reliably uses 'yes' and 'no' in response to questions
- whether visual aids (e.g. gestures, pictures, signing) are necessary to help the child understand directions
- whether there are idiosyncratic uses of language that may sabotage the session. For example, if the word 'finished' has a specific meaning for a specific child, such as 'it is time to go', it should not be used at the completion of individual tasks, but rather at the end of the entire testing session.

It is helpful for the parent(s) or a teacher to be present during the assessment itself, as they can verify and review the examiner's results. Professionals should try to develop a relationship with the child before the standardized testing begins. This may be accomplished by a visit to the home (or classroom) for an introduction. In addition, when the child enters the room where the testing will occur, he or she should be allowed to explore the room. The observations obtained during this time are no less important for the assessment than the standardized results.

Particularly in the assessment of language skills, it is important to administer a variety of tests that will span both the upper and lower limits of the child's ability. Cards and paper should be available to provide visual aids if necessary. Presenting a broad range of tasks and beginning at a point well below the child's ability will ensure success and minimize frustration. Conforming to standardized procedures gives one type of information. Afterwards, it is helpful to determine the type and level of support the child needs to respond correctly, without maintaining standardized procedures. This can be ascertained by checking the child's responses to attempts by the examiner to teach the child new skills or to be sure that the child understands what is being requested. While any modification in standardized procedures negates the meaning of the standardized scores, modifications are likely to produce the most valid and useful information. The importance of establishing good attending skills to adult-directed tasks cannot be underestimated. This sometimes requires frequent and immediate use of reinforcements. For basic attending tasks, such as sitting in a chair or completing an item, reinforcement can be given for compliance and not for correct performance. This is one method for maintaining standardized procedures while providing necessary reinforcement to the child.

As a general rule, children with autism are not manipulative, negative, or deliberately resistant. If children clearly understand the requests, they will generally be more likely to respond with fewer negative behaviors. A trained and experienced examiner can elicit a broad range of information from the testing procedures. It is important to remember that it is difficult to determine what children with autism really know, and results must be interpreted with caution. Reliance on full-scale scores (e.g. IQ scores or cumulative language scores) may mask the true nature of the individual's abilities. Analysis of performance on each task or subtest and of the overall profile will allow professionals to pinpoint learning strengths and weaknesses in order to develop appropriate instruction and treatment goals.

Communicating the results
Parental reactions to the diagnosis of autism

The evaluation process provides a unique opportunity for professionals to establish a relationship of trust and collaboration with the parents of the child. It is important to remember, however, that the period of diagnosis is often extremely stressful for parents, who may have difficulty dealing with the uncertainty of the process. The combination of poor resource availability, professional skepticism, indifferent awareness, and subsequent lack of information has been shown to distress even the strongest families. Parents have reported that when these issues are addressed in a professional and competent manner they experience some relief.

Professionals sometimes hedge the terminology that they use in diagnosing a child because autism has become a 'loaded' diagnosis (Siegel 1996) and they are concerned with the stigma that may be associated with it. Unfortunately, because of the variability of symptoms, there is a proliferation of alternative terms such as 'autistic tendencies' and 'autistic-like developmental delay' that can be quite confusing to parents. There is no justification for referring to 'autistic tendencies' or 'partial autism', as autism is a reasonably clearly defined syndrome. There are behavioral criteria (e.g. APA 1994; WHO 1992) to ascertain if there is enough evidence to establish the diagnosis or not. If not, then the diagnosis should not be given and another explanation for the child's presenting problems should be found. Lack of awareness of the broad nature of autism should not be a reason for labeling the mild end of autism 'autistic tendencies' rather than autism. Terms such as 'semantic pragmatic disorder' and 'hyperlexia' refer to specific aspects of impairments associated with autism spectrum disorders and are not diagnostically valid and reliable. They describe symptoms but have not been found to be separate and differentiated from autism.

Once the diagnosis of autism has been established, it is important for professionals to direct parents to useful resources, which imparts a feeling that there is 'something to do'. Parents should be helped to understand the specific manifestations of their child's autism, and encouraged to return to the professional who gave them the diagnosis with questions regarding the diagnosis. Parents can also be encouraged to read books, such as narrative accounts about families and individuals with autism (e.g. Grandin and Scariano 1986; Hart 1989; Stehli 1991), and to talk to other families who have a child with autism. The field of autism is constantly changing, and parents should be encouraged to continue to learn as much as possible about autism. In addition, families should be encouraged to contact the nearest branch of the Autism Society, and get onto waiting lists for services. Even if those services are not incorporated in future treatment programs, at least it imparts the feeling that options exist and something can be done (Moreno 1991; see also Chapter 11).

While parents are searching for things to do, it is also crucial to allow them to grieve following a diagnosis of autism. Although the child remains the same, parents may view the child differently once they have received the diagnosis. Some of their dreams and plans are lost and it will take time for new plans and dreams to replace them. Some parents actually experience relief because they were already aware that there was something wrong with their child. It may be helpful to determine what is useful to them and assist them in their search for support and comfort during this difficult period. It is important for professionals to stress that autism is just a label and can become a motivator to do things. An example of a practical proposition is to suggest that the family begin videotaping the child. In addition to documenting progress after treatment has begun, it can also be immediately helpful in viewing the child after receiving the autism diagnosis and verifying the behavioral manifestations of autism (Tommasone and Tommasone 2000).

Stressors unique to families of children with autism

Parents of autistic children face a number of special stresses because of their child's autism. The diagnostic confusion that many parents experience can create stress. Parents too often are not given an accurate, clear and informative description of their child's problems. Often parents suspect early on that a problem exists, but professionals do not support them. Later, as the problems escalate, they may blame themselves for not having been more assertive in obtaining professional assistance and guidance. In addition, as younger and younger children are being diagnosed, the diagnosis of autism is often subsumed in more generic, and less helpful, diagnoses such as pervasive developmental disorders, communication disorders, language impairments or developmental delays in the area of social development. The failure to establish a diagnosis of autism or to communicate that diagnosis may contribute to the stress of coping with difficult behaviors and the unique learning problems typically found in children with autism.

Another unique stress factor for parents is that for the most part children with autism appear physically normal. Because these children do not stand out from their peers, their parents often experience additional frustration and stress when their child engages in unusual or inappropriate behavior. When a child with an observable disability acts inappropriately, people usually respond with tolerance, since they are aware of the existence of a problem. In contrast, autism is invisible; accordingly children with autism often face expectations for normal behavior that are rarely met. This incongruity between expectations and the reality of the disability often becomes most problematic for parents when they are in public places where the child's behavior may be subject to criticism from strangers. Parents may be embarrassed by their child's behavior that may be disruptive, and they may be worried about being judged by others (Tunali and Power 1993). The parental anxiety level is often highest before they have received a diagnosis, as they have no explanation for the unpredictability of their child's responses in public places.

Particularly at young ages, autism is typically associated with an uneven developmental profile and unusual course of development. Often there are visual, spatial, and motor skills that remain relatively intact, or are even superior, alongside significant deficits in language, social, and problem-solving skills. Autism is often marked by delays and deviance in development that cut across a variety of areas of functioning. Development may appear normal in early stages and may then plateau or be characterized by regression, or may be generally slow with gradual unfolding of autism characteristics (Lord 1995). This variability can be quite frustrating and often confusing to parents, who see the slowing down as temporary, particularly if it is concomitantly accompanied by the birth of a sibling or within accepted norms of development.

Parents are also faced with many dilemmas in behavior intervention, particularly since children with autism, for the most part, do not respond to accepted, tried and true techniques of child-raising. This can shatter parents' confidence in their parental instincts. Professionals can help parents assess and understand why their child behaves in a certain manner. Recognizing the reasons governing their child's behavior can help restore the parents' confidence and empower them as well. One of the most common dilemmas for parents involves the willfulness of the child (Glenn 1996). Often it is difficult to differentiate between situations when children with autism can do something but choose not to, and when they truly cannot do what is required of them because of a lack of understanding of the demand or the situation. This question of inability versus refusal is compounded by the inconsistent manner in which children with autism perform skills, since something that they perform spontaneously in one context may not necessarily be repeated when it is requested. Parents may assume that their child is being stubborn or that it is a question of motivation. When parents assume that their child is being willful and obstinate, discipline techniques may become confrontational and negative, as opposed to firmly directing the child to the appropriate, required behavior. Parents may require professional guidance in order to begin to recognize the origins of behaviors and to choose appropriate intervention strategies (Powers 1988).

After obtaining a diagnosis, many parents often confront disagreements among professionals as to the best course of treatment for their child. This is partially a function of the complexity of autism, which affects multiple aspects of development, and partially fueled by professional 'turfism', with practitioners from different disciplines seeing things differently, stressing different goals and urging the use of different techniques. Naturally, parents may latch onto programs espousing 'cures' for autism. Some of these programs require parents to totally reorganize their home lives in order to work with the child intensively, at great financial and emotional cost. While parents should have control over decisions about their own child, they seem to be particularly vulnerable to quick resolutions or promises of miracle cures during these first years. Popular literature and news media often fail to evaluate claims of success critically, and when parents turn to professionals for advice regarding the best available services, it is important for professionals to be aware of developments in the field and to handle questions in a frank but nonjudgmental manner. The desire of parents to find an answer or a solution should be acknowledged, without encouraging them to pursue actively every lead or unsubstantiated promise of cure. Professionals can help by providing empirically based information about such claims (see Chapter 5). Similarly, some treatment strategies, such as sensory integration therapy, may focus on specific manifestations of autism without taking the total picture into consideration. Parental stress is compounded by the fact that parents often find themselves forced to choose between methods, because professionals are committed to specific intervention techniques and do not necessarily work collaboratively with others.

Moving from diagnosis to treatment

Parental and professional roles

All intervention strategies must involve parents in the treatment process, particularly since parents often feel overwhelmed and helpless at the time of diagnosis, and need to feel involved in the decision-making process in order to translate what they hear about their child into practical intervention strategies. While professionals should provide the initial momentum, parents should be given as much responsibility as possible. Minimally, they need to be informed about any therapeutic decisions and any additional diagnostic procedures, such as additional medical tests; maximally, their feelings and opinions about such procedures should be actively solicited. During this first stage, most families are eager for maximum participation. Parents of young children are usually young themselves and they have energy and are full of hope. It is crucial to capitalize on normal reactions (e.g. 'What can we do?') upon hearing the diagnosis.

Regardless of the specific methodology and context chosen for the treatment program, direct parental involvement is critical for success. One option for involving parents is participation in training programs (Briesmeister and Schaefer 1998). Parents are no longer seen as the cause of their child's autism and are now recognized as playing a key role in effective treatment (e.g. Blackwell 1978). The parent–child relationship is seen as interactional or transactional and patterns of behavior are established and maintained over time through a cycle of mutual influences.

Diagnosis as a base for treatment

A comprehensive assessment that elicits the unique profile of strengths and areas of impairment for each child is the base from which to ensure that an intervention program will meet the needs of children with autism. Parents and professionals feel pressure to accomplish goals quickly, but although it is necessary to focus on goals and structure, taking the time to assess, plan, and proactively set up appropriate treatment environments is no less vital to the success of the intervention chosen for the child with autism. A well-balanced program includes work and play, individual and group work, structured learning and natural settings. Parents and professionals should work together in a collaborative fashion to develop a systematic plan of action that will strengthen the child's competencies and address areas of impairment. The concepts underlying all therapies included in such programs must be based on an underlying understanding of autism as a developmental disability (Siegel 1996) and must stress the importance of structure and consistency as a predictable base from which to understand the world (Mesibov, Schopler and Hearsey 1994). The intervention program should be based on individualized assessment and rooted in developmental principles which attribute the child's behavior to its place on the developmental continuum. (For more complete information regarding treatment, see Chapter 5.)

An important concern in deciding on treatment placement and programming is the manner in which the setting can support learning and encourage productive behavior in the child. This is crucial because children with autism often become confused and anxious when critical supports are missing, and this can lead to behavior problems. When deciding where to place a child with autism and what intervention strategy to employ, it is important to take into account the unique strengths and interests, past experiences and patterns of development of the child with autism. The goals of any program should include teaching children with autism to interact intentionally, to communicate effectively, and to develop flexibility and tolerance of change. Independent functioning is a long-term goal with short-term applications. Finally, learning to monitor and manage stress becomes increasingly important as the demands placed on the individual with autism increase (Quill 1993).

Establishing collaboration between parents and professionals

Partnership between parents and professionals is crucial for addressing the needs of children with autism. An effective team must be based on supportive, non-threatening relationships that encourage open discussion regarding problems and include mechanisms for positive feedback. Active involvement in such a team provides many opportunities for personal and professional growth (Coling 1991). The collaborative treatment team should include parents and an autism specialist or treatment coordinator as core participants, while others, such as principals, teachers, and therapists, can be added to the team as needed, based on the child's needs, the decision to be made, and the specific presenting problems. The autism specialist or treatment coordinator is an important resource with specialized training and experience in treating individuals with autism. This experience enables autism specialists to explain the world of autism to the team members, while they attempt to find methods to interpret the world for the individual with autism. The autism specialist should help team members adapt strategies and materials to match the child's needs, while providing training, feedback, and support to those involved in the treatment of the child, and should serve as a resource for parents and professionals (Janzen 1996).

The support team's responsibilities include performing periodic formal and informal assessments as a basis for intervention. Likewise, the support team should facilitate collaboration and integration of all therapies into a total and unified program. One of the results of collaborative work of this type is coordination of observations and anecdotal records, which should be systematically collected and shared among participants. The team supports family and professional members in the development of strategies and related services. In order to develop balanced treatment programs, it is necessary to work on life routines and set specific goals and priorities that are related to the child's autism. (See Chapter 5 for more information about setting up a collaborative treatment approach.)

Parent training

Standard parent-training goals are clearly applicable to autism (Kozloff 2000). They include decreasing inappropriate behavior and improving the quality of parent–child relationships, as well as involving the parents in the change process. Parent-training programs have several advantages. For example, it has been shown that teaching parents to be active change agents has positive effects above and beyond the teaching of specific skills (Turnbull and Turnbull 1990). Parents develop feelings of competence and self-efficacy as a result of successfully intervening with their child with autism (Howlin 1998). Thus, the potential for treatment gains to be maintained and generalized over time and over context is increased. Treatment of specific behavior problems may favorably influence other behaviors, not specifically targeted. Parents who are involved in parent training programs often also report a favorable influence on other children in the house. In the final analysis, parent training is a relatively cost-effective treatment approach, with parents spending the most time with their child and the home being the most inclusive social setting in which the child functions and with which the child must cope. It has been shown that the child's condition improves when the parents are successfully trained (Tunali and Power 1993). The distinctive element in adapting techniques of parent training for families with a child with autism involves the need to be trained in the unique characteristics associated with autism.

Conclusion

Identifying autism and assessing its unique manifestations in a particular child is the most important step when beginning to establish a treatment program for a child with autism. There are a number of autism-specific, diagnostic assessment instruments that have been developed since the 1990s and are available to professionals. A comprehensive diagnosis involves the use of such tools. Parents play an important role in both the diagnostic assessment and the treatment of their child. Although parents are often highly stressed during the evaluation, this process provides a unique opportunity for the professional to establish a cooperative relationship with the parents of a child with autism.

Developmental assessment procedures are also necessary in order to identify strengths and limitations in each child, as well as matching appropriate intervention strategies to a particular child with autism. Useful information can be obtained through modifications and informal tasks that can be added to the standardized battery of assessment tools.

The reality is that autism is too variable and complex a condition for any one treatment strategy possibly to address all cases. Ongoing assessment is essential for establishing effective intervention plans and for addressing challenging behaviors. Treatment plans need constant refinement to match the needs of the child at a particular time and in a particular setting. Appropriate diagnosis and ongoing assessment are inextricably related to the development of effective intervention strategies for children diagnosed with autism.

References

American Psychiatric Association (1994) *Diagnostic and Statistical Manual of Mental Disorders (DSM-IV)*, 4th edn. Washington, DC: APA.

Baird, G., Charman, T., Baron-Cohen, S., Cox, A., Swettenham, J., Wheelwright, S. and Drew, A. (2000) 'A screening instrument for autism at 18 months of age: a 6-year follow-up study.' *Journal of the American Academy of Child and Adolescent Psychiatry 39*, 694–702.

Baranek, G. (1999) 'Autism during infancy: a retrospective video analysis of sensory motor and social behaviors at 9–12 months of age.' *Journal of Autism and Developmental Disorders 29*, 213–224.

Baron-Cohen, S., Allen, J. and Gillberg, C. (1992) 'Can autism be detected at 18 months? The needle, the haystack and the CHAT.' *British Journal of Psychiatry 161*, 839–843.

Baron-Cohen, S., Cox, A., Baird, G., Swettenham, J., Nighingale, N., Morgan, K., Drew, A. and Charman, T. (1996) 'Psychological markers in the detection of autism in infancy in a large population.' *British Journal of Psychiatry 168*, 158–163.

Berument, S.K., Rutter, M., Lord, C., Pickles, A. and Bailey, A. (1999) 'Autism Screening Questionnaire: diagnostic validity.' *British Journal of Psychiatry 175*, 444–451.

Bishop, D.M.V. (1994) 'Developmental disorders of speech and language.' In M. Rutter, E. Taylor and L. Hersov (eds) *Child and Adolescent Psychiatry*, 3rd edn. Oxford: Blackwell Scientific.

Blackwell, L. (1978) *Judevine Training System: Competency Based Training for Parents and Professionals*. St Louis, MO: Judevine Center for Autism.

Briesmeister, J. and Schaefer, C. (1998) *Handbook of Parent Training: Parents as Co-therapists for Children's Behavior Problems*, 2nd edn. New York: Wiley.

Bristol, M.M. (1985) 'Designing programs for young developmentally disabled children: a family systems approach to autism.' *Remedial and Special Education (RASE) 6*, 4, 46–53.

Bristol-Power, M. and Spinella, G. (1999) 'Research on screening and diagnosis in autism: a work in progress.' *Journal of Autism and Developmental Disorders 29*, 435–438.

Capps, L., Kasari, C., Yirmiya, N. and Sigman, M. (1993) 'Parental perception of emotional expressiveness in children with autism.' *Journal of Consulting and Clinical Psychology 61*, 475–484.

Capps, L., Sigman, M. and Mundy, P. (1994) 'Attachment security in children with autism.' *Development and Psychopathology 6*, 249–261.

Capps, L., Sigman, M. and Yirmiya, N. (1995) 'Self-competence and emotional understanding in high functioning children with autism.' *Development and Psychopathology 7*, 137–149.

Charman, T., Baron-Cohen, S., Baird, G., Cox, A., Wheelwright, S., Swettenham, J. and Drew, A. (2001) 'Commentary: the modified checklist for autism in toddlers.' *Journal of Autism and Developmental Disorders 31*, 145–148.

Coling, M.C. (1991) *Developing Integrated Programs: A Transdisciplinary Approach for Early Intervention*. Tucson, AZ: Therapy Skill Builders.

DeLong, G.R. (1999) 'Autism: new data suggest a new hypothesis.' *Neurology 52*, 911–916.

Eaves, R. and Milner, B. (1993) 'The criteria-related validity of the Childhood Autism Rating Scale and the Autism Behavior Checklist.' *Journal of Abnormal Psychology 21*, 481–491.

Filipek, P.A., Accardo, P.J., Ashwal, S., Baranek, G.T., Cook, Jr, E.H., Dawson, G., Gordon, B., Gravel, J.S., Johnson, C.O., Kallen, R.J., Levey, S.E., Minshew, N.J., Ozonoff, S.,

Prizant, B.M., Rapin, I., Rogers, S.J., Stone, W.L., Teplin, S.W., Tuchman, R.F. and Volkmar, F.R. (1999) 'The screening and diagnosis of autistic spectrum disorders.' *Journal of Autism and Developmental Disorders 29*, 439–484.

Glenn, M. (1996) 'The effects of social subtypes of autism on the psychological functioning of the family.' *Dissertation Abstracts International 56*, 3078.

Grandin, T. and Scariano, M.M. (1986) *Emergence: Labeled Autistic.* Novato, CA: Arena.

Hart, C. (1989) *Without Reason: A Family Copes with Two Generations of Autism.* New York: Signet.

Howlin, P. (1998) *Children with Autism and Asperger Syndrome: A Guide for Practitioners and Carers.* Chichester: Wiley.

Howlin, P. and Yates, P. (1989) 'Treating autistic children at home: a London based programme.' In C. Gillberg (ed) *Diagnosis and Treatment of Autism.* New York: Plenum.

Janzen, J. (1996) *Understanding the Nature of Autism: A Practical Guide.* San Antonio, TX: Therapy Skill Builders.

Jarrold, C., Boucher, J. and Smith, P. (1993) 'Symbolic play in autism: a review.' *Journal of Autism and Developmental Disorders 23*, 281–307.

Johnson, M.H., Siddons, F., Frith, U. and Morton, J. (1992) 'Can autism be predicted on the basis of infant screening tests?' *Developmental Medicine and Child Neurology 34*, 316–320.

Kozloff, M. (2000) *Reaching the Autistic Child: A Parent Training Program*, 2nd edn. Champaign, IL: Research Press.

Krug, D.A., Arick, J.R. and Almond, P.J. (1980) *Autism Screening Instrument for Educational Planning.* Portland, OR: ASIEPed.

Lister-Brook, S. (1992) 'The early detection of autism.' Unpublished doctoral dissertation, University of London.

Lord, C. (1991) 'Methods and measures of behavior in the diagnosis of autism and related disorders.' *Psychiatric Clinics of North America 14*, 69–80.

Lord, C. (1994) 'The complexity of social behavior in autism.' In S. Baron-Cohen, H. Tager-Flusberg and D. Cohen (eds) *Understanding Others' Minds: Perspectives from Autism.* New York: Oxford University Press.

Lord, C. (1995) 'Follow-up of two year olds referred for possible autism.' *Journal of Child Psychology and Psychiatry 36*, 1365–1382.

Lord, C. and Pickles, A. (1996) 'Language level and nonverbal social communicative behaviors in autistic and language delayed children.' *Journal of the American Academy of Child and Adolescent Psychiatry 35*, 1542–1550.

Lord, C., Pickles, A., McLennan, M., Rutter, M., Bregman, J., Folstein, S., Fombonne, E., Leboyer, M. and Minshew, N. (1997) 'Diagnosing autism: analysis of data from the Autism Diagnostic Interview.' *Journal of Autism and Developmental Disorders 27*, 501–517.

Lord, C. and Risi, S. (2000) 'Diagnosis of autism spectrum disorders in young children.' In A. Wetherby and B. Prizant (eds) *Autism Spectrum Disorders: A Transactional Developmental Perspective.* Baltimore, MD: Paul H. Brookes.

Lord, C., Risi, S., Lambrecht, L., Cook, E., Leventhal, B., Dilavore, P., Pickles, A. and Rutter, M. (2000) 'The Autism Diagnostic Observation Schedule – Generic: a standard measure of social and communication deficits associated with the spectrum of autism.' *Journal of Autism and Developmental Disorders 30*, 205–223.

Lord, C., Rutter, M. and LeCouteur, A. (1994) 'Autism Diagnostic Interview – Revised: a revised version of a diagnostic interview for caregivers of individuals with possible pervasive developmental disorders.' *Journal of Autism and Developmental Disorders 24*, 659–685.

Mesibov, G., Schopler, E. and Hearsey, K. (1994) 'Structured teaching.' In E. Schopler and G. Mesibov (eds) *Behavioral Issues in Autism.* New York: Plenum.

Moreno, S. (1991) *High functioning individuals with autism: advice for parents and others who care.* Crown Point, IN: MAAP Services.

Powers, M.D. (1988) 'Behavioral assessment of autism.' In E. Schopler and G. Mesibov (eds) *Diagnosis and Assessment in Autism.* New York: Plenum.

Prizant, B. and Wetherby, A. (1989) 'Providing services to children with autism (ages 0–2) and their families.' *Focus on Autistic Behavior 4*, 16–39.

Quill, K.A. (1993) 'Methods to enhance learning in students with autism.' Poster at International Conference on Autism, Arlington, TX, Summer.

Roeyers, H. and van Berckelaer, I. (1994) 'Play in autistic children.' *Communication and Cognition 27*, 349–359.

Rutter, M. and Schopler, E. (1992) 'Classification of pervasive developmental disorders: some concepts and practical considerations.' *Journal of Autism and Developmental Disorders 22*, 459–482.

Schopler, E., Reichler, R., DeVillis, R. and Daly, K. (1980) 'Toward objective classification of childhood autism: Childhood Autism Rating Scale (CARS).' *Journal of Autism and Developmental Disorders 10*, 91–103.

Shulman, C., Tidhar, S. and Bukai, O. (2001) 'A comparison of parental perceptions of their autistic children's behavior and the results of clinical testing.' Poster session presented at the Society for Research of Child Development, Minneapolis, MN, April.

Siegel, B. (1996) *The World of the Autistic Child.* New York: Oxford University Press.

Sigman, M. (1994) 'What are the core deficits in autism?' In S. Broman and J. Grafman (eds) *Atypical Cognitive Deficits in Developmental Disorders: Implications for Brain Function.* Hillsdale, NJ: Erlbaum.

Stehli, A. (1991) *The Sound of a Miracle.* New York: Doubleday.

Sturmey, P., Matson, J. and Sevin, J. (1992) 'Analysis of the internal consistency of three autism scales.' *Journal of Autism and Developmental Disorders 22*, 321–328.

Tommasone, L. and Tommasone, J. (2000) 'Adjusting to your child's diagnosis.' In M.D. Powers (ed) *Children with Autism: A Parent's Guide*, 2nd edn. Bethesda, MD: Woodbine House.

Travis, L. and Sigman, M. (1998) 'Social deficits and interpersonal relationships in autism.' *Mental Retardation and Developmental Disabilities Research Reviews 4*, 65–72.

Tunali, B. and Power, T. (1993) 'Creating satisfaction: a psychological perspective on stress and coping in families of handicapped children.' *Journal of Child Psychology and Psychiatry 34*, 945–957.

Turnbull, A. and Turnbull, H. (1990) *Families, Professionals and Exceptionality: A Special Partnership.* Columbus, OH: Merrill.

Volkmar, F., Cicchetti, D., Dykens, E., Sparrow, S., Leckman, J. and Cohen, D. (1988) 'An evaluation of the Autism Behavior Checklist.' *Journal of Autism and Developmental Disorders 18*, 81–97.

Volkmar, F. and Lord, C. (1998) 'Diagnosis and definition of autism and other pervasive developmental disorders.' In F. Volkmar (ed) *Autism and Pervasive Developmental Disorders.* New York: Cambridge University Press.

Wadden, N.P., Bryson, S. and Rodger, R. (1991) 'A closer look at the Autism Behavior Checklist: discriminant validity and factor structure.' *Journal of Autism and Developmental Disorders 21*, 529–541.

Watson, L., Lord, C., Schaffer, B. and Schopler, E. (1989) *Teaching Spontaneous Communication to Autistic and Developmentally Handicapped Children.* New York: Irvington.

World Health Organization (WHO) (1992) *International Classification of Diseases* (ICD-10), 10th edn. Geneva: WHO.

CHAPTER 3

Neuropsychology of Autism

Research, Theory, and Practical Implications

Dina E. Hill and Piyadasa Kodituwakku

An understanding of brain–behavior relationships is crucial to the development of effective treatments and effective environmental accommodations. (Maurer 1997, p.3)

Neuropsychology is 'an applied science concerned with the behavioral expression of brain dysfunction' (Lezak 1983, p.7), or the study of brain–behavior relationships. Research in this field has taken two directions: clinical and research investigations using neuropsychological assessment, and the more direct study of the brain through the use of neuroimaging. This chapter describes assessment considerations with children who have autism, introduces research on the neuropsychological profiles observed in children with autism, presents cognitive theories of autism, and reviews recent neuroanatomical studies. The chapter concludes with comments on integrating neuropsychological research and clinical findings into individual treatment plans.

Neuropsychological assessment considerations

Information obtained during a neuropsychological assessment may be used to assist in developing diagnostic impressions. However, the results are more commonly used for education and treatment planning, including describing a child's learning style, identifying cognitive strengths and weaknesses, and providing information to qualify the child for special educational services and state programs (Ozonoff 1997a). Typically, a neuropsychological assessment will address the cognitive domains of intelligence, academic achievement, attention, executive functioning, memory and learning, language, visual processing, motor skills, and adaptive functioning. Table 3.1 provides an overview of the neuropsychological domains, observed strengths and weaknesses in the autism population for each domain, and a selection of assessment tools.

The neuropsychological assessment of children with autism is often challenging because of the heterogeneity of behavioral expression in this population, including widely varying language, cognitive, and social skills (Dawson 1996). Communication factors must be considered when administering neuropsychological tests and when interpreting the test results. The vast majority of standardized cognitive tests require the understanding of verbal instructions and may also require a verbal response. Those tests that do not rely on verbal instructions or verbal responses, such as the Leiter International Performance Scale – Revised (Leiter – R: Roid and Miller 1997), a test of nonverbal intelligence, instead may require pointing for responding, a nonverbal gesture often absent in children with autism. Children with autism tend to demonstrate deficits in fine motor skills, and may be unwilling to attempt tasks requiring a written response. Children with autism may also engage in maladaptive behaviors in unfamiliar settings, with unfamiliar people, or when task demands exceed their cognitive capacity. It is essential that clinicians recognize these challenges and expand testing beyond standardized methods in order to obtain the most accurate picture of the child's cognitive abilities. Experienced examiners are often able to adapt tests to obtain useful information. For example, the use of visual cues, gestures and modeling, the use of reinforcement for on-task behavior, and accommodating alternative methods of responding (e.g. placing a token on the chosen response instead of pointing) may increase cooperation and participation by the child. Use of test modifications is not part of standard administration, and any modifications used should be noted in the report.

Table 3.1 Neuropsychological profiles and assessment tools

Neuropsychological domain	Relative strengths	Relative weaknesses	Assessment tools
Intelligence	Performance IQ, Visuospatial subtests, Rote Memory subtests	Verbal IQ, Verbal Comprehension, Verbal Abstract Concept Formation, Visual/Verbal Sequencing	Wechsler Intelligence Scales (WISC III, WPPSI-R, WAIS III, WASI), Leiter – R, Stanford Binet, Differential Abilities Scale (DAS), Mullen Scales of Early Learning, Bayley Infant Development Scales
Academic achievement	Reading: phonics and decoding Arithmetic: calculations	Reading: comprehension Arithmetic: math concepts	Woodcock Johnson – III Tests of Achievement, Psychoeducational Profile – Revised (PEP-R), Wechsler Individual Achievement Test (WIAT)
Attention	Sustained Attention Focusing	Orienting, Shifting, Selective Attention	Conners' Continuous Performance Test (CPT), Matching Familiar Figures Test, Symbol Digits Modalities Test (SDMT)
Executive functioning	Inhibition High Functioning Individuals: Planning and Set Shifting, Working Memory	Working Memory Cognitive Flexibility Low Functioning Individuals: Set Shifting, Planning, Organization	Category Test, Design Fluency Test, Stroop Test, Wisconsin Card Sorting Test, Tower of Hanoi/London, NEPSY Tower subtest, Trail Making Test

Domain			Tests
Memory and learning	Auditory Rote Memory, Immediate/Delayed Visual Memory, Paired Associative Learning, Discriminative Learning, Operant Learning	Long-Term Memory, Metamemory Skills, Declarative Memory, Sequential Memory	California Verbal Learning Test, Wide Range Assessment of Memory and Learning, Test of Memory and Learning, NEPSY Memory subtests, Rey Complex Figure Test, Auditory Consonant Trigrams, Benton Visual Retention Test, Wechsler Memory Scale
Language	Phonology, Syntax	Pragmatics, Prosody, Comprehension of Complex Material, Expressive and Receptive Language Skills	Preschool Language Scale, Clinical Evaluation of Language Fundamentals, Expressive One-Word Picture Vocabulary Test, Peabody Picture Vocabulary Test, Controlled Oral Word Association, Multilingual Aphasia Examination, Token Test
Visual processing	Visual Matching, Visuospatial Problem-solving	Visual–Motor Integration	Developmental Test of Visual-Motor Integration, Developmental Test of Visual Processing, Block Design, Wide Range Assessment of Visual Motor Abilities, Test of Visual-Perceptual Skills
Motor skills	Inconsistent findings of relative strengths in gross motor skills	Fine Motor, Eye–Hand Coordination, Visual–Motor Integration	Grooved Pegboard Test, Developmental Test of Motor Coordination, Finger Tapping Test
Adaptive functioning	Motor skills and daily living skills	Adaptive communication and social skills	Vineland Adaptive Behavior Scales, Scales of Independent Behavior – Revised (SIB-R)

Sources: Adapted in part from Ozonoff (1997a) and Dawson (1996)

Neuropsychological profiles

Intellectual and academic functioning

Developmental and intelligence testing establishes a child's current level of overall cognitive functioning. Test results may be used in part to diagnose mental retardation or other learning disorders. Cognitive testing is essential, as research indicates that approximately 70–75 per cent of children diagnosed with autism will also be diagnosed with mental retardation (Happé and Frith 1996). Research on intellectual profiles of children with autism indicates a mixed performance across the subtests of intelligence tests (Happé and Frith 1996). A common misperception is that children with autism tend to demonstrate a pattern of higher nonverbal skills than verbal skills. It is the case, however, that children with autism are likely to perform best on tests of visuospatial problem-solving (nonverbal subtest) and on measures of rote learning and memory (verbal subtest) than on measures of visually sequencing social stimuli (nonverbal subtest) and measures of verbal comprehension (verbal subtest). In general, these children perform better on tasks that are less abstract in nature. A thorough evaluation of intellectual functioning is necessary in order for caregivers and clinicians neither to overestimate nor to underestimate the child's capacity. An accurate picture of intellectual functioning will aid in the development of effective treatment plans.

Academic achievement is varied in this population as well, and is closely related to overall intelligence. Ozonoff (1997a) noted that in reading, phonics and decoding skills tend to be spared but that comprehension is often impaired in this population. Professionals may encounter hyperlexia in children with autism in that they are able to decode words at or above expectations, but with little understanding of what was read. Ozonoff also noted that in mathematics, calculation skills are an area of relative strength, whereas arithmetic concepts are an area of relative weakness.

There are few assessment tools that were designed for or standardized with children with autism. One exception is the Psychoeducational Profile – Revised (PEP-R). The PEP-R is a standardized measure of behaviors and skills used with children aged 6 months to 7 years. Development skills in the areas of imitation, perception, fine motor and gross motor skills, eye–hand integration, cognitive performance (nonverbal), and cognitive verbal are evaluated using toys and learning materials (Schopler et al. 1990). As noted in the manual, the PEP-R was designed for planning individualized intervention and to identify cognitive areas of strengths and weaknesses.

Attention and executive functioning

Attention, including sustained, selective, divided, and focused attention, 'enables people to respond to particular information while either consciously or unconsciously ignoring other potential stimuli' (Cohen, Malloy and Jenkins 1998, p.542). Thus, learning new information requires adequate attention to the task at hand. Research indicates that rapid shifting of attention and divided attention are impaired in individuals with autism (Happé and Frith 1996). In contrast, research suggests that focused and sustained attention are relatively intact, at least in children with average intellectual abilities. Executive functions include at least four components: goal formulation, planning, carrying out goal-directed plans, and effective performance (Lezak 1983, p.507). Executive functions are hypothesized to be under frontal lobe control (Duncan 1986). The majority of research in executive functioning in children with autism has been with high functioning individuals (i.e. Performance IQ scores of 80 or higher). A review of the research suggests weaknesses in cognitive flexibility, verbal reasoning, planning and organization, and self-monitoring (see Liss *et al.* 2001a). In contrast, motor inhibition is thought to be relatively intact (Ozonoff 1997b). Deficits in executive functioning may underlie, in part, behaviors observed in children with autism such as perseverative responding and inflexible adherence to routines. Possible intervention strategies to address attention and executive function deficits in children with autism include:

- reducing unnecessary environmental stimuli
- organizing activities and transitions with visual cues and schedules
- allowing wait time for responding
- teaching self-management programs including independent monitoring of on-task behaviors.

Memory functioning

Memory is described as 'the means by which an organism registers some previous exposure to an event or experience' (Lezak 1983, p.414). Neuropsychological assessment of memory generally includes evaluation of the encoding, retention, immediate and delayed retrieval, and recognition of information. Research suggests that children with autism demonstrate a mixed performance on tests of memory. Rote memory and short-term memory skills tend to be areas of relative strength. In contrast, recall of recent events

(Boucher 1981), inefficient use of encoding and retrieval strategies (Ozonoff 1997b), free recall, and autobiographical memory are areas of relative weakness. Mottron, Morasse and Belleville (2001) pointed out that memory skills in this population appear to be related, in some part, to level of intellectual functioning. Children with high functioning autism may demonstrate intact immediate and delayed recognition of visually presented items, intact delayed non-matching to sample, and intact long-term recognition, cued recall, and new learning, but show deficits in working memory or the encoding of complex verbal information (Dawson 1996). Low functioning children with autism may demonstrate impairments in basic memory functioning, including immediate and delayed recall and recognition, but may retain abilities in rote learning. It can be concluded that memory functioning is highly variable and dependent, in part, on level of intellectual functioning. Suggested intervention strategies (Ozonoff 1997a) that take advantage of areas of strength and address areas of weakness in memory include:

- using concrete visual cues to aid in retrieval of information
- using repetition to teach new skills
- using assignment logs, day planners, and checklists to aid memory.

Language abilities

A review of language skills in children with autism also indicates a mixed profile with some areas preserved and other areas impaired. Impaired social use of language is a core deficit in children with autism, as well as part of the diagnostic criteria. Additionally, 25 per cent of children with autism do not have functional verbal or nonverbal language skills (Bryson, Clark and Smith 1988). Stereotypic use of language, pronoun reversal, echolalia, and idiosyncratic vocalizations characterize many children with autism. In children with autism who use verbal language to communicate, impaired pragmatics, unusual prosody and intonation, poor coordination of spoken language and nonverbal communication (e.g. gestures, eye gaze, facial expressions), and limited use and understanding of figurative language are often reported (Happé and Frith 1996). Communication skills and treatment interventions for children with autism are further discussed in Chapter 6.

Visuospatial skills and motor functioning

Visuospatial, visual organization, and visual matching skills are reported as a cognitive area of strength for this population (Ozonoff 1997a). However, visual-motor integration skills, such as drawing or copying, are often impaired due to fine motor deficits. Gross motor skills are relatively intact, although a significant number of children with autism demonstrate poor posture, hypertonia, and poor bilateral coordination (Bauman 1999). Fine motor skills are often significantly impaired in this population. Motor imitation and execution of skilled motor tasks are also areas of significant difficulty for children with autism (Rapin 1991). Research and treatment interventions in the area of motor functioning are further discussed in Chapter 7.

Adaptive functioning

Adaptive functioning refers to an individual's effectiveness in 'meeting the standards expected for his or her age by his or her cultural group' (*DSM-IV*: APA 1994, p.46). Tests of adaptive functioning, such as the Vineland Adaptive Behavior Scales (Sparrow, Balla and Cicchetti 1984) and the Scales of Independent Behavior – Revised (Bruininks *et al.* 1996), usually evaluate the areas of communication, social skills, and daily living skills. Children with autism demonstrate not only deficits in cognitive functioning, but also deficits in adaptive functioning. However, in contrast to the extensive research in the area of cognitive functioning, there has been little research in the specific correlates of adaptive functioning (Liss *et al.* 2001b). A review of available research indicates that children with autism demonstrate adaptive functioning deficits that exceed their cognitive deficits, and that adaptive social skills are specifically impaired (Liss *et al.* 2001b). Assessment of adaptive functioning is necessary not only for treatment planning, but also as part of the diagnostic criteria for mental retardation.

Conclusion

Identification of a child's neuropsychological pattern of strengths and weaknesses aids in the development of appropriate educational plans and treatment interventions. In addition, neuropsychological research has identified areas of strengths and weaknesses in this population, as well as offering insight into the underlying causes of behaviors observed in children with autism.

Psychological theories of autism

Since the pioneering studies of cognitive functions in children with autism by Hermelin and O'Connor (1970), a host of psychological and neuropsychological theories have been advanced to explain autism. These theories have sought to explain the primary characteristics of autism in terms of a core deficit. Described below are those theories or conceptual frameworks that have generated considerable research since the 1980s. These include theory of mind, executive functions, central coherence, and social impairments.

Theory of mind

The phrase 'theory of mind' refers to the ability to appreciate the mental states (beliefs, desires) of oneself and others; and to understand and predict behavior in terms of these states (Baron-Cohen and Swettenham 1997). Wimmer and Perner (1983) reported that typically developing 4-year-olds are able to predict another person's behavior utilizing information on mental states, as reflected by their performance on a false belief task. In this task, children see a girl (doll) named Sally hide a marble in a basket and then leave the room. Unbeknown to Sally, Anne (another doll) moves the marble to a box. The critical test question in this task is: where will Sally look for the marble? Baron-Cohen, Leslie and Frith (1985) found that, unlike typically developing 4-year-olds or children with Down syndrome, a large majority of children with autism failed this test. This result was taken as evidence for a deficient theory of mind or 'mentalizing' ability, as children with autism failed to make a mental-state-based prediction regarding another person's behavior.

The finding that children with autism are impaired in mentalizing ability has since been supported by results from widely different experimental paradigms. For example, the majority of children with autism do not demonstrate a clear understanding of how physical objects differ from thoughts about objects (Baron-Cohen 1989); they produce a limited range of mental state words in spontaneous speech (Tager-Flusberg 1992); and they fail to recognize that 'seeing leads to knowing' (Leslie and Frith 1988). More importantly, the theory of mind hypothesis has been at least partially successful in accounting for the triad of core impairments (socialization, imagination, and communication) found in autism (Frith 1989). It has also been partially successful in explaining the uneven profiles of abilities commonly found in individuals with autism. For example, the majority of children with autism who have good skills in rote language are often impaired in the social use of language or pragmatics (Tager-Flusberg 1993). In the socialization domain, children with autism are specifically impaired in behaviors that involve mentalizing ability (e.g. taking a hint), whereas they are unimpaired at tasks that do not require this ability (e.g. signaling to come).

Some researchers have challenged the theory of mind account of autism. Russell and his colleagues (Hughes and Russell 1993; Russell, Saltmarsh and Hill 1999) proposed that failure on false belief tasks reflects 'an inability to disengage from the object' (suppression of one's own true belief that the object is in the new location), rather than a deficient mentalizing ability. Researchers have also pointed out that theory of mind and executive function tasks both involve common cognitive processes such as sequential analysis of information and embedded rule use (Ozonoff 1997c). Thus, failure on false belief tasks could be indicative of defective general information processing rather than a modular deficit in mentalizing. Klin and colleagues (Klin 2000; Klin, Volkmar and Sparrow 1992) have argued that even though mentalizing deficits exist in individuals with autism, these deficits are not sufficient to account for social deficits in these individuals. Klin (2000) found that a task devised to measure social attribution discriminated individuals with autism who passed false belief tasks from typical individuals. Thus, false belief tasks were not sufficiently sensitive to detect social deficits in these individuals. Klin *et al.* (1992) reported that early social behaviors that emerge prior to mentalizing ability are also impaired in children with autism. Therefore, deficient mentalizing ability does not appear to account fully for the social impairments in autism.

Executive functioning

Damasio and Maurer (1978) drew a parallel between stereotyped and ritualistic strategies observed in patients with frontal lobe damage and repetitive patterns of behavior found in people with autism. Neuropsychological studies of autism have revealed that individuals with autism are indeed impaired in executive function tasks that involve the prefrontal cortex. Ozonoff, Pennington and Rogers (1991) reported that children with autism of normal intellectual ability were markedly impaired relative to control children on tests measuring planning and set shifting. Ozonoff *et al.* (1993) reported that tests measuring executive function also discriminated between siblings of individuals with autism and siblings of individuals with learning disorders.

It should be noted, however, that executive dysfunction is found in a range of neurodevelopmental disorders, including schizophrenia (Liddle 2000), treated phenylketonuria (PKU) (Diamond *et al.* 1997), Tourette Syndrome (Baron-Cohen and Robertson 1995) and Attention Deficit and Hyperactivity Disorder (ADHD) (Clark, Prior and Kinsella 2000). Given that individuals with these disorders do not have autism, executive dysfunction is neither necessary nor sufficient to produce autistic symptoms. Even though there is evidence that component skills of executive functioning may be selectively impaired in neurodevelopmental disorders (Ozonoff 1997c), a profile of executive dysfunction unique to autism is yet to be determined. Ozonoff and Strayer (1997) reported that children with autism were unimpaired on two tests of inhibition, whereas they were impaired at a test of cognitive flexibility. A comparable pattern of performance is also seen in children with prenatal alcohol exposure (Kodituwakku, Kalberg and May 2001).

Central coherence

Frith (1989) proposed that people with autism show evidence of weak central coherence. Central coherence refers to the normal tendency to extract meaning or the gestalt of a situation in order to process information. This hypothesis attempts to account for not only deficient performance of individuals with autism, but also their exceptionally good performance on specific tasks. For example, individuals with autism perform exceptionally well on tests in which they are able to utilize piecemeal or detail-oriented strategies, for example the Block Design Test and the Embedded Figures Test. However, the piecemeal strategy can hinder their performance on tests such as pronunciation of homographs (i.e. two or more words with the same spelling but different meaning or pronounciation) (Happé 1997), as accurate pronunciation is context dependent. Happé, Briskmann and Frith (2001) found that fathers of boys with autism show evidence of weak coherence as reflected by their piecemeal approach to problem-solving. However, it has not been fully established that people with autism utilize a piecemeal approach to problems across the board. Baron-Cohen and Swettenham (1997) pointed out that children with autism perform in the normal range on a number of tasks that would seem to involve the integration of information (e.g. transitive inference, analogic reasoning).

Social impairments

There exists a vast body of literature on social impairments of people with autism. Hobson (1986) underscored the lack of social relatedness in children with autism. In Hobson's view, failure to coordinate affective perspectives is at the root of the deficient social interactions of autistic children. Hobson, Ousten and Lee (1988) reported that children with autism were impaired relative to controls at cross-modal matching of emotions, but were unimpaired at matching non-emotional stimuli. However, Ozonoff, Pennington and Rogers (1990) failed to find differences between children with autism and normal control children in facial affect identification after adjusting for their verbal ability.

Researchers have also reported that children with autism are impaired in imitation, which is believed to be a precursor to social competence. DeMyer *et al.* (1972) found that individuals with autism were impaired in imitation of both body movements and actions on objects. Hammes and Langdell (1981) reported that children with autism were successful in imitating simple actions, but were impaired in imitating symbolic gestures. Meltzoff and Gopnick (1993) hypothesize a link between early imitation deficits and a failure to develop a theory of mind in children with autism. However, some researchers have failed to find evidence for deficient imitation in children with autism. For example, Charman and Baron-Cohen (1994) found intact gesture and procedural imitation (manipulation of objects) in this population.

There is substantial evidence that children with autism are impaired, relative to control children, in joint attention. Joint attention refers to the sharing of an experience of an object or an event with another person through alternating eye gaze or pointing. An infant pointing at a toy and simultaneously alternating gaze between the toy and the mother is an example of joint attention. Researchers have obtained evidence that children with autism are deficient in their ability to use eye gaze or pointing in a communicative manner (Mundy, Sigman and Kasari 1994). Charman and Baron-Cohen (1994) suggested that joint attention might be a precursor to the theory of mind deficit in autism. The above theories of social impairments in autism do not claim to explain other features associated with autism.

Conclusion

No single psychological theory has been successful in accounting fully for all the features associated with autism. There is an emerging consensus among researchers that a given theory or conceptual framework may sufficiently account for only some domains of the cognitive profile associated with autism. For example, the theory of mind hypothesis seems to explain deficits in socialization, communication, and imagination; the central coherence theory provides a tenable explanation for the piecemeal approach to problem-solving, specifically in perceptual processing; the executive functioning framework accounts for repetitive behaviors and cognitive inflexibility in individuals with autism well; and the theories of social impairments have delineated unique patterns of social dysfunction. Baron-Cohen and Swettenham (1997) raised the question of whether there are subtypes of autism, based on combinations of these deficit patterns (e.g. theory of mind plus executive functioning; theory of mind plus central coherence). If such subtypes of autism exist, then intervention methods can be developed to address specific patterns of difficulties observed in children with autism.

Brain–behavior relationships in autism

Although neuroimaging procedures are not routinely recommended as part of the diagnostic work-up, professionals who work with children with autism should be familiar with the published research regarding brain morphology and physiology. Parents are often aware of the brain-imaging research, but may be unclear of its relevance to their child's treatment. The following review is not meant to be comprehensive, but rather an overview of general findings and possible practical implications of group differences to the development of individual treatment plans.

Researchers have used both neuropathological (brain autopsy) studies and non-invasive neuroimaging (magnetic resonance imaging or MRI) to examine the structure of the brain in the autism population. Neuropathological studies have been limited by the small number of brains that have been examined. Rapin and Katzman (1998) reported that fewer than 35 brains of individuals diagnosed with autism have undergone histological examination, and 'none with state-of-the-art immunocytochemical techniques for synaptic, cytoskeletal, or glial markers' (Rapin and Katzman 1998, p.9). MRI technology allows for in vivo morphometric analysis of the brain, as well as volumetric analysis of specific areas of the brain. Using both of these techniques, two regions of the brain, the cerebellum and the limbic system, have been identified as abnormal in this population. Neuropathological studies have confirmed cerebellar and limbic abnormalities in individuals with autism (Bauman and Kemper 1994). Other brain regions, including the corpus callosum, brainstem, and the parietal lobe, have also been studied, but the results have been inconsistent (Bauman 1999).

Cerebellar findings

The cerebellum is a hindbrain structure with connections to both the vestibular system and the neocortex (for further discussion see Kandel, Schwartz and Jessell 1991; see also Figure 3.1). Damage to the cerebellum has been associated with impaired equilibrium and postural defects, as well as impaired skilled motor movements (Kandell *et al.* 1991). Autopsy evidence from Bauman and Kemper (1985, 1994) suggests significantly reduced numbers of Purkinje neurons in the hemispheres of the cerebellum, predominantly in the postereolateral neocerebellar cortex and the adjacent archicerebellar cortex, without changes in the cerebellar vermis (Kemper and Bauman 1998). The inferior olive, a brainstem structure with neuronal connections to the cerebellum, was found to be essentially intact (Bauman 1999). When taken together, a marked reduction in Purkinje cells but preserved cells in the inferior olive suggests that the etiology of the Purkinji cell loss occurs prior to 30 weeks' gestation.

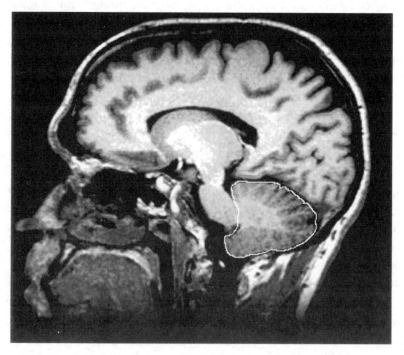

Figure 3.1 MRI scan of the cerebellum

MRI findings of cerebellar abnormalities in autism have not been consistent (for a review, see Bauman 1999). In some of the earliest MRI studies in autism, Courchesne and colleagues (1987, 1988, 1994) reported hypoplasia (i.e. incomplete development) of the neocerebellar vermis (Lobules VI–VII) as measured from a midsaggital slice. On further analyses, Courchesne and colleagues found that while in the majority of cases, the cerebellar vermis was hypoplastic (i.e. smaller) in this population, in a small proportion, it was hyperplastic (i.e. enlarged). They suggested that this finding could account for the lack of significant results in other studies (e.g. Filipek *et al.* 1992; Piven *et al.* 1992).

Bauman (1999) reviewed human and non-human research on the cerebellum and found it to be implicated in cognitive activities such as aspects of language processing, mental imagery, voluntary shifting of attention, and cognitive planning. Bauman notes that 'a growing body of evidence suggests that the cerebellum is important in the regulation of the speed, consistency, and appropriateness of mental and cognitive processes and in the control of motor and sensory information and activity' (Bauman 1999, p.393). Possible behavioral implications of abnormalities in this area include difficulties adjusting attention, following rapidly changing stimuli, responding to instructions, and predicting events. In summary, abnormalities in this brain region likely contribute to the behavioral and cognitive profiles of children with autism. However, the exact relationship between cerebellar abnormalities and autistic behaviors has yet to be determined.

Limbic system findings

The limbic system is comprised in part of the hippocampus, the septum, the cingulate gyrus, and the amygdala (see Figure 3.2). Bauman and Kemper (1994) detected increased cell packing density due to stunted dendritic arbors and small cell bodies in autopsy findings in individuals with autism. These findings were identified in the hippocampus, subiculum, entorhinal cortex, amygdala, mammillary body, anterior cingulate cortex and the septum (Bauman 1999), and are consistent with developmental curtailment.

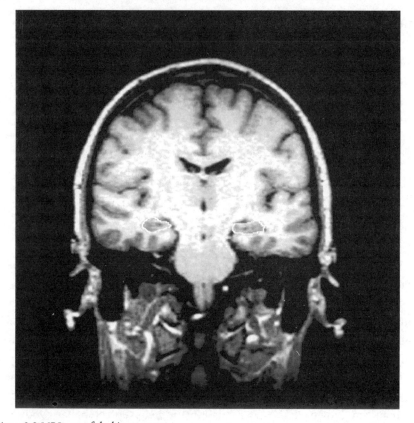

Figure 3.2 MRI scan of the hippocampus

The hippocampus is a gray-tissue area within the medial temporal lobe caudal to the amygdala (Kandel *et al.* 1991). The hippocampus is thought to be an essential component of the declarative memory system. As noted above, histological analyses have identified abnormalities in this structure. However, MRI studies (e.g. Haznedar *et al.* 2000; Piven *et al.* 1998; but also see Aylward *et al.* 1999) have not found consistent abnormal hippocampal volumes in this population. Rapin and Katzman (1998) suggest that an increased number of smaller, tightly packed cells (histological findings) in a typical volume (MRI findings) may result from an increased number of abnormally wired cells. The amygdala is also a gray-tissue area within the medial temporal lobe. The amygdala is thought to be involved critically in emotions. Histological and MRI findings in the amygdala mirror hippocampal findings.

Bauman (1999) reviewed implications of limbic system abnormalities in children with autism through a review of human and non-human animal literature. Lesions in the mesial temporal lobe in non-human animals result in 'pronounced effects on emotion, behavior, motivation, and learning' (Bauman 1999, p.390). Of interest, the animals were noted to engage in 'purposeless hyperactivity, severe impairment in social relatedness, hyperexploratory behavior, and the inability to remember or recognize the significance of visually or manually examined objects' (Bauman 1999, p.391). Additionally, human and non-human primate research supports two hypothesized memory systems: representational memory and habit memory. Representational memory concerns memory of facts, experiences, and events, and is thought to be critically related to intact limbic system, an area noted to be abnormal in children with autism. Habit memory concerns skill learning and is thought to be mediated by the striatum and neocortex, areas thought to be unaffected in this population. Thus, the difficulties in understanding and controlling emotions, learning from experience, and storing, processing, and retrieving information observed in children with autism may be related to early damage to the limbic system.

The study of brain morphology, through neuroimaging and autopsy, and its relationship to cognitive and behavioral profiles in autism, is in its infancy. This exciting field is constantly generating new insights into our understanding of autism. Additionally, other neuroimaging techniques, including functional magnetic resonance imaging (fMRI: Baron-Cohen et al. 1999), positron emission tomography (PET: Haznedar et al. 2000; Zilbovicius et al. 2000), magnetoencephalography (MEG: Lewine et al. under review), and magnetic resonance spectroscopy (MRS: Chugani et al. 1999; Minshew et al. 1993), are providing new insights into autism. An in-depth discussion of these techniques is beyond the scope of this chapter, and the reader is referred to the suggested articles.

Although of interest to many families and professionals working in this field, the implications of group research findings in neuroimaging for the individual child with autism is not clear. Thus, parents and professionals need to exercise caution in requesting extensive neuroimaging studies for children with autism.

Conclusion

Researchers have made significant progress in elucidating the cognitive processes underlying autistic symptoms and the neurobiological basis of these processes. Theoretical debates among researchers have generated new assessment procedures and interesting data. There still exists, however, a wide gap between theory and practice in the field of autism. Perusal of published materials in the popular press and the World Wide Web reveals that parents and teachers are feeling desperate about managing children with autism. There are also numerous success stories about various therapeutic methods. These methods vary from vitamin therapy to behavioral management. Unfortunately, most of these reports are not based on systematic outcome studies. Researchers have also not demonstrated the utility of theories in the development of intervention methods. For example, it is unknown if training in theory of mind or executive control will improve social interaction or communication skills in people with autism.

The foregoing comments are not meant to imply that theories are of limited use for developing intervention methods. Rather, we assert that theories are indeed needed for developing methods of intervention for people with autism. As Kazdin (2001) has elegantly argued, a theory can inform practice in a number of ways. First, theory can explain the mechanisms common to several techniques, thus bringing order and parsimony to the field of interventions for autism. For example, sensory integration, auditory integration, and behavior modification may also involve a single mechanism such as deconditioning. Second, the effectiveness of a treatment may depend on a range of moderator variables (e.g. age, intellectual ability, language etc.). Theory can guide interventions by specifying the way in which moderator variables contribute to the effects of therapy. Third, theory can account for the underlying mechanisms of therapeutic change. For example, in Rapport's (2001) view, neurobiological substrate is presumed to be responsible for the core deficits of a disorder. Rapport's model posits that these core deficits lead to secondary disabilities such as academic difficulties. Therefore, it seems reasonable to conclude that most significant advances in the development of interventions for autism require guidance from sound theories and carefully designed outcome studies.

References

American Psychiatric Association (1994) *Diagnostic and Statistical Manual of Mental Disorders (DSM-IV)*, 4th edn. Washington, DC: APA.

Aylward, E.H., Minshew, N.J., Goldstein, G., Honeycutt, N.A., Augustine, A.M., Yates, K.O., Barta, P.E. and Pearlson, G.D. (1999) 'MRI volumes of amygdala and hippocampus in non-mentally retarded autistic adolescents and adults.' *Neurology 53*, 2145–2150.

Baron-Cohen, S. (1989) 'Are autistic children behaviorists? An examination of their mental–physical and appearance–reality distinctions.' *Journal of Autism and Developmental Disorders 19*, 579–600.

Baron-Cohen, S., Leslie, A.M. and Frith, U. (1985) 'Does the autistic child have a "theory of mind?"' *Cognition 21*, 37–46.

Baron-Cohen, S., Ring, H.A., Wheelwright, S., Bullmore, E.T., Brammer, M.J., Simmons, A. and Williams, S.C. (1999) 'Social intelligence in the normal and autistic brain: an fMRI study.' *European Journal of Neuroscience 11*, 1891–1898.

Baron-Cohen, S. and Robertson, M. (1995) 'Children with either autism, Gilles de la Tourette syndrome or both: mapping cognition to specific syndromes.' *Neurocase 1*, 101–104.

Baron-Cohen, S. and Swettenham, J. (1997) 'Theory of mind in autism: its relationship to executive function and central coherence.' In D.J. Cohen and F.R. Volkmar (eds) *Handbook of Autism and Pervasive Developmental Disorders*, 2nd edn. New York: Wiley.

Bauman, M.L. (1999) 'Autism: clinical features and neurobiological observations.' In H. Tager-Flusberg (ed) *Neurodevelopmental Disorders*. Cambridge, MA: MIT Press.

Bauman, M.L. and Kemper, T.L. (1985) 'Histoanatomic observations of the brain in early infantile autism.' *Neurology 35*, 866–874.

Bauman, M.L. and Kemper, T.L. (1994) *The Neurobiology of Autism*. Baltimore, MD: Johns Hopkins University Press.

Boucher, J. (1981) 'Memory for recent events in autistic children.' *Journal of Autism and Developmental Disorders 11*, 293–301.

Bruininks, R.H., Woodcock, R.W., Weatherman, R.F. and Hill, B.K. (1996) *SIB-R: Scales of Independent Behavior – Revised Comprehensive Manual*. Chicago: Riverside.

Bryson, S.E., Clark, B.S. and Smith, I.M. (1988) 'First report of a Canadian epidemiological study of autistic syndromes.' *Journal of Child Psychology and Psychiatry 29*, 433–445.

Charman, T. and Baron-Cohen, S. (1994) 'Another look at imitation in autism.' *Development and Psychopathology 6*, 403–413.

Chugani, D.C., Sundram, B.S., Behen, M., Lee, M-L. and Moore, G.J. (1999) 'Evidence of altered energy metabolism in autistic children.' *Progress in Neuro-Psychopharmacology and Biological Psychiatry 23*, 4, 635–641.

Clark, C., Prior, M. and Kinsella, G.J. (2000) 'Do executive function deficits differentiate between adolescents with ADHD and oppositional/defiant conduct disorder? A neuropsychological study using the Six Elements Test and Hayling Sentence Completion Test.' *Journal of Abnormal Child Psychology 28*, 403–414.

Cohen, R.A., Malloy, R.F. and Jenkins, M.A. (1998) 'Disorders of attention.' In P.J. Snyder and P.D. Nussbaum (eds) *Clinical Neuropsychology: A Pocket Handbook for Assessment*. Washington, DC: APA.

Courchesne, E., Hesselink, J.R., Jernigan, T.L. and Yeung-Courchesne, R. (1987) 'Abnormal neuroanatomy in a nonretarded person with autism: unusual findings with magnetic resonance imaging.' *Archives of Neurology 44*, 335–341.

Courchesne, E., Saitoh, O., Yeung-Courchesne, R., Press, G.A., Lincoln, A.J., Hass, R.H. and Schreibman, L. (1994) 'Abnormality of cerebellar vermian lobules VI and VII in patients with infantile autism: identification of hypoplastic and hyperplastic subgroups with MR imaging.' *American Journal of Roentgenology 162*, 123–130.

Courchesne, E., Yeung-Courchesne, R., Press, G.A., Hesselink, J.R. and Jernigan, R.L. (1988) 'Hypoplasia of cerebellar vermal lobules VI and VII in autism.' *New England Journal of Medicine 318*, 1349–1354.

Damasio, A.R. and Maurer, R.G. (1978) 'A neurological model of childhood autism.' *Archives of Neurology 35*, 777–786.

Dawson, G. (1996) 'Brief report: neuropsychology of autism: a report on the state of the science.' *Journal of Autism and Developmental Disorders 26*, 179–184.

DeMyer, M.K., Alpern, G.D., Barton, S., DeMyer, W.E., Churchill, D.W., Hingtgen, J.H., Bryson, C.Q., Pontius, W. and Kimberlin, C. (1972) 'Imitation, in autistic, early schizophrenic, and non-psychotic subnormal children.' *Journal of Autism and Childhood Schizophrenia 2*, 264–287.

Diamond, A., Prevor, M.B., Callender, G. and Druin, D.P. (1997) 'Prefrontal cortex cognitive deficits in children treated early and continuously for PKU.' *Monograph of the Society for Research in Child Development 62*, 1–208.

Duncan, J. (1986) 'Disorganization of behavior after frontal lobe damage.' *Cognitive Neuropsychology 3*, 271–290.

Filipek, P.A., Richelme, C., Kennedy, C.N., Rademacher, J., Pitcher, D.A., Zidel, S. and Caviness, V.S. (1992) 'Morphometric analysis of the brain in developmental language disorder and autism.' *Annals of Neurology 32*, 475 (Abstract).

Frith, U. (1989) *Autism: Explaining the Enigma.* Oxford: Basil Blackwell.

Hammes, J.G.W. and Langdell, T. (1981) 'Precursors of symbol formation and childhood autism.' *Journal of Autism and Developmental Disorders 11*, 331–346.

Happé, F. (1997) 'Central coherence and theory of mind in autism: Reading homographs in context.' *British Journal of Developmental Psychology 15*, 1–12.

Happé, F., Briskman, J. and Frith, U. (2001) 'Exploring the cognitive phenotype of autism: weak "central coherence" in parents and siblings of children with autism: 1. experimental tests.' *Journal of Child Psychology and Psychiatry 42*, 299–307.

Happé, F. and Frith, U. (1996) 'The neuropsychology of autism.' *Brain 119*, 1377–1400.

Haznedar, M.M., Buchsbaum, M.S., Wei, T., Hof, P.R., Cartwright, C., Bienstock, C.A. and Hollander, E. (2000) 'Limbic circuitry in patients with autism spectrum disorders studied with positron emission tomography and magnetic resonance imaging.' *American Journal of Psychiatry 157*, 1994–2001.

Hermelin, B. and O'Connor, N. (1970) *Psychological Experiments with Autistic Children.* Oxford: Pergamon.

Hobson, R.P. (1986) 'The autistic child's appraisal of expression of emotion.' *Journal of Child Psychology and Psychiatry 27*, 321–342.

Hobson, R.P., Ousten, J. and Lee, A. (1988) 'What is in a face? The case of autism.' *British Journal of Psychology 79*, 441–453.

Hughes, C. and Russell, J. (1993) 'Autistic children's difficulty with mental disengagement from an object: its implications for theories of autism.' *Developmental Psychology 29*, 498–510.

Kandel, E.R., Schwartz, J.H. and Jessell, T.M. (1991) *Principles of Neural Science,* 3rd edn. Norwalk, CT: Appleton and Lange.

Kazdin, A.E. (2001) 'Bridging the enormous gaps of theory with therapy research and practice.' *Journal of Clinical Child Psychology 30*, 59–66.

Kemper, T.L. and Bauman, M. (1998) 'Neuropathology of infantile autism.' *Journal of Neuropathology and Experimental Neurology 57*, 645–652.

Klin, A. (2000) 'Attributing social meaning to ambiguous visual stimuli in higher-functioning autism and Asperger syndrome: the Social Attribution Task.' *Journal of Child Psychology and Psychiatry 41*, 831–846.

Klin, A., Volkmar, F.R. and Sparrow, S.S. (1992) 'Autistic social dysfunction: some limitations of the theory of mind hypothesis.' *Journal of Child Psychology and Psychiatry 33*, 861–876.

Kodituwakku, P.W., Kalberg, W. and May, P.A. (2001) 'The effects of prenatal alcohol exposure on executive functioning.' *Alcohol Research and Health 25*, 192–198.

Leslie, A.M. and Frith, U. (1988) 'Autistic children's understanding of seeing, knowing, and believing.' *British Journal of Developmental Psychology 6*, 315–324.

Lewine, J.D., Provencal, S., Hill, D., Davis, J., Funke, M., Huang, M., Thoma, R., Orrison, W., Johnson, M., Paulson, K., Hatch, K. and Detmers, D. (under review) 'Magnetic source imaging of epileptiform activity in autism: developmental delay versus regressive profiles.'

Lezak, M.D. (1983) *Neuropsychological Assessment*, 2nd edn. New York: Oxford University Press.

Liddle, P.F. (2000) 'Cognitive impairment in schizophrenia: its impact on social functioning.' *Acta Psychiatrica Scandinavica Supplementum 400*, 11–16.

Liss, M., Fein, D., Allen, D., Dunn, M., Feinstein, C., Morris, R., Waterhouse, L. and Rapin, I. (2001a) 'Executive functioning in high-functioning children with autism.' *Journal of Child Psychology and Psychiatry 42*, 261–270.

Liss, M., Harel, B., Fein, D., Allen, D., Dunn, M., Feinstein, C., Morris, R., Waterhouse, L. and Rapin, I. (2001b) 'Predictors and correlates of adaptive functioning in children with developmental disorders.' *Journal of Autism and Developmental Disorders 31*, 2, 219–230.

Maurer, R. (1997) *Report to the NIH Autism Coordinating Committee: Directions for Future Research.* Washington, DC: National Institutes of Health.

Meltzoff, A.N. and Gopnick, A. (1993) 'The role of imitation in understanding persons and developing theories of mind.' In S. Baron-Cohen, H. Tager-Flusberg and D. Cohen (eds) *Understanding Other Minds: Perspectives from Autism.* Oxford: Oxford University Press.

Minshew, N.J., Goldstein, G., Dombrowski, S.M., Panchalingam, K. and Pettegrew, J.W. (1993) 'Preliminary −3-1P MRS study of autism: evidence for undersynthesis and increased degradation of brain membranes.' *Biological Psychiatry 33*, 762–773.

Mottron, L., Morasse, K. and Belleville, S. (2001) 'A study of memory functioning in individuals with autism.' *Journal of Child Psychology and Psychiatry 42*, 253–260.

Mundy, P., Sigman, M. and Kasari, C. (1994) 'Joint attention, developmental level, and symptom presentation in autism.' *Development and Psychopathology 6*, 389–401.

Ozonoff, S. (1997a) Neuropsychological Assessment and Treatment Strategies. Presented at the Eighteenth Annual TEACCH Conference, May.

Ozonoff, S. (1997b) 'Components of executive functioning in autism and other disorders.' In J. Russell (ed) *Autism as an Executive Disorder.* New York: Oxford University Press.

Ozonoff, S. (1997c) 'Causal mechanisms of autism: unifying perspectives from an information-processing framework.' In D.J. Cohen and F.R. Volkmar (eds) *Handbook of Autism and Pervasive Developmental Disorders*, 2nd edn. New York: Wiley.

Ozonoff, S., Pennington, B.F. and Rogers, S.J. (1990) 'Are there emotion perception deficits in young autistic children?' *Journal of Child Psychology and Psychiatry 31*, 343–361.

Ozonoff, S., Pennington, B.F. and Rogers, S.J. (1991) 'Executive function deficits in high-functioning autistic individuals: relationship to theory of mind.' *Journal of Child Psychology and Psychiatry 32*, 1081–1105.

Ozonoff, S., Rogers, S.J., Farnham, J.M. and Pennington, B.F. (1993) 'Can standard measures identify subclinical markers of autism?' *Journal of Autism and Developmental Disorders 23*, 429–441.

Ozonoff, S. and Strayer, D.L. (1997) 'Inhibitory function in nonretarded children with autism.' *Journal of Autism and Developmental Disorders 27*, 59–77.

Piven, J., Bailey, J., Ranson, B.J. and Arndt, S. (1998) 'No differences in hippocampus volume detected on magnetic resonance imaging in autistic individuals.' *Journal of Autism and Developmental Disorders 28*, 105–110.

Piven, J., Nehme, E., Simon, J., Barta, P., Pearlson, G. and Folstein, S.F. (1992) 'Magnetic resonance imaging in autism: measurement of the cerebellum, pons, and fourth ventricle.' *Biological Psychiatry 31*, 491–504.

Rapin, I. (1991) 'Autistic children: diagnosis and clinical features.' *Pediatrics 87* (suppl.), 473–500.

Rapin, I. and Katzman, R. (1998) 'Neurobiology of autism.' *Annals of Neurology 43*, 7–14.

Rapport, M.D. (2001) 'Bridging theory and practice: conceptual understanding of treatments for children with attention deficit hyperactivity disorder (ADHD), obsessive-compulsive disorder (OCD), autism, and depression.' *Journal of Clinical Child Psychology 30*, 3–7.

Roid, G.H. and Miller, L.J. (1997) *Leiter International Performance Scale – Revised Examiners' Manual.* Wood Dale, IL: Stoelting.

Russell, J., Saltmarsh, R. and Hill, E. (1999) 'What do executive factors contribute to the failure on false belief tasks by children with autism?' *Journal of Child Psychology and Psychiatry 40*, 859–868.

Schopler, E., Reichler, R.J., Bashford, A., Lansing, M.D. and Marcus, L.M. (1990) *Individualized Assessment and Treatment for Autistic and Developmentally Disabled Children: Volume 1 – Psychoeducational Profile – Revised (PEP-R).* Austin, TX: PRO-ED.

Sparrow, S.S., Balla, D.A. and Cicchetti, D.V. (1984) *Vineland Adaptive Behavior Scales.* Circle Pines, MN: American Guidance Service.

Tager-Flusberg, H. (1992) 'Autistic children's talk about psychological states: deficits in the early acquisition of a theory of mind.' *Child Development 63*, 161–172.

Tager-Flusberg, H. (1993) 'What language reveals about the understanding of minds in children with autism.' In S. Baron-Cohen and H. Tager-Flusberg (eds) *Understanding Other Minds: Perspectives from Autism.* Oxford: Oxford University Press.

Wimmer, H. and Perner, J. (1983) 'Beliefs about beliefs: representation and constraining function of wrong beliefs in young children's understanding of deception.' *Cognition 13*, 103–128.

Zilbovicius, M., Boddaert, N., Belin, P., Poline, J-B., Remy, P., Mangin, J-F., Thivard, L., Barthelemy, C. and Samson, Y. (2000) 'Temporal lobe dysfunction in childhood autism: a PET study.' *American Journal of Psychiatry 157*, 1988–1993.

CHAPTER 4

Medical Aspects of Childhood Autism

Edward Goldson

The much-needed integration of clinical, genetic, neuropsychological, and neurobiological perspectives in autism may at last be on the horizon. (Rutter 1999, p.181)

Childhood autism is one of the more common behavioral disorders encountered in pediatrics. In the past it was considered to be a rare disorder, but current figures place its prevalence at one or two in a thousand live births (Fombonne 1999; Gillberg and Coleman 2000). Historically, it was considered to be a purely psychiatric disorder, as first described by Leo Kanner in the 1940s (Kanner 1943). More recently it has been stripped of its psychiatric imprimatur and etiology and is now considered to be a neurodevelopmental disorder: 'autism is a behavioral symptom constellation signaling underlying nervous system dysfunction' (Aicardi 1998, p.827). Another way of describing autism is that it is a 'disorder of brain development with a strong genetic basis' (American Academy of Pediatrics (AAP) 2001, p.1221). Although autism is considered to be a neurologic disorder, it is nevertheless described in behavioral terms. Drawing on the classification in the fourth edition of the *Diagnostic and Statistical Manual of Mental Disorders* (*DSM-IV*: APA 2000), children with autism are characterized as having three core impairments that are manifested in a multitude of behaviors. These impairments are well characterized in the manual and are discussed and described in other chapters of this book. They include qualitative impairments in social interaction, qualitative impairments in communication, and restricted, repetitive, and stereotyped patterns of behavior, interests, and activities. Wing and Gould (1979) condensed these three disturbances into what they call the

triad of social impairment or the triad of social, communication, and imagination impairments (Wing's triad).

The focus of this chapter is the discussion of the medical aspects of
childhood autism. The chapter will cover some of the theories of autism
etiology, the genetics of the disorder, and medical problems associated with
autism, as well as some strategies for medical management, including psycho-
pharmacological interventions and alternative methods of treatment. This
chapter also emphasizes the fact that children with autism *are* children; they
have the same needs as typical children. Finally, it is proposed that the
management of children with autism must incorporate collaboration between
medicine and allied disciplines.

Theories of the etiology of autism

There are a number of theories postulated for the cause of autism. Central to
the issue is the presence of a genetic disturbance. There may be any number of
defective genes that influence brain development, signaling, transport or cell
structure. But to date, no pathognomonic abnormality has been identified. It
is apparent from reports in the literature and clinical experience that the
spectrum of cognitive and emotional disturbances seen in children with
autism is suggestive of a disorder of interneuronal communication affecting
the neural networks that mediate social, cognitive, and language-based
behavior (Johnston 2000; Johnston and Harum 1999). Moreover, it is clear
that autism is neurologically based given that abnormalities in the mesial and
limbic cortical systems, in the frontal lobes and the cerebellum have been
identified in neuropathological studies (Rapin and Katzman 1998; see also
Chapter 3). It has also been noted that there is a greater incidence of
macrocephaly among children with autism as compared with the general
population and even to children with tuberous sclerosis, suggesting a
disturbance in brain maturation (Fidler, Bailey and Smalley 2000). Moreover,
there is a higher prevalence of macrocephaly in the first-degree relatives of
children suggesting a strong genetic component to autism. Having said this,
the question remains as to what are the more peripheral or physiologic
mechanisms leading to what is recognized as genetic autism, as opposed to
autism associated with specific chromosomal or metabolic disturbances.

Immunologic theory

It is suggested that the immune system plays a significant role in the pathogenesis of autism. Proponents of this theory maintain that there are perturbations in the immune system of children with autism. They suggest that mechanisms other than inflammation can lead to disturbances in the central nervous system (CNS) such as the production of cytokines and disorders of apoptosis. Opponents of this position note that there is no evidence for an inflammatory response which, it is maintained, would need to be present if there was an immunologic basis for autism. Needless to say there is much debate and ongoing research to determine the role of the immune system in autism (Gupta 2000).

Metabolic theory

Another mechanism that has been invoked as leading to autism is disturbances in metabolic pathways, often termed metabolic autism. There are a number of metabolic disorders that are associated with autistic-like features, but they differ from classical autism. These disorders include phenyl-ketonuria, disorders of purine metabolism and associated hyperuricosuria and nucleotidase-associated pervasive developmental disorder in which there is increased cellular purine and pyrimidine 5' nucleotidase activity (Page 2000a). A leap is then made that there may be forms of autism in which 'the genetic mechanism of transcriptional dysregulation can produce pathologic phenotypes that resemble metabolic disorders that stunt axonodentritic development, as well as psychomotor regression in the absence of true degeneration' (Page 2000b, p.472). On the other hand, metabolic abnormalities may simply be epiphenomena related to other genetic abnormalities unrelated to autism. This is an area that remains unclear and warrants intensive research.

Vitamin deficiency theory

Vitamin deficiencies have been postulated to cause autism. Research has been conducted on the use of pyridoxine in conjunction with magnesium as a treatment for autism. In some patients there seems to have been some improvement, although no specific vitamin deficiencies have been identified (Page 2000a). The mechanism for the positive responses remains unclear.

When considering the nutritional aspects of autism, dietary interventions also have been advocated to treat autism. It is postulated that certain proteins produce toxic peptides that can lead to autism. This view may have as a parallel the treatment of phenylketonuria, a metabolic disorder in which certain metabolic products are toxic to the central nervous system and is treatable with dietary restrictions. It is recognized that treatment of autism-associated phenylketonuria can prevent the autistic behaviors and mental retardation. Consequently, some researchers have proposed the use of other dietary manipulations, namely a low casein or gluten diet or both for the treatment of autism. In some circumstances this intervention has been found to be effective, but this is generally not the case. A somewhat similar perspective suggests an increase in gut permeability among children with autism. Thus, it is suggested that passage of toxic substances from the gut to the circulation can lead to autism and that by altering the diet one may be able to treat autism.

There are other hypotheses concerning the metabolic or gut association with autism. Unfortunately, the data remain unclear. Page (2000b) suggests that a more productive approach to assessing the metabolic basis of autism would be to identify a population of children with genetic autism (i.e. those children without any clearly defined underlying metabolic or chromosomal disorder) and perform a comprehensive metabolic evaluation in order to identify whether there are specific metabolic abnormalities common to these children and then treating and monitoring them. To date, no published research is available to answer these questions.

Genetics of autism

Although autism is described as if it were a single or unitary entity, the reality is that autism is a heterogeneous disorder with core genetic components (APA 1994). All children with autism demonstrate some degree of the behavioral disturbances described above, but there are qualitative and quantitative differences in the symptomatology. Consequently, autism is indeed a spectrum disorder with multiple etiologies. In the simplest and perhaps most complex formulation of the disorder, one can appreciate a powerful genetic component as well as what might be considered non-genetic contributors, such as infection and adverse perinatal events.

Among the major strategies for looking at the genetic component of autism are twin studies. Although there are differences in opinion in the literature, the consensus seems to be that there is significant concordance of symptoms between monozygotic (MZ) twins and very limited concordance between dizygotic (DZ) twins or siblings. However, there is an increased risk among family members in general, for autism. There is a 3 per cent to 7 per

.cent recurrence for isolated autism that represents a 50- to 100-fold increase in risk for siblings of children with autism as compared with children in the general population. Moreover, in the family histories of children with autism there is a considerable increase in the occurrence of cognitive and social disorders. Specific cognitive disabilities involve speech, language, and reading. What is of interest is that even among discordant MZ twins, cognitive and social deficits have been observed in the twin without autism but to a lesser degree, even in the presence of normal intelligence. Thus, an autism phenotype has been postulated that includes social characteristics, such as a lack of empathy, rapport, and emotional responsiveness, hypersensitivity, and single-minded pursuit of special interests and communication difficulties, including pragmatic deficiencies, over-communicativeness and under-communicativeness, excessive guardedness, and disinhibition. This phenotype differs from the traditional phenotype of autism in that there is a lack of non-pragmatic language features (echolalia, reversal of pronouns), less striking stereotypies and lack of an association with epilepsy (Rutter *et al.* 1997).

To date there is no clearly defined gene for autism. Indeed, most researchers in the field believe that the genetic component is multifocal and that many genes may be implicated in the etiology of autism. Nevertheless, there are numerous genetic disorders that are associated with autism. Indeed, with the exception of chromosome 14, disorders involving the remainder of the chromosomes have been reported to have some association with autism (Gillberg and Coleman 2000). Included in this list are conditions such as the fragile X syndrome, Rett's disorder, tuberous sclerosis, neurofibromatosis, and hypomelanosis of Ito, among others. One study noted a deletion on chromosome 15 in an autistic patient (Smith *et al.* 2000). Another report from a register-based study in Denmark identified a number of autosomal chromosome abnormalities associated with autism or autistic-like behaviors (Lauritsen *et al.* 1999).

The central discussions concerning the genetics of autism revolve around whether there is genetic heterogeneity. There is a general consensus that in genetic autism, namely that disorder not associated with a specific chromosomal abnormality, there is heterogeneity and that probably multiple genes are involved. The other issue concerns whether there are autism-specific factors (Rutter *et al.* 1997) or autism is no more than a final common pathway for a heterogeneous group of etiological processes (Gillberg, Gillberg and Steffenburg 1992). There are strong arguments that suggest there are autism-specific factors. Nevertheless, on this point there appears to be ongoing debate and it remains an area open for much further research.

Medical issues

Medical conditions overview

Major medical issues for professional consideration include the identification of other syndromes associated with autism. These associations introduce the concept of the double syndromes (Gillberg and Coleman 2000), namely, the presence of a known syndrome and the presence of autism or dual diagnosis. This is a useful formulation in that it directs the clinician to think broadly in the evaluation of children falling into the autism spectrum disorders. Other issues to consider include seizure disorders and the identification of cognitive and sensorimotor deficits. Another medical problem, not mentioned in reports on practice parameters, is gastrointestinal disturbances. Finally, case coordination, support and counseling are central to the pediatric care of the child with autism (American Academy of Pediatrics 2001).

There are perhaps two ways of viewing or addressing the medical aspects of childhood autism that might to be considered. First, clinicians need to consider conditions that may be associated with autism (double syndromes) and second, they need to evaluate the child for medical problems that may accompany autism. Steffenburg (1991), in a population-based study, found that the overwhelming majority of children meeting the criteria for autism had some associated brain abnormality. Based on this study Steffenburg identified several possible etiology groups including those with:

- non-specific signs of brain damage such as children with abnormal electroencephalograms (EEGs), computerized axial tomography (CAT/CT) scans, and epilepsy
- hereditary disorders such as fragile X syndrome and tuberous sclerosis
- other specific brain damage syndromes such as other chromosomal syndromes or Moebius syndrome
- other hereditary conditions such as Asperger syndrome
- no known associated brain damage or genetic factors.

Gillberg and Coleman (1996) reviewed the population studies in the English language and found that an average of 24.4 per cent of individuals with autism had associated medical conditions. Also included were syndromes and organic conditions (e.g. maternal rubella), neurocutaneous syndromes (e.g. tuberous sclerosis and neurofibromatosis), chromosomal abnormalities (e.g. fragile X syndrome and Williams syndrome), Rett's disorder, encephalitis and meningitis. Because of these associations it is recommended that any child meeting the criteria for autism deserves not only a complete developmental and psychological assessment, but also a comprehensive medical examination. This evaluation should include a meticulous physical examination (to identify neurocutaneous disorders, dysmorphic features, etc.), high resolution chromosomal analysis, fluorescent *in situ* hybridization (FISH) testing to rule out 15q duplication (a duplication of genetic material on the long arm of chromosome 15), DNA testing for fragile X syndrome, lead levels if there has been a history of pica, an EEG (for subclinical epilepsy), and a comprehensive metabolic evaluation, if indicated, along with ophthalmologic and auditory assessments (Aicardi 1998; Filipek *et al.* 1999; Gillberg and Coleman 2000; Mars, Mauk and Dowrick 1998). Some professionals suggest cerebral spinal fluid analysis (for encephalitis or progressive encephalopathies) although there is debate as to whether this study should be performed under all circumstances.

A thorough discussion of children with double syndromes, such as having autism and fragile X syndrome, is beyond the scope of this chapter but is covered in a number of textbooks and papers dealing with children with these syndromes (e.g. Gillberg and Coleman 2000; Hagerman 1999). Thus, the remainder of this chapter will focus on children who meet the criteria for autism, without other syndromes or conditions. In and of themselves, these children present many medical challenges.

Seizure disorders

Kanner (1943) in his original paper on children with autism identified a child with seizures and in his later follow-up study identified two children with seizures (Kanner 1971). Thus, seizures have been associated with autism from the inception of our recognition of this disorder and continue to play an important role in the lives of these children and their families. It has been recognized for some time that children with autism, independent of other associated medical conditions, are at increased risk for having seizures. About one-third of children with autism have some form of seizure disorder by adulthood (Rapin 1997) with a range, depending on the study, between 7 per cent and 42 per cent. Also of interest is the age distribution in the presentation of seizures with peaks in early childhood and in adolescence (Tuchman

2000). However, there is no one specific seizure type associated with autism (Gillberg and Coleman 2000). Rather, many patterns of seizures are seen in individuals with autism, including infantile spasms, atonic seizures, myoclonic seizures, atypical absence, complex partial seizures and generalized tonic-clonic seizures. Also, most known electro-encephalographic patterns are also found in this group of patients. Thus, there is no one specific treatment of these individuals. Instead, the seizure type needs to be identified and the appropriate anti-epileptic medication prescribed. As many of these children are quite complex and have other behavioral issues, the approach toward management should be interdisci-plinary and should, of course, include a neurologist as well as a primary care physician and mental health workers. It should also be remembered that in a small number of children with autism there is a metabolic etiology for the seizure disorder that should also be evaluated and appropriately treated (Page 2000b).

There are other conditions and circumstances that complicate the diagnosis and treatment of seizures in children with autism. Approximately one-third of parents of toddlers with autism report regression in language, sociability, play, and often cognition (Rapin 1995). The regression may be of an acute onset or may take place over a prolonged period of time with some spontaneous recovery, but rarely to the baseline level of functioning (Rapin 1995). Why this occurs is unknown, but it has been associated in a significant number of circumstances with an environmental stress such as a benign intercurrent illness, trivial physical trauma, the sudden absence of the mother or even moving the household (Rapin 1995). In a very small portion of children the regression has been associated with clinical seizures or a paroxysmal EEG or even status epilepticus in slow wave sleep (Gillberg and Coleman 2000). There continues to be debate as to the direct association between autistic regression and the presence of an abnormal EEG.

It is generally agreed upon that clinical seizures need to be treated, but it is unclear as to whether subclinical seizures should also be treated. When treatment is instituted it should be directed toward controlling the seizures and not toward necessarily improving the behavioral, cognitive, or linguistic regression. There may indeed be improvement in these domains, but the changes are probably the result of the seizure control and not any specific effect on the autism (Gillberg and Coleman 2000). There are fairly reasonable arguments suggesting that seizures are not the precipitating event for the regression, but are a reflection of the underlying neuropathology responsible for the cognitive and behavioral impairments as well (Rapin 1998). Of note, there is a much higher incidence of seizures and autistic regression among children with mental retardation than those with greater cognitive abilities (Tuchman and Rapin 1997). Finally, it should be recognized that autistic regression is not a particular risk factor for seizures.

An area of confusion is the association between what is known as the Landau-Kleffner syndrome (LKS) and autism (Landau and Kleffner 1957). LKS is a known, rare epileptic syndrome in which clinical seizures are not necessarily part of the diagnosis. Instead, there is an association between acquired aphasia and an epileptiform EEG demonstrating spikes or spike and wave discharges over the temporal and parietal brain regions. The clinical presentation and course of LKS is very different from that of epilepsy in children with autism or autistic regression, or both. In LKS the language regression starts later in childhood and may be more dramatic in onset. These children retain their social awareness, use of gestures and measured cognitive abilities. Also, they continue to retain their interest in toys, interactive games and imaginative play, as compared with children with autism (Mantovani 2000; Rapin 1995; Tuchman 2000). The EEG pattern is characterized by a centro-temporal spike while in autism the foci are more diffuse. Thus, LKS should not be confused with childhood autism and treatment strategies employed in LKS should not be generalized to the treatment of autistic regression (Mantovani 2000; Tuchman 2000). LKS and autistic regression are different entities, although it is worth including them, along with disintegrative epileptic regression under the umbrella term of acquired epileptiform aphasias (Tuchman 1997). This term acknowledges the electrophysiological similarities while still distinguishing the clinical characteristics of each entity (Mantovani 2000).

Gastrointestinal (GI) symptoms

GI symptoms have been associated with childhood autism (Quigley and Hurley 2000). There are often complaints of constipation, flatus or diarrhea. One entity that has been discussed is the autism/steatorrhea syndrome (Gillberg and Coleman 2000). No clear etiology for this disorder has been identified and there is no growth failure associated with the symptoms. At one time celiac disease was considered to be one possible cause for autism, but there has been no clear evidence for its association with autism. Nevertheless, numerous attempts have been made to treat this disorder as if it caused autism.

Elimination diets have been attempted, none of which have been clearly efficacious in the treatment of autism.

Wakefield and colleagues (1998) described several children with lymphoid nodular hyperplasia which, they proposed, was unique to autism. This has not been borne out by subsequent studies (Quigley and Hurley 2000). Nevertheless, the debate continues with the suggestion that there is evidence for gut epithelial dysfunction in autism (Furlano *et al.* 2001). The outcome of this discussion remains to be seen. Wakefield and colleagues also suggested that the lymphoid nodular hyperplasia was associated with the measles, mumps and rubella (MMR) vaccine. This association has been disavowed by a number of studies both in the United States and in the United Kingdom (Dales, Hammer and Smith 2001; Halsey *et al.* 2001; Taylor, Miller and Farrington 1999). Unfortunately, there are groups in both countries that have advocated for not immunizing children against these illnesses in order to prevent autism. This is a disturbing turn of events, as no association between immunization and autism has been demonstrated and children are placed at risk for contracting these diseases with all of the potential complications associated with these viral illnesses. Thus, the consensus is that children should continue to be immunized and that there is no association between autism and the MMR immunization.

Horvath and colleagues (1999) studied a group of children with autism with a variety of GI complaints including abdominal pain, chronic diarrhea, gaseous/bloating, and unexplained nighttime awakening. They found a significant number of these children had reflux esophagitis, disaccharide malabsorption and gastric and duodenal inflammation. These GI disorders are also found in children with other neurologic disorders and so it is difficult to determine how specific the findings are to children with autism. Nevertheless, these are signs and symptoms commonly seen in children with autism and need to be clinically managed.

These and previous findings have led to speculation as to the role played by secretin in contributing to these GI symptoms, as well as the etiologic role of secretin, a gut polypetide involved in digestion, in the neuropathology of autism. Horvath and colleagues (1998) reported that children with autism demonstrated dramatic improvements in language, social interaction, and cognitive functioning following the infusion of porcine-derived secretin. Subsequently, a number of double-blind, controlled studies have not demonstrated any positive effect with the use of secretin (Dunn-Geier *et al.* 2000; Owley *et al.* 1999; Roberts *et al.* 2001; Sandler *et al.* 1999). Thus, currently, secretin is not considered to be a treatment for autism. It must be acknowledged, however, that continued research is still indicated to determine whether there is a relationship between gastrointestinal and central nervous system polypetides and autism.

Mental retardation

There is a strong association between mental retardation and autism, independent of the presence of other syndromes. Between 67 and 88 per cent, depending on the study, of children with autism are also mentally retarded (Gillberg and Coleman 2000; Nordin and Gillberg 1996; Rapin 1997). There is a strong association between mental retardation, seizures, and motor difficulties. The question remains as to what are the mechanisms leading to mental retardation and why it occurs in some children with autism and not others.

Hearing impairment

For some unknown reason there is a higher incidence of hearing impairment among children with autism as compared with the general population. In a study of 1150 students assessed at a school for deaf children, 46 children met the criteria for autism. Of this group 50 per cent had known causes for the loss, including congenital rubella, pre-term birth, bacterial meningitis and malformation syndromes. The cause in the remainder was unknown in 37 per cent and genetic in 13 per cent (Jure, Rapin and Tuchman 1991).

In another study in Sweden, 199 children with autistic disorder were audiologically evaluated (Rosenhall *et al.* 1999). Mild to moderate sensorineural hearing loss was identified in 7.9 per cent of the children, unilateral hearing loss was identified in 1.9 per cent and pronounced to profound hearing loss was identified in 3.5 per cent of cases, with a total of 13.3 per cent of the population having some form of sensorineural hearing loss. In addition, 23.5 per cent of the population had serous otitis media, of whom 18.3 per cent had conductive hearing loss.

Children with autism are not an easy population to evaluate. Often the usual behavioral measures employed to assess hearing cannot be performed. Regardless of this difficulty, all children with autism should have their hearing tested, as early as is possible. The most effective and reliable measure is the auditory brainstem response (ABR) examination. In this procedure children are presented with several distinct tones. Their response to these tones is an electrical pattern in the brain, which is measured using an electroencephalogram. The nature and degree of hearing loss can be quite accurately determined with this method and appropriate interventions then utilized.

Co-morbid conditions

There are a number of co-morbid psychiatric conditions associated with autism including affective disorders, obsessive compulsive disorder, anxiety and attention deficit and hyperactivity disorder (ADHD). In this section, ADHD will be discussed as it is one of the most common problems presented to the pediatrician. A detailed discussion of the treatment of all these disorders is beyond the scope of this chapter. Thus, several reviews addressing the pharmacologic treatment of children with autism and co-morbid psychiatric disorders are recommended to the reader for further reference (Aman *et al.* 1995; Gilman and Tuchman 1995; McDougle, Price and Volkmar 1994).

Attention deficit and hyperactivity disorder

The exact incidence of ADHD among children with autism is unknown. Aman and colleagues (1995) reviewed the literature and found that about 12 per cent of children with autism spectrum disorders (ASD) were treated with stimulant medications, suggesting that this constellation of symptoms is frequently identified and treated with drugs. However, there is a paucity of research about the efficacy of these medications in ameliorating ADHD symptoms (King 2000). Aman and Langworthy (2000) reviewed the literature on pharmacotherapy for hyperactivity in children with autism and found some evidence to support the efficacy of the use of stimulants and naltrexone. Campbell and colleagues (1993) and Kolmen and colleagues (1995) found that naltrexone improved attention and decreased hyperactivity, but had little effect on the core symptoms of autism. One of the side-effects of naltrexone was mild sedation. Consequently, it remains somewhat unclear whether the symptom control was the result of sedation or of some other effect. Nevertheless, naltrexone should be included in the pharmacologic armamentarium in the treatment of ADHD symptoms among child with autism. Handen, Johnson and Lubetsry (2000) performed a double-blind study using methylphenidate to treat ADHD symptoms and found some improvement in behavior. However, they also noted significant negative side-effects including increases in lethargy, irritability, stereotypy, hyperactivity, and inappropriate speech. Thus, there is a cost/benefit ratio to be considered when using this or any other drug (i.e. there may be positive effects in one behavioral domain with the risk of negative effects elsewhere). Furthermore, it is almost impossible to predict how the individual child will respond. Nevertheless, the consensus seems to be that this medication should also be included in the treatment armamentarium with the recognition that there is the risk of adverse effects and that the drug may need to be discontinued. Finally, there is a degree of trial and error in the use of this or any psychotropic medication with this population; these medications should be prescribed and closely monitored by a physician with expertise in the care of children with autism.

Treatment: medications, behavioral interventions, and alternative treatments

There are numerous treatments for children with autism. One approach to management has been pharmacological treatment. For example, Fluoxetine has been found to be somewhat effective for some children (DeLong, Teague and Kamran 1998). Serotonin reuptake inhibitors have also been found to be helpful for some children (McDougle, Kresch and Posey 2000). However, the major focus for most, if not all, children in this population is behavioral intervention, based on what is understood of the neuropsychology of children with autism (see Chapter 2). It is recognized that the earlier the diagnosis is made, the sooner interventions can be instituted. With early intervention, the more likely there will be a more positive outcome (see also other chapters in this volume). But behavioral interventions take time and children with autism can be difficult to care for and their behaviors may be disruptive to their families, schools, and communities. Consequently, there are enormous stresses, and frequently there is the urge for parents to move away from conventional and more rigorously evaluated treatments and towards alternative treatments. As physicians often do not fully understand autism or the stresses families are under, they may not be responsive to parents' needs and requests. Consequently parents may reach out to or respond to promises of non-traditional or alternative therapies in the hope that their child might be 'cured' or at least helped (Nickel 1996).

Over the years, there have been numerous alternative drugs and therapies that have been touted as 'the treatment' for autism. Gerlach (1998) assembled a guide of autism treatments that includes 12 known complementary or controversial therapies. Some of these therapies have been evaluated and have been found not to be effective (Nickel 1996; Silver 1995), while others have never been rigorously tested. Needless to say, there are and will be new 'therapies' that emerge to which desperate parents will gravitate. Currently, the use of secretin is one such therapy (see the section on gastrointestinal symptoms above) and there has also been increasing interest in immunological therapies. To date, secretin has not been found to be effective, and other immunological therapies are currently under investigation (Gupta 2000). Finally, it is important that clinicians be aware of these therapies, understand or are willing to learn about them and be willing to listen to and support families as they grapple with decisions about whether or not to embark on such interventions (Committee on Children with Disabilities 2001; Hyman and Levy 2000).

Conclusion

Children with autism represent a spectrum of very complex disorders. Even setting aside those children with double diagnoses, there is a broad range of clinical findings including a broad range of associated medical conditions within this population. This is what makes these children so unique and separates them from children who have other neurodevelopmental disorders. In this chapter, medical issues have been discussed including seizures, gastrointestinal disorders, hearing loss, mental retardation, and ADHD, all of which occur more commonly among children with autism than in the general population. However, practitioners must never forget that children with autism have the same health needs as typically developing children as well as similar medical problems encountered among typical children. They get colds, they can get pneumonia, and they may have illnesses affecting other organ systems, just as do other children. It is important that they receive the same kind of medical surveillance as do other children, and that they are not treated differently from other children. They should be immunized, their weight, linear growth, and head circumference should be monitored, and they should receive the same basic health care received by other children.

Having stated the above, professionals need to remember, however, that these children have special needs. The comprehensive evaluation of a child with autism requires a multidisciplinary team with the ability and expertise to evaluate children with special needs. However, the medical care of such children still falls to the physician and requires skill, knowledge, and resources. In order to meet these needs and those of the family, an interdisciplinary perspective within the context of a medical home is essential. The concept of a medical home, as put forward by the American Academy of

Pediatrics, is a model that is well worth heeding (Ad Hoc Task Force on Definition of the Medical Home 1992; American Academy of Pediatrics 1993; Committee on Children with Disabilities 1997, 1999). The medical home is a family-centered practice that is able to provide accessible care, accepts all insurance and provides continuity of care. Moreover, such a practice needs physicians and other personnel who are able to provide comprehensive care and are skilled in identifying the need for specialty services. The practice needs to have the capacity to make appropriate referrals for services as well as the ability to interpret diagnostic and treatment information to parents and to participate in care coordination. It is a practice that is able to interact with educational systems and other community services and is compassionate and culturally competent, which is essential to the care of children with disabilities. One of the greatest problems in the care of children with disabilities is the fragmentation of services and the failure to integrate all of the components of care into an effective delivery system. The establishment and maintenance of such systems is one of our current challenges.

Children with autism are a unique but heterogeneous group. These children are not easy to care for, yet their care can be extraordinarily rewarding. In order to care successfully for children with autism and their families, flexibility, understanding, access to resources, and patience are essential. To combine these traits within a family-centered practice is one of the major challenges now confronting pediatricians and others involved in the care of children with autism.

References

Ad Hoc Task Force on Definition of the Medical Home (American Academy of Pediatrics) (1992) 'The medical home.' *Pediatrics 90,* 774.

Aicardi, J. (1998) 'Autism and autistic-like conditions.' In J. Aicardi, *Diseases of the Nervous System in Children,* 2nd edn. Cambridge: Cambridge University Press.

Aman, M.G. and Langworthy, K.S (2000) 'Pharmacotherapy for hyperactivity in children with autism and other pervasive developmental disorders.' *Journal of Autism and Developmental Disorders 30,* 451–459.

Aman, M.G., Van Bourgondien, M.E., Wolford, P. and Sarphare, G. (1995) 'Psychotropic and anticonvulsant drugs in subjects with autism: prevalence and patterns of use.' *Journal of the American Academy of Child and Adolescent Psychiatry 34,* 1672–1681.

American Academy of Pediatrics (1993) 'The medical home statement addendum: pediatric primary health care.' *AAP News 11,* 93.

American Academy of Pediatrics (2001) 'The pediatrician's role in the diagnosis and management of autistic spectrum disorder in children.' *Pediatrics 107,* 1221–1226.

American Psychiatric Association (1994) *Diagnostic and Statistical Manual of Mental Disorder, (DSM-IV)*, 4th edn. Washington, DC: APA.

Campbell, M., Anderson, L.T., Small, A.M., Adams, P., Gonzalez, N.M. and Ernst, M. (1993) 'Naltrexone in autistic children: behavioral symptoms and attentional learning.' *Journal of the American Academy of Child and Adolescent Psychiatry 32*, 1283–1291.

Committee on Children with Disabilities (American Academy of Pediatrics) (1997) 'General principles in the care of children and adolescents with genetic disorders and other chronic health conditions.' *Pediatrics 99*, 643–644.

Committee on Children with Disabilities (American Academy of Pediatrics) (1999) 'Care coordination: health and related systems of care for children with special health care needs.' *Pediatrics 104*, 978–981.

Committee on Children with Disabilities (American Academy of Pediatrics) (2001) 'Counseling families who choose complementary and alternative medicine for their child with chronic illness or disability.' *Pediatrics 107*, 598–601.

Dales, L., Hammer, S.J. and Smith, N.J. (2001) 'Time trends in autism and MMR immunization coverage in California.' *Journal of the American Medical Association 285*, 1183–1185.

DeLong, G.R., Teague, L.A. and Kamran, M.M. (1998) 'Effects of fluoxetine treatment in young children with idiopathic autism.' *Developmental Medicine and Child Neurology 40*, 551–562.

Dunn-Geier, J., Ho, H.H., Auersperg, E., Doyle, D., Eaves, L., Matsuba, C., Orrbine, E., Pham B. and Whiting, W. (2000) 'Effect of secretin on children with autism: a randomized control.' *Developmental Medicine and Child Neurology 42*, 796–802.

Fidler, D.J., Bailey, J.N. and Smalley, S.L. (2000) 'Macrocephaly in autism and other developmental disorders.' *Developmental Medicine and Child Neurology 42*, 737–740.

Filipek, P.A., Accardo, P.J., Ashwal, S., Baranek, G.T., Cook, Jr, E.H., Dawson, G., Gordon, B., Gravel, J.S., Johnson, C.O., Kallen, R.J., Levey, S.E., Minshew, N.J., Ozonoff, S., Prizant, B.M., Rapin, I., Rogers, S.J., Stone, W.L., Teplin, S.W., Tuchman, R.F. and Volkmar, F.R. (1999) 'The screening and diagnosis of autistic spectrum disorders.' *Journal of Autism and Developmental Disorders 29*, 439–484.

Fombonne, E. (1999) 'The epidemiology of autism: a review.' *Psychological Medicine 29*, 769–786.

Furlano, R.I., Anthony, A., Day, R., Brown, A., McGarvey, L., Thomson, M.A., Davies, S.E., Berelowitz, M., Forbes, A., Wakefield, A.J., Walker-Smith, J.A. and Murch, S.H. (2001) 'Colonic CD8 and gamma theta T-cell infiltration with epithelial damage in children with autism.' *Journal of Pediatrics 138*, 366–372.

Gerlach, E.K. (1998) *Autism Treatment Guide.* Eugene, OR: Four Leaf Press.

Gillberg, C. and Coleman, M. (1996) 'Autism and medical disorders: a review of the literature.' *Developmental Medicine and Child Neurology 38*, 191–202.

Gillberg, C. and Coleman, M. (2000) *The Biology of the Autistic Syndromes.* London: MacKeith.

Gillberg, C., Gillberg, I.C. and Steffenburg, S. (1992) 'Siblings and parents of children with autism: a controlled population-based study.' *Developmental Medicine and Child Neurology 34*, 389–398.

Gilman, J.T. and Tuchman, R.F. (1995) 'Autism and associated behavioral disorders: pharmacotherapeutic intervention.' *Annals of Pharmacotherapy 29*, 47–56.

Gupta, S. (2000) 'Immunological treatments for autism.' *Journal of Autism and Developmental Disorders 30*, 475–479.

Hagerman, R.J. (1999) *Neurodevelopmental Disorders: Diagnosis and Treatment.* New York: Oxford University Press.

Halsey, N.A., Hyman, S.L. and Conference Writing Panel (2001) [Electronic article] 'Measles-mumps-rubella vaccine and autistic spectrum disorder.' Report from the New Challenges in Childhood Immunization Conference convened in Oak Brook, IL, 12–13 June, 2000. *Pediatrics 107*, e84.

Handen, B.J., Johnson, C.R. and Lubetsry, M. (2000) 'Efficacy of methylphenidate among children with autism and symptoms of attention-deficit hyperactivity disorder.' *Journal of Autism and Developmental Disorders 30*, 245–255.

Horvath, K., Papadimitriou, J.C., Rabsztyn, A., Drachenberg, C. and Tildon, J.T. (1999) 'Gastrointestinal abnormalities in children with autistic disorder.' *Journal of Pediatrics 135*, 559–563.

Horvath, K., Stefanatos, G., Sokolski, K., Wachtel, R., Nabors, L. and Tildon, J.T. (1998) 'Improved social and language skills after secretin administration in patients with autism spectrum disorders.' *Journal of the Association of Academic Minority Physicians 9*, 9–15.

Hyman, S.L. and Levy, S.E. (2000) 'Autistic spectrum disorders: when traditional medicine is not enough.' *Contemporary Pediatrics 17*, 101–116.

Johnston, M.V. (2000) 'Commentary: Potential neurobiologic mechanisms through which metabolic disorders could relate to autism.' *Journal of Autism and Developmental Disorders 30*, 471–473.

Johnston, W.V. and Harum, K.H. (1999) 'Recent progress in the neurology of learning: memory molecules in the developing brain.' *Journal of Developmental and Behavioral Pediatrics 20*, 50–56.

Jure, R., Rapin, I. and Tuchman, R.F. (1991) 'Hearing-impaired autistic children.' *Developmental Medicine and Child Neurology 33*, 1062–1072.

Kanner, L. (1943) 'Autistic disturbances of affective contact.' *Nervous Child 2*, 217–250.

Kanner, L. (1971) 'Follow-up study of eleven children originally reported in 1943.' *Journal of Autism and Childhood Schizophrenia 1*, 119–145.

King, B.H. (2000) 'Pharmacological treatment of mood disturbances, aggression, and self-injury in persons with pervasive developmental disorders.' *Journal of Autism and Developmental Disorders 30*, 439–445.

Kolmen, B., Feldman, H.M., Handen, B.J. and Janosky, J.E. (1995) 'Naltrexone in young autistic children: a double-blind, placebo-controlled cross-over study.' *Journal of the American Academy of Child and Adolescent Psychiatry 34*, 223–231.

Landau, W.M. and Kleffner, F. (1957) 'Syndrome of acquired aphasia with convulsive disorder in children.' *Neurology 7*, 523–530.

Lauritsen, M., Mors, O., Mortensen, P.B. and Ewald, H. (1999) 'Infantile autism and associated chromosome abnormalities: a register-based study and a literature survey.' *Journal of Child Psychology and Psychiatry 40*, 335–345.

McDougle, C.J., Price, L.H. and Volkmar, F.R. (1994) 'Recent advances in the pharmacotherapy of autism and related conditions.' *Child and Adolescent Clinics of North America 3*, 71–89.

McDougle, C.J., Kresch, L.E. and Posey, D.J. (2000) 'Repetitive thoughts and behavior in pervasive developmental disorders: treatment with serotonic reuptake inhibitors.' *Journal of Autism and Developmental Disorders 30*, 427–435.

Mantovani, J.F. (2000) 'Autistic regression and Landau-Kleffner syndrome: progress or confusion.' *Developmental Medicine and Child Neurology 42*, 349–353.

Mars, A.E., Mauk, J.E. and Dowrick, P.W. (1998) 'Symptoms of pervasive developmental disorders as observed in prediagnostic home videos of infants and toddlers.' *Journal of Pediatrics 132*, 500–504.

Nickel, R.E. (1996) 'Controversial therapies for young children with developmental disabilities.' *Infants and Young Children 8*, 29–40.

Nordin, V. and Gillberg, C. (1996) 'Autism spectrum disorders in children with physical or mental disability or both. I: Clinical and epidemiological aspects.' *Developmental Medicine and Child Neurology 38*, 297–313.

Owley, T., Steele, E., Corsello, C., Risi, S., McKaig, K., Lord, C., Leventhal, B.L. and Cook, Jr, E.H. (1999) 'A double-blind, placebo-controlled trial of secretin for the treatment of autistic disorder.' *MedGenMed*, October 6.

Page, T. (2000a) 'Metabolic approaches to the treatment of autism spectrum disorders.' *Journal of Autism and Developmental Disorders 30*, 463–469.

Page, T. (2000b) 'Commentary: potential neurobiologic mechanisms through which metabolic disorders could related to autism.' *Journal of Autism and Developmental Disorders 30*, 471–473.

Quigley, E.M. and Hurley, D. (2000) 'Autism and the gastrointestinal tract.' *American Journal of Gastroenterology 95*, 2154–2156.

Rapin, I. (1995) 'Autistic regression and disintegrative disorder: how important is the role of epilepsy?' *Seminars in Pediatric Neurology 24*, 278–285.

Rapin, I. (1997) 'Autism.' *New England Journal of Medicine 337*, 97–103.

Rapin, I. (1998) 'Neurobiology of autism.' *Annals of Neurology 47*, 7–14.

Rapin, I. and Katzman, R. (1998) 'Neurobiology of autism.' *Annals of Neurology 43*, 7–14.

Roberts, W., Weaver, L., Brian, J., Bryson, W., Emellianova, S., Griffiths, A.M., MacKinnon, B., Yim, C., Wolpin, J. and Koren, G. (2001) 'Repeated doses of porcine secretin in the treatment of autism: a randomized, placebo-control trial.' *Pediatrics 107*, e71.

Rosenhall, U., Nordin, V., Sandstrom, M., Ahlsen, G. and Gillberg, C. (1999) 'Autism and hearing loss.' *Journal of Autism and Developmental Disorders 29*, 349–357.

Rutter, M. (1999) 'The Emanuel Miller memorial lecture 1998. Autism: two-way interplay between research and clinical work.' *Journal of Child Psychology and Psychiatry 40*, 2, 169–188.

Rutter, M., Bailey, A., Simonoff, E. and Pickles, A. (1997) 'Genetic influences and autism.' In D.J. Cohen and F.R. Volkmar (eds) *Handbook of Autism and Pervasive Developmental Disorders*, 2nd edn. New York: Wiley.

Sandler, A.D., Sutton, K.A., DeWeese, J., Girardi, M.A., Sheppard, V. and Bodfish, J. (1999) 'Lack of benefit of a single dose of synthetic human secretin in the treatment of autism and pervasive developmental disorders.' *New England Journal of Medicine 341*, 1801–1806.

Silver, L.B. (1995) 'Controversial therapies.' *Journal of Child Neurology 10*, suppl. 1, S96–S100.

Smith, M., Filipek, P.A., Wu, C., Bocian, M., Hamim, S., Modahl, C. and Spence, M.A. (2000) 'Analysis of a 1-megabase deletion in 15q22–123 in an autistic patient: identification of candidate genes for autism and of homologous DNA segments in 15q22–q23 and 15q11–q13.' *American Journal of Medical Genetics 96*, 765–770.

Steffenburg, S. (1991) 'Neuropsychiatric assessment of children with autism: a population-based study.' *Developmental Medicine and Child Neurology 33*, 495–501.

Taylor, B., Miller, E. and Farrington, C.P. (1999) 'Autism and measles, mumps and rubella vaccine: no epidemiologic evidence for a causal association.' *Lancet 353*, 2026–2029.

Tuchman, R. (1997) 'Acquired epileptiform aphasias.' *Seminars in Pediatric Neurology 4*, 93–101.

Tuchman, R. (2000) 'Treatment of seizure disorders and EEG abnormalities in children with autism spectrum disorders.' *Journal of Autism and Developmental Disorders 30*, 485–489.

Tuchman, R. and Rapin, I. (1997) 'Regression in pervasive developmental disorders: seizures and epileptiform electroencephalogram correlates.' *Pediatrics 99*, 560–566.

Wakefield, A.J., Murch, S.H., Anthony, A., Linnell, J., Casson, D.M., Malik, M., Berelowitz, M., Dhillon, A.P., Murch, S.H., Harvey, P., Valentine, A., Davies, S.E. and Walker-Smith, J.A. (1998) 'Ileal-lymphoid-nodular hyperplasia, non-specific colitis and pervasive-developmental disorder in children.' *Lancet 351*, 637–641.

Wing, L. and Gould, J. (1979) 'Severe impairments of social interaction and associated abnormalities in children: epidemiology and classification.' *Journal of Autism and Developmental Disorders 9*, 11–29.

Part II
Child-Centered Interventions

CHAPTER 5

Therapy

Laying the Foundation for Individual and Family Growth

Robin L. Gabriels

If these [learning disabilities] do not cause the child to lose his zeal or do not force him to flee from them, but activate him, then they will lead to a roundabout path of development. Lev Semenovich Vygotsky, The Collected Works of L.S. Vygotsky (Rieber and Carton 1993, p.131)

These words by L.S. Vygotsky, founder of Soviet cognitive developmental psychology in the 1920s and 1930s, are remarkably consistent with the current thinking of clinicians and researchers in the field of treating children who have autism. Vygotsky advocated for a shift from the hopeless thinking about educating children 'who were physically handicapped or difficult to educate' to an educational approach that tailored developmental teaching curricula and techniques to children's unique strengths in order to provide a means for compensating for their disabilities (Rieber and Carlton 1993, p.3). He also believed that the variable outcomes of a child's capacity to compensate depended on a combination of the individual child's strengths and the social environment (Rieber and Carlton 1993).

Currently, programs and techniques for ameliorating the symptoms and behaviors of individuals who have autism are plentiful. However, crucial questions remain to be explored regarding individuals' unique responses to treatment and the effectiveness of certain treatment components over others (Schreibman 2000). This issue tends to fuel 'controversy, divisiveness, and rather blind preference for one approach over another' without considering the individual child's strengths and needs (Siegel 1999, p.35). The wealth of treatment information presents a challenge for practitioners entering the autism field who want to develop effective individualized programs for young children with autism. Therefore, it is the goal of this chapter to provide a method for understanding the major autism treatment modalities available and to suggest a process for implementing an individualized, family-centered treatment program. This will be accomplished by providing:

- a brief overview of autism treatment outcome research
- a discussion of the role of psychological theory in guiding treatment and the contributions of three diverse autism treatment models
- a rationale for initially targeting specific developmental foundation skills
- suggestions for initiating and engaging in home therapy with families of children who have autism.

Overview: autism treatment outcome research

A review of autism intervention research indicates that early intervention (i.e. treating children prior to age 5) can have a positive impact on short and long-term developmental gains (Connor 1998; Rogers 1998). Positive outcomes have been demonstrated in young children with autism through programs targeting single aspects of autism-specific difficulties as well as through comprehensive programs that simultaneously target multiple autism-specific deficits (Rogers 1998). Treatments derived from behavior learning theory have been the most extensively researched, evidencing effective outcomes in addressing a variety of the skill deficits and behavior problems associated with individuals who have autism (e.g. Connor 1998; Lovaas 1987; McEachin, Smith and Lovaas 1993; Matson *et al.* 1996; Rogers 1998). However, despite these positive findings, no one type of behavior program has proved superior over another for all children with autism and it is still unknown how to combine and tailor approaches to best impact treatment outcomes (Schreibman 2000).

Variability in outcomes for different subgroups of children who have autism (i.e. some children making great progress and others making little, as measured by developmental cognitive ability), regardless of the type and intensity of intervention, complicates the autism outcome research (Gabriels *et al.* 2001; Luiselli *et al.* 2000; Sheinkopf and Siegel 1998; Stevens *et al.* 2000). Outcome variability suggests the possibility that there are other factors, besides program type, that contribute to treatment effectiveness. Some factors may include age of treatment onset (Harris and Handleman 2000), pretreatment intelligence (Stevens *et al.* 2000), pretreatment language levels (Lord and Schopler 1989), rate of cognitive processing speed (Scheuffgen *et al.* 2000), autism symptom severity (Szatmari *et al.* 2000), co-morbid conditions including mental retardation, medical syndromes, and neurological conditions (Nordin and Gillberg 1998), and parent–family factors such as amount of parental involvement in incidental teaching throughout the child's day (Luiselli *et al.* 2000) and parental stress (Gabriels *et al.* 2001; Ozonoff and Cathcart 1998).

In an attempt to identify possible characteristics contributing to treatment effectiveness, Dawson and Osterling (1997) reviewed eight different model preschool programs for children with autism utilizing a variety of behavioral and developmental approaches. Outcome data were available for most of these programs, with similar positive outcomes observed across programs. Common elements among these programs included:

- focusing core curricula to address the areas of attending, imitation, communication, play, and social skills

- initially teaching core skills in one-to-one structured teaching sessions with the child and then generalizing to natural settings

- implementing predictable routines with visual cues to assist children with transitions between activities

- utilizing proactive behavior management strategies (e.g. use of high-interest activities, structure, child-choice, and encouragement of independence) to help prevent behavior problems

- employing functional assessment techniques to increase staff understanding of child problem behaviors and teaching the child alternative coping behaviors

- encouraging family involvement and educating parents about how to engage and teach their child with autism.

Role of psychological theory in guiding treatment

Theories play an important role in providing clinicians as well as researchers with a context to organize therapy and techniques. Theories help explain why a certain therapy or technique works and how it contributes to a desired outcome. This process in turn allows for theoretical and therapeutic modifications to be made in order to 'identify what is necessary, sufficient, or facilitative for therapeutic change' (Kazdin 2001, p.63). The revision of theory and therapeutic approaches in light of new knowledge can be seen in the evolution of autism theory and treatment over time. For example, initial psychogenic theorizing in the 1940s and 1950s deemed a child with autism to be the product of extreme parental rejection and lack of maternal bonding (Kanner 1949). This view was fueled in part by the fact that children with autism appeared physically normal and not all had severe intellectual impairments (Frith 1993). The psychodynamic therapies that stemmed from this philosophy advocated for children to be placed out of their homes and into residential settings (Mesibov 1991), and blamed parents for causing their child's symptoms of autism (Frith 1993). However, empirical findings did not support these theories and approaches to autism, leading researchers to search for alternative explanations (Frith 1993). To date, there has been substantial scientific evidence to support the current understanding that autism is a neurodevelopmental disorder involving various biologic and brain irregularities. These impairments have implications for the patterns of behaviors and learning styles associated with this population (Whaley and Shaw 1999; see also Chapter 3 for more information).

In light of the current neurodevelopmental understanding of autism, specific treatment models and teaching techniques have emerged since the 1960s (Campbell *et al.* 1996). These treatments are derived from a variety of theoretical frameworks, the two major orientations being behavioral learning theory and developmental theory. There has been a discussion in the literature that both orientations have considerable implications for the treatment of children with autism (Erba 2000; Prizant and Wetherby 1998; Quill 2000; Schreibman and Anderson 2001; Siegel 1999). It is important for providers to understand these two philosophies and be informed about the research in these areas so that treatment techniques can be knowledgeably applied as needed to individualize treatment, rather than rigidly adhering to one approach over another. This is a crucial issue because choosing an interesting technique without truly comprehending its purpose can risk muddling treatment. It is the goal of this section to provide a theoretical frame of reference for three well-known autism treatment approaches and to identify the implications of their techniques for initiating clinic and home-based treatment with young children who have autism. However, it is beyond the scope of this chapter to provide an extensive review of all the autism treatment models or hybrid approaches currently available. It is also not the intent of this chapter to teach the application of the techniques discussed. It is recommended that providers seek specialized supervision and training to learn how to utilize effectively the approaches identified in this chapter.

Behavior learning theory

Behaviorism, introduced at the onset of the twentieth century, is a philosophy of science with the objective of observing and measuring lawful relationships between behavior and the environment in an effort to improve society and human behavior (Krasner 1988). Ivan P. Pavlov (Russian physiologist) and John B. Watson (American psychologist), two early behaviorists, focused on classical conditioning principles, the objective study of the conditions that preceded (antecedents) and thus predicted a behavioral response (Reese, Howard and Reese 1966). This classical conditioning model was later thought to be too limited in its explanation of the causes of behavior, as it did not consider other contextual influences (Todd and Morris 1992). Therefore, several shifts occurred within the behavioral paradigm in an attempt to apply the understanding of behavior learning theory across a wider range of contexts and make its scientifically derived principles more useful in therapeutic practice (Krasner 1988).

Operant conditioning theory

B.F. Skinner (1953) introduced the first shift in behaviorism by examining how antecedents not only influenced behaviors but also the resulting consequences. Operant conditioning theory provided a foundation for understanding the cause-and-effect learning process common in daily life and offered numerous possibilities for education and therapy. Ferster (1961) introduced an explanation of how Skinner's operant conditioning principles might contribute to the development of the specific behaviors identified in children with autism. Specifically, Ferster (1961) hypothesized that children with autism may have difficulty learning from social consequences (e.g. attention and praise) in natural environments and may learn better when operant learning principles are applied. As previously mentioned, research has indicated that operant conditioning techniques have positive implications for modifying behavior and motivating individuals with autism to attend and learn in a variety of therapy, school, and natural living settings (Rogers 1998). Operant conditioning techniques derived from Skinner's original work include backward chaining, errorless learning, positive reinforcement, prompting and modeling, and shaping, along with rules of generalization.

(See Appendix 5.1 for specific definitions of these techniques.) The process of therapeutically applying and routinely evaluating the effectiveness of these scientifically derived learning principles is often referred to as applied behavioral analysis (ABA: Wolery, Bailey and Sugai 1988).

Several educational treatment programs have been developed for individuals with autism using the direct application of operant conditioning principles in a range of settings (e.g. naturalistic to highly structured) to modify behaviors and teach specific skills in the areas of communication, socialization, academics, cognition, play, and imitation (Schreibman 2000). O. Ivar Lovaas introduced one of the most highly structured, comprehensive models derived from operant learning principles. The model evolved from the 1960s approach of teaching children within institutional settings with minimal parental involvement to teaching children within their home and school environments with parents and paraprofessionals acting as the child's primary teachers (Lovaas 1981). The first stage of this approach advocates for intensive (i.e. an average of 40 hours per week), discrete trial, one-to-one home-based instruction to teach developmental skills. This is based on the Lovaas and Smith (1989) discrete-trial training (DTT) theory that identifies this particular method of teaching as more conducive to the initial skill learning needs of a child with autism than natural learning environments. Discrete trials are carefully implemented learning sequences that target single aspects of skill areas (e.g. imitation of one body movement). The teaching sequence involves providing a specific instruction to the child (i.e. stimulus), a behavior response from the child (i.e. response), followed by positive reinforcement (i.e. consequence), and then a brief pause (including clearing the table of any task materials) before the next instruction (Anderson, Taras and Cannon 1996). The second stage of this program combines one-to-one discrete-trial teaching with an introduction of the child into school and other social settings (Lovaas 1981). Of note, 'other programs use DTT as a key method of delivering direct instruction, but also include other methods, do not necessarily prescribe a certain number of hours, and utilize a classroom setting' (Marcus, Garfinkle and Wolery 2001, p.178).

Cognitive social learning theory

Cognitive social learning theory represented another outgrowth of behaviorism and was developed and researched by Albert Bandura and colleagues (Bandura and Walters 1963). Cognitive social learning theory combines cognitive and social learning strategies with operant behavioral techniques in order to develop effective learning environments that maximize a person's sense of competency, thus decreasing undesirable behavior and affect (Kendall and Bacon 1988). This theory considers the effect of individuals' perception of their ability to master or cope with a task on their motivation to carry out that task successfully (Erwin 1988). The role of modeling and imitation, including the social perceptions of others, is also considered to facilitate the learning process (Bandura and Walters 1963).

The TEACCH (Treatment and Education of Autistic and Related Communication Handicapped Children) model, founded by Eric Schopler in the 1970s at the University of North Carolina at Chapel Hill, is a statewide parent–professional collaborative program that serves individuals with autism (Mesibov 1996). The TEACCH program combines behavioral techniques and cognitive social learning strategies (i.e. environmental modifications) within a developmental framework to address autism-specific needs (Mesibov 2000). The model advocates for simultaneously teaching skill acquisition along with making environmental modifications specific to the individual child's developmental needs and abilities. Modifications include the use of visually clear physical boundaries, schedules, and work systems to assist comprehension of task expectations (e.g. tasks need to have a clear beginning and end and visually cue the child to the answers to the questions 'What do I do?', 'How much work needs to be done?', and 'When am I done?'). Environmental modifications decrease the individual's need for verbal or physical direction from others. The goals of TEACCH are to create work and leisure environments that decrease behavioral problems related to poor understanding of task expectations and increase independent behavior along with quality of life (Schopler 2001; Schopler, Mesibov and Hearsey 1995).

Developmental theory

Developmental theory focuses on the importance of the developmental patterns or stages that children go through, leading them to acquire increasingly more complex and abstract cognitive abilities. Jean Piaget (1970), a Swiss psychologist, influenced this theory by identifying specific biologically determined stages of cognitive development for the typical child. Piaget (1970) asserted that it is essential for children to progress through preliminary levels of cognitive understanding before moving on to more abstract concepts, to prevent the learning of concepts only on a surface level. Developmental research has provided considerable information about the process of typical development across overlapping skill domains along with the prerequisite skills needed to master more complex skills (Schreibman and Anderson 2001).

Stanley Greenspan's Floor-Time model is an example of a developmental approach that attempts to address the biological processing delays of children with autism within a social-relational framework. Greenspan (1992) addresses how these delays can influence the way children with autism respond to others within their social environment. Important stages of learning may be thwarted by the challenging interaction patterns that result from caregivers' lack of awareness of how to respond or relate to their children. The Floor-Time model provides techniques for helping parents and therapists take advantage of cause-and-effect teaching opportunities within the context of the child's interests in order to motivate the child to engage and learn (Greenspan and Wieder 1998). The model recognizes the need for teaching a developmental sequence of new skills that build upon each other, leading to more complex thought. The model also acknowledges the need to make use of specialized therapists to teach the child core developmental skills and then bring these skills to the parent–child interaction Floor-Time experience, thus avoiding simply rote-learning of 'splinter' skills (Greenspan 1992, p.5; Greenspan and Wieder 1998). Techniques include following the child's lead and building on the child's interests in a 'playfully obstructive' way in order to 'create an interaction' (Greenspan and Wieder 1998, p.124). For example, an adult can actively get in the way of the child or a child-desired object in order to instigate a 'spontaneous, self-motivated interaction' from the child that will help restart a developmentally appropriate social interaction process (Greenspan 1992, p.4).

Combining treatment approaches to target foundation skills

Young children with autism may present to treatment with a host of varying abilities and difficulties in areas such as attention, communication, motor imitation, cognition, and play (Dawson 1996). For this reason, Siegel (1999, p.34) recommends taking 'a kind of systematic eclecticism' to developing individualized treatment programs. This involves emphasizing various treatment models at different times throughout the treatment process in order to match the child's ever-changing needs and developing strengths (Siegel 1999). This process requires flexibility and creativity on the part of the therapist as well as a detailed understanding of theoretical models. The therapist must know how to make learning tasks meaningful as well as how and when to transition a child from discrete-trial teaching activities to using mastery skills in daily living settings. The Denver model is one example of an approach that advocates for practitioners to 'be familiar with a very wide range of intervention techniques, ranging across theoretical orientations and educational practices, in order to maximize the learning rate and repertoire of each child' (Rogers *et al.* 2000, p.110).

Target areas needing to be addressed initially in treatment can be viewed as foundation skills required for the acquisition of later functional life skills. As previously indicated, young children with autism may vary in their ability levels. Therefore, practitioners will need to evaluate, formally or informally, where to begin treatment. (See Chapters 2 and 3 for assessment information.) The information that follows is an overview of rationales for initially targeting foundation skills in the treatment of young children diagnosed with autism along with suggestions for how to teach these skills using techniques derived from behavioral and development research and autism treatment models. The following discussion is not a comprehensive list of starting points or next steps for therapy, and there are a number of valuable resources available that provide extensive details on specific teaching goals and intervention strategies across all areas of development (e.g. Greenspan and Wieder 1998; Gutstein 2000; Johnson-Martin *et al.* 1995; Lovaas 1981; Maurice, Green and Luce 1996; Murray-Slutsky and Paris 2000; Schopler, Reichler and Lansing 1980; Schopler *et al.* 1983).

Attending

In order to learn, individuals must first be able to attend selectively to relevant information. Typically developing children are able to engage in 'focused or selective attention [which] is the capacity to highlight one or two important stimuli or ideas being dealt with while suppressing awareness of competing distractions' (Lezak 1995, pp.39–40). The attentional abilities of individuals with autism are thus impacted by their tendencies to be either hyper- or hypo-responsive to environmental stimuli (Dawson and Watling 2000) and to over-focus on specific idiosyncratic details rather than scanning the environment for relevant information (Lovaas, Koegel and Schreibman 1979). The following teaching strategies derived from general cognitive research have implications for increasing attention and learning in children who have autism.

1. Create an environment with minimal sensory distractions.

2. Use familiar and interesting materials or activities to teach new information.

3. Provide regular and routine opportunities for learning and practice.

4. Break down complex tasks into smaller parts, initially providing easier tasks, or alternating between easy (i.e. previously mastered) and more difficult tasks (Bruning, Schraw and Ronning 1990).

Additionally, intervention research indicates that children with autism may attend better to tasks when presented with powerful primary reinforcements that can compete with their idiosyncratic behavior preferences (Garretson, Fein and Waterhouse 1990).

Teaching children with autism to attend while sitting on a chair and later at a table is an important life skill that affects their ability to engage with others and in activities, such as eating and working. Having the child sit at eye-level in front of an adult helps the child know where to focus his or her attention (Janzen 1999). Operant teaching techniques combined with environmental modification strategies can facilitate a child's acquisition of this important life skill. The following is an example of the process involved in initially teaching this skill to a young child with autism.

1. Focus the environment by placing the only interesting toy(s) on a table near the child's chair. Table 5.1 includes a list of suggested toys and activities to help attract a child's interest and motivate him or her to sit and engage in an activity with another person.

2. Reinforce sitting behavior by allowing a child to engage with the toy of interest only when he or she is seated.

3. Initially, a child should be expected to sit and engage only for brief periods (i.e. one to two minutes). This ensures that the experience of sitting and attending to another person is a positive one for the child.

4. After this brief engagement in the chair, the adult should prompt the child to 'Stand up' and 'Take a break'. Gradually, time sitting and attending can be increased.

5. Providing interesting materials only in the area of the child's chair and table can entice a wandering child back to the table and chair to continue with sitting and attending.

Table 5.1: Suggested attending/interaction cause-and-effect sensory toys and activities

Balloons: adult blows up balloon and then lets child hold the balloon as it deflates. Adult prompts child to give the balloon then repeats this sequence.

Small spin top (without a stable base): child can be prompted to give the top to an adult for assistance to activate.

Bubbles and bubble toys (preferably electronic): child can be prompted to give toy to an adult to activate.

Vibrating toys: small massagers, vibrating stuffed animals, or vibrating pens. Adult intermittently turns off the toy to motivate the child to give the object to the adult for help to activate the toy again.

Any toys that are activated by pushing knobs: pop-n-pals or other infant-type tabletop push toys that spin, pop, or make sound/music. These toys can be eventually used for turn-taking games.

Plastic accordion type tubes: child holds both sides of the tube and then the adult waits for a child to give eye contact before pulling the tube apart with the child.

Self-contained ramp toys: animals, cars, or balls that travel down a winding ramp to the bottom. Adult prompts child to give the object to request more of this activity.

Musical and sound toys: Jack-in-the-box, drum, or xylophone. These toys can be eventually used for turn-taking games.

6. Resistance behaviors, such as screaming and crying, may appear as the child begins to understand the rules and limits implicit in this interaction (i.e. 'First sit down, then you can do this'). This can be minimized or avoided by paying attention to the child's need to disengage, and by prompting the child to 'Stand up' long before he or she protests.

7. If the child protests, briefly ignore the child by avoiding eye contact, then immediately re-engage the child in a brief interaction when he or she is calm. Following this, prompt the child to 'Take a break'.

This sequence helps the child to begin to understand positive contingency affect modulation (e.g. 'If I am calm, then I can engage in something fun and get what I want'). It is important to be consistent with this approach to unwanted behaviors so as not to reward negative behaviors inadvertently (Murray-Slutsky 2000). See Lovaas (1981), Lovaas and Smith (1989) and Murray-Slutsky and Paris (2000) for more information on contingency behavior management.

Communication

Developing communication skills has important implications for understanding, regulating, and engaging others, which can in turn influence a child's behavior and ability to learn (Koegel 2000). Developmental research describes how the repeated process of infants' exposure to the association of caregivers' responses to their behaviors helps them develop an understanding of the function of communication, including the understanding that communication can be instrumental (child can get something), regulatory (regulate the behaviors of others), and engaging (the back and forth turn-taking of playful interactions) (Black, Puckett and Bell 1992). Gestures are the origins of communication and include making eye contact, reaching, grasping, touching or tapping objects, pushing objects away, grasping and giving objects, pointing, or any other purposeful, controlled, and coordinated movement (Zinober and Martlew 1985). Children with autism tend to lack spontaneity and coordinated use of gestures, as well as the verbal means to communicate. Additionally, when these children do initiate communication, a majority of their communicative attempts are focused on requesting objects or protesting, rather than on using communication to share social experiences with another person (joint attention) (Stone et al. 1997b). The outcomes of joint attention include an 'ability to understand the thoughts, intentions, and behaviors of oneself and others' (Black et al. 1992, p.159). Joint attention has been identified as an important prelinguistic developmental ability that is intrinsically and socially motivated (Bates, Thal and Marchman 1991) and considered to be developmentally more advanced than simply communicating wants and needs (Koegel 2000).

Helping a child with autism develop an understanding of the function of communication begins with teaching a child to use communicative gestures to obtain a desired object or event, and by engaging the child in the back and forth gestural and vocal turn-taking of social routines (Rollins et al. 1998). The use of communicative gestures teaches children that they can use their behavior to direct another person's attention to get what they need or want (Rollins *et al.* 1998). For example, caretakers can wait for the child to look at them before continuing an activity that the child desires, such as pushing the child on a swing. It is recommended that intentional gestures be taught in a developmental sequence. More complex gestures, such as pointing, may be difficult for the child to achieve, depending on the child's level of motor coordination skill development (Zinober and Martlew 1985). Pivotal Response Training (PRT) strategies, which apply operant teaching principles within naturalistic and child-choice directed teaching settings, can be employed to increase a child's motivation to use communicative gestures (e.g. pointing) to request (Koegel, O'Dell and Koegel 1987). For example, one can use a desired object when teaching a child to point, then give the desired object to the child each time he or she points to the object. The Picture Exchange Communication System (PECS) also provides a method for teaching young children with autism how to use communicative strategies by having the child give objects or a picture of desired objects to make requests (Bondy and Frost 1994). Engaging a child in back and forth turn-taking activities within a socially motivating format can increase a child's desire to use vocalizations and gestures as a means for engaging (joint attention) and continuing social interactions (Rollins *et al.* 1998). Social interactions can include games, such as 'Peek-a-boo', where the adult can use pauses within the interaction sequence to elicit a child's gesture (e.g. child reaches to pull down the blanket) that will then continue the interaction. (See Chapter 6 for more information on communication intervention.)

Motor imitation

The ability to imitate has implications for social learning and the development of crucial life skills in areas such as socialization, cognition, and communication (Bandura and Walters 1963). Young children with autism have more difficulty imitating body movements of others than imitating actions on objects. It is also more difficult for these children to imitate non-meaningful (e.g. unrelated to a context) than meaningful actions (Stone, Ousley and Littleford 1997a). This is an important concept to remember when determining how best to teach a young child the initial concept of imitation. For example, based on a 'child's level and understanding of the process', it may be better to teach the child by imitating his or her behaviors and having him or her imitate meaningful actions (e.g. within the context of songs), rather than expecting a child to copy repetitive meaningless actions (Marcus *et al.*

2001, p.175). However, with these concepts in mind, research has found that individuals who have difficulty spontaneously imitating others can be successfully taught to imitate using operant techniques, such as reinforcement of targeted imitative behaviors cued by simple verbal ('Do this') and physical (as needed) prompts, along with modeling. After imitation skills have been taught using these techniques, rates of imitative responding have been found to increase and generalize to the imitation of other non-reinforced imitative behaviors (Rimm and Masters 1979). Occupational therapy may provide children with autism an initial arena in which to practice motor coordination skills and to begin to imitate. (See Chapter 7 for more information regarding motor skill intervention.)

Cognition

Cognitive development involves a lifelong process of acquiring, modifying, storing, retrieving, and using information necessary for understanding the world (Lerner 1985). Typically this process begins with gradual learning about 'objects and events' through the second year of life (Bloom, Lifter and Broughton 1985, p.153). This period is often referred to as Piaget's sensorimotor stage, learning through cause-and-effect sensory experiences within the environment. During Piaget's second period of development, the preoperational stage, children develop further understanding of previous cause-and-effect experiences, use beginning problem-solving strategies, and develop simple mental representations of objects and events. The child's beginning use of words to represent objects facilitates this initial process of conceptualizing and categorizing objects and events (Wadsworth 1978). Lovaas (1981) recommends initially teaching categorization concepts without the use of word labels. This strategy can help avoid confusing a young child with autism who has limited receptive language skills. For example, practitioners can instruct a child to 'Put same with same' and later, as a child learns the concept of same versus different, teach the labels for objects and categories (e.g. colors, shapes, numbers, letters etc.) (Lovaas 1981, p.73).

Play

Play provides child-centered avenues for children to learn about the world and develop cognitive concepts, language skills, and social-emotional skills. Developmental research indicates that within the first three years of life, typical children follow a progressive sequence of play, moving from sensory exploration of objects to more advanced functional and symbolic use of objects combined with social and cooperative play (Fewell and Kaminski 1988). As previously discussed, children with autism have difficulties in the areas of attention, communication, imitation, and cognition, all requirements for functional symbolic and social play. Williams, Costall and Reddy (1999) reviewed the autism object-play research and identified several notable tendencies in young children with autism that are not explained by their developmental mental age. These included a persistence in undifferentiated object manipulation beyond the age of what is typically expected, a preference for exploring the sensory aspects of objects, and a tendency to use objects in stereotypical ways, such as lining them up or focusing on parts of objects rather than using an object for its intended function. Although children with autism have been found to engage in functional play with objects and toys, their play tends to be more repetitive and simplistic than typically developing peers and peers with Down syndrome (Williams, Reddy and Costall 2001).

Research suggests that engaging children with autism in child-preferred activities and using PRT techniques derived from behavior learning theories can help to sustain their attention and increase their motivation to learn and socialize (Koegel, Dyer and Bell, 1987; Stahmer 1999). Developmentally oriented interventions, such as Floor-Time, also provide useful strategies to encourage play skills with children who have autism (Greenspan and Wieder 1998). For example, persisting in pursuing and engaging the child who tends to run away, treating unintentional behaviors or comments as intentional and then incorporating them into the play theme, and expanding a child's perseverative play by actively introducing how to play in different ways with the same materials (Greenspan and Wieder 1998). Appendix 5.2 describes a step-by-step process for introducing and teaching play after a child has learned some basic social imitation skills.

Tables 5.2 to 5.6 outline autism strengths and needs in relation to suggested initial early intervention goals and associated techniques for teaching and generalization.

Table 5.2: Attending skills

Autism areas of strength and need	Foundation skill area	Teaching targets (Targets are listed in a suggested sequential teaching order)	Suggested techniques to apply	Child's skill outcome objectives
Distractible (Garretson et al. 1990) Preference for routines, consistency, and sameness (DSM-IV: APA 1994)	Attending skills	Sit on child-sized chair and engage with an adult at eye-level. Child's feet should touch the ground to minimize sensory distraction. Sit at child-sized table and engage with an adult with a variety of work and sensory play tasks. Sit on floor with an adult. Once a child is attending to an adult, it is important to help the child generalize these attending skills to sitting and attending in a variety of settings (e.g. on the floor) with materials previously mastered at the table.	Provide predictable environment with minimal clutter and sensory distractions, clear visual boundaries, and simple verbal instructions. Provide child-preferred activities to sustain a child's attention and desire to sit on a chair facing and engaging with an adult. Use operant teaching techniques (e.g. verbal and physical prompting to sit and positive reinforcement for sitting). Keep the attending experience positive.	Increase child's awareness and mastery over how to engage with others, learning materials, and toys.

Sources: Adapted from Lovaas (1987), Floor-Time (Greenspan and Wieder 1998), TEACCH (Schopler et al. 1980, 1983), and Denver model (Rogers 2000) programs

Table 5.3 Communication skills

Autism areas of strength and need	Foundation skill area	Teaching targets (Targets are listed in a suggested sequential teaching order)	Suggested techniques to apply	Child's skill outcome objectives
Minimal or lack of coordinated use of nonverbal gestures to communicate needs and regulate social interactions (*DSM-IV*: APA 1994)	Communication skills	Nonverbal communicative gestures to request and regulate interactions: • use of eye contact • reaching towards and grasping objects • tapping or touching desired objects or people • giving objects then later bringing objects to request help or more of an interaction • pointing proximally then distally to desired objects	Provide repetition and practice within both daily living and one-to-one discrete trial settings to clearly teach the cause-and-effect relationship of using gestures. Use operant teaching techniques (e.g. positive reinforcement, shaping and prompting). Use playful obstruction techniques (e.g. put desired objects in clear container with childproof lid). Use a visual target/cue (e.g. sticker dots) on desired objects when initially teaching a child how to point, to increase task objective understanding (i.e. use one finger to point to a concrete target). Later, fade dot cue away. Engage child in a variety of sensory motivating social routines and turn-taking games.	Increase child's understanding and use of nonverbal communication strategies to get needs met, regulate interactions, and engage others.

Sources: Adapted from Lovaas (1987), Floor-Time (Greenspan and Wieder 1998), TEACCH (Schopler et al. 1980, 1983), and Denver model (Rogers 2000) programs

Table 5.4 Imitation skills

Autism areas of strength and need	Foundation skill area	Teaching targets (Targets are listed in a suggested sequential teaching order)	Suggested techniques to apply	Child's skill outcome objectives
Difficulties in capacity to imitate and plan/coordinate motor movements (Stone *et al.* 1997a) Lack of social imitative play (*DSM-IV*: APA 1994)	Imitation skills	• Imitation of one-step meaningful actions on objects (e.g. pat drum or table with hand, put block in cup, shake maracas, tap spoon on table, etc.) • Imitation of simple motor movements. Begin with teaching movements easily visible to a child (e.g. clap hands, blow a kiss, and wave bye-bye), then move to more complex (i.e. less visible) movements, like hands on head. • Imitation of one-step block designs. Begin with stacking two differently colored blocks, then gradually advance to creating more complex multi-block designs. Later, generalize this skill to imitating from picture models, using other building materials, and playing turn-taking building games.	Reinforce imitation concept by imitating the child's actions or vocalizations and making imitation tasks meaningful. Teach body movement imitation within naturally motivating activities (e.g. within the context of songs). Provide repetition and practice in a discrete trial format to increase motor coordination and planning. Use operant teaching techniques (e.g. positive reinforcement, shaping, prompting, modeling, and errorless learning). Initially, keep verbal prompts simple and consistent ('Do this') then generalize to other prompts such as, 'Do what I do' or 'Make this'. After body movement imitation concept is mastered, use instruction labels for prompts to expand receptive vocabulary (e.g. 'Wave bye-bye'). Make task expectations visually clear. For example, have two sets of identical objects for each imitation task.	Increase motor planning/coordination skills so child can use these skills to imitate play, social, and communication behaviors of others.

Sources: Adapted from Lovaas (1987), Floor-Time (Greenspan and Wieder 1998), TEACCH (Schopler et al. 1980, 1983), and Denver model (Rogers 2000) programs

Table 5.5: Cognitive skills

Autism areas of strength and need	Foundation skill area	Teaching targets (Targets are listed in a suggested sequential teaching order)	Suggested techniques to apply	Child's skill outcome objectives
Strengths in tasks requiring visual/manipulation skills (Ozonoff 1997) Difficulties with tasks requiring symbolic/abstract thought and sequential logic (Liss et al. 2001)	Cognitive skills	Sorting and matching skills: • identical object to object match, then later sort identical objects • identical picture to picture match, then later teach picture-matching games like Memory • object to picture match • match shapes, colors, upper case ABCs, numbers, quantities, numbers to quantities, upper to lower-case letters, and pictures to words • sort object categories (e.g. toy food, people, animals, cars)	Provide repetition and practice in discrete trial format. Use operant teaching techniques (e.g. errorless learning, prompting, positive reinforcement). Initially, keep verbal prompts simple and consistent (e.g. 'Put same with same') then generalize to other prompts, such as 'Sort' or 'Match'. After matching concept is mastered, use item labels for prompts to expand receptive vocabulary (e.g. 'Put yellow with yellow'). Generalize mastered skills to meaningful sorting activities. Provide predictable environment with minimal clutter and sensory distractions. Engage child in preferred visual/manipulation activities (e.g. puzzles) that provide exposure to cognitive concepts in meaningful and fun ways. Alternate these activities with more difficult work tasks.	Development of conceptual and categorical problem-solving knowledge needed for: • functional play • simple social matching games • category/sort in clean-up and other in daily living activities. • academics

Sources: Adapted from Lovaas (1987), Floor-Time (Greenspan and Wieder 1998), TEACCH (Schopler et al. 1980, 1983), and Denver model (Rogers 2000) programs

Table 5.6 Play skills

Autism areas of strength and need	Foundation skill area	Teaching targets (Targets are listed in a suggested sequential teaching order)	Suggested techniques to apply	Child's skill outcome objectives
Tendency to become preoccupied with certain features (e.g. sensory) of objects or toys rather than using them for their intended purpose. (*DSM-IV:* APA 1994)	Play skills	• Engage in a variety of sensory mediums (e.g. dry rice or beans, sand, water, play dough, shaving cream, cornstarch mixed with water, musical instruments). • Engage in sensory play turn-taking schemas (e.g. take turns with scoop to pour material on each other's hands or into a common container, or take turns playing a musical instrument.) • Engage in toy play imitation with sensory materials and toys. (See imitation tasks above and Appendix 2.5.)	Use naturally reinforcing sensory materials to introduce and teach social/play skills. Make sensory play environment clutter-free, so activity focus is between the child and adult. Keep verbal prompts simple and consistent at first ('Do this') then generalize to other prompts such as 'Do what I do' or 'Make this'. Use operant teaching techniques (e.g. shaping, prompting, and modeling) to encourage social engagement. Reinforce imitation concept by imitating the child's actions and making imitation tasks meaningful.	Expand child's ability to play functionally with a variety of toys both independently and with others.

Sources: Adapted from Lovaas (1987), Floor-Time (Greenspan and Wieder 1998), TEACCH (Schopler *et al.* 1980, 1983), and Denver model (Rogers 2000) programs

Nuts and bolts of the therapy process within the family context: role of the educational coordinator/family therapist

There is a wealth of information available to professionals concerning the importance of taking a family-centered approach that is 'consumer driven and competency enhancing' with families who have a child with special needs (Hecimovic, Powell and Christensen 1999, p.267). However, it can be difficult for professionals to put this approach into practice given the unique challenges presented by each family. Several overall guiding principles may assist professionals in providing a successful family-centered approach.

First, professionals should consider the assumptions of family systems theory, which values the uniqueness of each family and recognizes the fact that 'each member contributes to the overall composition and thus influences all aspects of the family' (Hecimovic *et al.* 1999, p.273). Families are also impacted by extended family members, as well as by their community system (Hecimovic *et al.* 1999). Acknowledging this assumption can help professionals be mindful of the *quality* versus the *quantity* of supportive services available to individual families and recommend system adjustments as needed.

Second, professionals need to be aware of the inherent power in their role and its impact on the family. Professionals need to be constantly alert to the potential harm to the family due to loss of professional objectivity resulting from blurred boundaries and role conflicts with family members, exploitation of power by the professional, and insensitivity to the importance of confidentiality (Kitchener 1988). The ethics code of the American Psychological Association (1992) can provide professionals with guidance on these issues of potential harm.

The following section lists key considerations for professionals throughout the phases of treatment with families of children who have autism. Depending on individual family situations and stress levels, it may be necessary for the family to have either one or two coordinating professionals managing the child's educational programming at home and school and mental health family support needs. If only one professional assumes the role of providing educational coordination and support to families in relation to coping with their child who has autism, it is recommended that this professional be a trained mental health professional.

Alliance formation

Initial sessions with the parent(s) and child involve not only gathering pertinent information about child and family needs, but also joining with the family to understand their perspectives in order to clarify treatment goals and expectations. It may be helpful to meet initially with the child and family in their home to gain a better understanding of environmental factors that can influence treatment. Even if a formal assessment has been completed previously, the professional should formally or informally assess the child's current strengths and needs and observe parent–child interactions in order to determine appropriate skills to target in treatment. (See Chapters 2 and 3 for a list of assessment tools.)

Issues for therapists to explain to parents during initial sessions about the process of therapy include:

1. Where therapy will take place (e.g. at client's home, in the therapist's office, or a combination).

2. The role of the educational coordinator or family support therapist (this can include developing and monitoring a child's educational and behavioral treatment plan as well as providing family support, training, and education about how to live with and teach their child with autism on a daily basis).

3. How the coordinator role differs from the role of other therapists and school personnel involved with the child and family, along with how collaboration will occur with these other professionals.

4. The treatment contributions of major autism therapy models, in order to help parents avoid the temptation to seek out excessive quantities of treatment rather than focus on systematically designing quality treatment programs.

5. How frequently the meetings with the child and family will occur and when this will decrease based on the child's requirements for consultation with home and school teaching programs.

6. The role of a home trainer, and when (or if) to introduce a home trainer into the treatment program. (Having a home trainer can be an economical way to provide the continuous and consistent rote practice a child may need to develop foundation skills and later functional academic, daily living, advanced communication, and social/play skills. Home trainers consult with the educational

treatment coordinator about treatment goals and keep data on the child's progress. These data can be useful to insurance companies or school programs that require documentation of a child's progress to help determine necessity of reimbursement for service delivery.)

Issues to discuss with and inquire of parents during initial sessions include:

1. The process the family engaged in prior to coming for treatment (e.g. previous evaluations leading up to their child's diagnosis and prior experiences with professionals).

2. Child's previous and current therapy services.

3. Child's areas of strengths and interests, including unique ways the parent(s) have found to engage their child.

4. Current issues of concern and how these issues impact family life (parents may require help sorting through the pile of issues needing to be addressed).

Issues of concern may include:

1. Issues of child related to safety, self-care, and daily living (e.g. dental care, sleep, impulsivity, bathing, aggression, eating, and toileting). Some of these issues may require a referral to a physician or psychiatrist to rule out the possible need for medication or other medical interventions (see Chapter 4). Also, a *functional analysis* may help determine the function of the child's behaviors in order to develop an appropriate behavior modification plan (O'Neill *et al.* 1990). For more information on helping children who have special needs with sleep problems see Durand (1998).

2. Issues of parent depression and/or couple's problems that have been exacerbated by the child's new diagnosis and related behaviors. Parents may need to be referred for individual or couples therapy. Make it clear that the role of the family therapist is to support the parents in relation to the child's needs, but not to be their personal therapist, as there is a danger of focusing too much on the couple or individual parent problems and neglecting the child's treatment needs.

3. Issues of sibling frustration, anger, or embarrassment with their brother or sister who has autism. Siblings may be confused about how to understand or engage effectively with their sibling who has

autism. Siblings may benefit from a referral to individual or support group therapies. (See Chapter 9 for more information regarding sibling interventions.)

Finally, specific type, frequency, and intensity of service provision is often a question initially posed by parents when they are desperately trying to determine what is in the best interest of their young child with autism. As previously discussed, treatment outcome research in the field of autism has not yet identified one magic formula to answer these questions. This factor combined with the variable outcome results in autism treatment research indicates that it may be prudent for practitioners to 'acknowledge that complex issues cannot always be resolved with a one-size-fits-all solution' (Hanft and Feinberg 1997, p.28). Indeed, practitioners need to listen to the diverse needs of the child and family and then develop appropriate therapeutic approaches, rather than simply placing a specific treatment model on a family. Quality and value of services is also a consideration that needs to be tied to family priorities regarding desired outcomes for their child (Hanft and Feinberg 1997). For example, if a child has a particular interest in music, as evidenced by their increased social responsiveness while listening to music, a family may consider providing music therapy for their child as well as encouraging the use of music strategies in other therapies to introduce and teach new skills in areas such as communication and functional academics. Along with intensity of professional service provision, parents may need help recognizing that their daily interactions with their child are valuable contributions to intervention intensity.

Therapeutic relationship

The therapeutic relationship is an important component of treatment after initial alliances have been formed when treatment work begins to focus on targeting defined goals with the child and family along with collaborating with a variety of service professionals. This collaboration process is easier discussed than put into practice, as professionals may have their own personal agendas that can thwart the collaboration process. To assist in this process, Bruder (1996) identified several elements of effective interdisciplinary team collaboration. These elements include the team's need to:

- have a common understanding of treatment goals and purpose for working together
- be willing to work collaboratively and creatively together to resolve problems and come up with solutions
- make a commitment to trust each other, including having 'honesty, openness, consistency, and respect', for team members (Bruder 1996, p.31)
- have a team leader (i.e. treatment coordinator) who can effectively 'establish a vision, create change, and unleash talent' among team members (p.32).

Bruder (1996) also differentiated between the terms multidisciplinary, inter-disciplinary, and transdisciplinary teams, the latter involving the highest level of integration and collaboration among diverse professional disciplines.

The following is a list of considerations for the treatment coordinator during the therapeutic relationship process.

1. *Teach foundation skills* (see Tables 5.2, 5.3, 5.4, 5.5, and 5.6) relevant to the child's specific strengths and needs within a safe, predictable, enjoyable, and understandable therapeutic environment. This will help the child develop an understanding of the expectations of therapy. After the child has learned to attend to adult-directed table tasks, the child may begin to want to explore his or her environment in a goal-directed manner. The therapist needs to be aware of this developmental progress and build in opportunities to follow the child's lead. It may help to schedule a time into the therapy sessions for play exploration. Setting containers filled with various learning toys around the room can allow the child to explore toys in a planful manner and generalize the skills learned during one-to-one table time.

2. *Address behavior problems* using functional analysis techniques to help understand the purpose of the child's behaviors and develop any needed environmental modifications and coping strategies for the child (O'Neill *et al.* 1990).

3. *Engage parents in the process of teaching their child* to ensure that therapeutic teaching will carry over outside therapy sessions.

4. *Teach siblings basic behavioral intervention strategies* so they can have positive interaction experiences with their brother or sister who has

autism. (See Chapter 9 for more information regarding sibling interventions.)

5. *Consult and overlap sessions* with other professionals working with the child to facilitate treatment focus and direction.

6. *Make appropriate referrals to other processionals* to address specific areas of concern as they become apparent. Ancillary creative therapies, including art and music therapy, can provide a means to support comprehensive treatment programs by using attractive sensory materials and strategies to enhance skill development and generalization. For example, individual and group music therapy sessions can encourage social-emotional communication skill development along with fine and gross motor coordination (Trevarthen *et al.* 1998; Whitaker-Haun and Haun 1997). Additionally, art therapy can offer opportunities for children to work with inherently reinforcing sensory art media in both individual and group (e.g. school art classes) settings to address functional academic and social skills (Gabriels 2002).

Termination of previous ways of working: moving into new directions

Finally, despite the concern that autism can require lifelong intervention, it is unrealistic for parents and therapists to expect that the same therapist will always be able to provide what is needed to the child and family throughout the child's lifetime. Therefore, it is the therapist's role to assess continuously the child's needs for different treatment focus, therapists, or therapy structure, and to help parents feel 'OK' about making changes.

Conclusion

Professionals face a myriad of information and 'helpful' advice through which to sort in an effort to provide successful individualized, and family-centered treatment within the autism population. Given this, it is important for professionals to be aware of current research and have an understanding of the theories that underlie the major treatment models in order to know how to individualize treatment systematically for a young child who has autism. Additionally, a successful family-centered approach requires that professionals have knowledge of family systems theory and mental health therapy along with a 'healthy' respect for professional ethics and standards.

APPENDIX 5.1

Behavioral Techniques to Enhance Learning

Note: The definitions of these techniques are brief and are intended only to provide the reader with a conceptual overview. For more comprehensive information about the application of these and other techniques see Lovaas 1981; Maurice *et al.* 1996; O'Neill *et al.* 1990; Reese *et al.* 1966; Wolery *et al.* 1988.

Backward chaining is a technique used to teach a complex chain of behaviors, such as self-care skills. Each behavior is taught starting with the last step in the chain that the person is able to complete independently. The accomplishment of the last step is then reinforced (Reese *et al.* 1966). For example, to teach a child to put on a sock, initially put the sock on almost over the child's heel, encourage the child to finish pulling up the sock, and then provide reinforcement. After sufficient repetitions, the next step back is introduced. For example, place the sock over the child's toes and prompt the child to pull the sock over his or her heel and then pull it all the way on. Another example is to teach a child to complete a six-piece non-inset puzzle by providing the child with the puzzle completed except for the last piece, and then rewarding the child for putting in this final piece. Next, the child is given the last two pieces of the puzzle to put in before being rewarded. Gradually, the child is given more pieces to complete the puzzle.

Errorless learning is one technique used in discrete-trial teaching to decrease the high error rates that can have detrimental effects (e.g. impaired retention rates) on the process of learning new information. If a child is continually getting a response wrong, he or she may quickly lose interest in learning the new task or, worse, begin to develop a variety of negative behaviors (e.g. biting, screaming, or hitting) to try to avoid the distressing situation. Errorless learning involves high-lighting the correct response in some way so that a person is less likely to respond incorrectly and then gradually introducing incorrect response choices to increase task complexity (Wolery *et al.* 1988). For example, to teach a child to match identical objects, first present only the correct object in front of the child. Then, gradually introduce an incorrect choice into the child's field of vision during each response trial so that eventually the child is faced with having to choose the initially learned correct response in the presence of an incorrect choice. Another example of errorless learning is to teach a child initially to put shapes into a shape sorter by adapting a container to have only one opening (e.g. a circle) that is large enough for the child easily to place a circular shape into the corresponding hole of the container. The errorless learning techniques in this example involve providing only one choice (circle shape and hole) and making the opening large enough to require minimal motor coordination from the child to ensure success. The opening can later be made smaller as the child develops more visual and motor control.

Functional analysis is a process of 'gathering information that can be used to build effective behavioral support plans' (O'Neill *et al.* 1990, p.3). The data gathered provide a better understanding of the targeted problem behaviors, including the functions of these behaviors and the circumstances that maintain their occurrence (O'Neill *et al.* 1990).

Generalization of skills across environments and materials is a critical issue for providers to consider in order for individuals to maintain and use therapeutically targeted learned behaviors within the context of their daily lives. Ferster (1961, p.452) discussed how sudden exposure to novel environments might cause 'gross emotional and autonomic responses' within the child with autism that can interfere with his or her ability to perform. To address this issue, a gradual and systematic transfer of the child from one situation to another is recommended. This involves being aware of the effect of changing too many variables at one time and only changing one of the following: the teaching materials, interaction partner, physical environment, directions or prompts, child's targeted behavior, or the consequences that result from the child's targeted behavior, until the child is able to engage successfully in the targeted new activity with a previously mastered skill (Wolery *et al.* 1988).

Positive reinforcement is a procedure used to increase the frequency of a behavior. There are various types of positive reinforcement (i.e. primary and secondary/generalized) as well as various schedules of reinforcement that can strengthen behaviors. Reinforcements should be continuously identified for each individual because preferences vary and change. Teaching programs usually begin with primary reinforcements such as favored toys, foods, and events (e.g. sensory and social activities). Primary reinforcements can be initially paired with social praise or tokens, which will allow for the gradual shift away from primary reinforcements to these types of secondary/generalized reinforcements (e.g. tokens earned can be exchanged later for primary reinforcements). Primary reinforcements have been found to work well for individuals who are not initially affected by social reinforcement, such as in the case of autism (Reese *et al.* 1966). Learning rates are more rapid when a behavior is initially reinforced immediately following each time it occurs (contingent reinforcement). After a behavior is learned, continuous reinforcement is not necessary and an intermittent schedule of reinforcement should be introduced to maintain the behavior (Wolery *et al.* 1988).

Prompting and modeling involve providing cues that are either verbal, physical, or both, to assist the individual in approximating a desired behavior. The prompts should be systematically faded as the individual develops mastery of the desired skill (Reese *et al.* 1966). Gradually fading prompts or doing less modeling decreases the individual's reliance on others and thus increases independence. For children with autism, the fading sequence can go from initially pairing a simple verbal instruction with a gesture or physical prompt to just using physical prompts, gradually fading them away from a full physical assist to a tap on the elbow, then simply pointing to the object of reference.

Shaping a behavior involves reinforcing each approximation of the desired behavior until the goal behavior is attained (Wolery *et al.* 1988). For example, to teach a child to clap his or her hands, reinforce the child's approximation of imitating clapping (e.g. child independently moves his or her hands in the direction of putting them together) to establish a contingent relationship between clapping behavior and reward. Then after this relationship has been established, expect a higher level of performance (e.g. child independently moves his or her hands together) before providing reinforcement.

APPENDIX 5.2

Step-By-Step Beginning Play Strategies

Strategies are adapted in part from Greenspan and Wieder (1998) and are more likely to be successful if used with a child who has first developed foundation imitation skills.

1. Offer the child a choice of two play materials or two sets of toys (e.g. container of blocks and cars or container of play dough, baby doll, utensils, and plates).

2. Allow the child to choose one; if the child cannot choose, choose one for him or her.

3. Take out all toys and initially observe the child's play and the direction the child may go with the toys. Pay attention to any spontaneous vocalizations and comments made by the child. These may provide child-directed clues for the adult to emphasize in order to encourage or lead the child's play direction.

4. Begin to engage with the child and toys by taking ideas from the child's comments and/or initial responses with the toys.

5. *Exaggerate* and be *dramatic* with play demonstrations to catch the child's attention.

6. Use object substitutions whenever possible (e.g. use cylinder blocks to represent people).

7. Pair verbal comments with actions to increase language knowledge. Alternate/pair natural language with familiar simple and concrete language to increase language knowledge. Also, use the child's familiar language paired with play actions to bridge the child's understanding to more complex language concepts.

8. Be assertive with play introductions. Do not ask the child if he or she wants to do something, as the child may not comply because of not understanding the request. Just state what is happening with the toys while providing a demonstration. Following this, wait for spontaneous

imitation from the child and then, if necessary, physically prompt the child to imitate the play actions demonstrated. Encourage the repetition of this newly learned play action. Following this, link this play action to another related play schema. For example, teach the child to have a character knock on the door of a house. Then, have another character open the door in response to the child's character knocking and say 'Hello'. Then, close door and repeat the sequence several more times. Next, demonstrate and prompt the child to have his or her character come inside the house to eat dinner after they knock on the door and say 'Hello'.

References

American Psychiatric Association (1994) *Diagnostic and Statistical Manual of Mental Disorders (DSM-IV)*, 4th edn. Washington, DC: APA.

American Psychological Association (1992) 'Ethical principles of psychologists and code of conduct.' *American Psychologist 47*, 1597–1611.

Anderson, S.R., Taras, M. and Cannon, B.O. (1996) 'Teaching new skills to young children with autism.' In C. Maurice, G. Green and S.C. Luce (eds) *Behavioral Intervention for Young Children with Autism: A Manual for Parents and Professionals.* Austin, TX: PRO-ED.

Bandura, A. and Walters, R.H. (1963) *Social Learning and Personality Development.* New York: Holt, Rinehart and Winston.

Bates, E., Thal, O. and Marchman, V. (1991) 'Symbols and syntax: a Darwinian approach to language development.' In N.A. Krasnegor and D.M. Rumbaugh (eds) *Biological and Behavioral Determinants of Language Development.* Hillsdale, NJ: Erlbaum.

Black, J., Puckett, M. and Bell, M. (1992) *The Young Child: Development from Prebirth through Age Eight.* New York: Macmillan.

Bloom, L., Lifter, K. and Broughton, J. (1985) 'The convergence of early cognition and language in the second year of life: problems in conceptualization and measurement.' In M.D. Barrett (ed) *Children's Single-Word Speech.* New York: Wiley.

Bondy, A. and Frost, L. (1994) 'The picture exchange communication system.' *Focus on Autistic Behaviour 9*, 3, 1–9.

Bruder, M.B. (1996) 'Interdisciplinary collaboration in service delivery.' In R.A. McWilliam (ed) *Rethinking Pull-Out Services in Early Intervention: A Professional Resource.* Baltimore, MD: Paul H. Brookes.

Bruning, R.H., Schraw, G.J. and Ronning, R.R. (1990) *Cognitive Psychology and Instruction*, 2nd edn. Englewood Cliffs, NJ: Prentice-Hall.

Campbell, M., Schopler, E., Cueva, J.E. and Hallin, A. (1996) 'Treatment of autistic disorder.' *Journal of the American Academy of Child and Adolescent Psychiatry 35*, 2, 134–143.

Connor, M. (1998) 'A review of behavioural early intervention programs for children with autism.' *Educational Psychology in Practice 14*, 109–117.

Dawson, G. (1996) 'Brief report: neuropsychology of autism:a report on the state of the science.' *Journal of Autism and Developmental Disorders 26*, 2, 179–184.

Dawson, G. and Osterling, J. (1997) 'Early intervention in autism.' In M.J. Guralnick (ed) *The Effectiveness of Early Intervention.* Baltimore, MD: Paul H. Brookes.

Dawson, G. and Watling, R. (2000) 'Interventions to facilitate auditory, visual, and motor integration in autism: a review of the evidence.' *Journal of Autism and Developmental Disorders 30,* 5, 415–421.

Durand, V.M. (1998) *Sleep Better! A Guide to Improving Sleep for Children with Special Needs.* Baltimore, MD: Paul H. Brookes.

Erba, H.W. (2000) 'Early intervention programs for children with autism: conceptual frameworks for implementation.' *American Journal of Orthopsychiatry 70,* 1, 82–94.

Erwin, E. (1988) 'Cognitivist and behaviorist paradigms in clinical psychology.' In D.B. Fishman, F. Rotgers and C.M. Franks (eds) *Paradigms in Behavior Therapy: Present and Promise.* New York: Springer.

Ferster, C.B. (1961) 'Positive reinforcement and behavioral deficits of autistic children.' *Child Development 32,* 437–456.

Fewell, R.R. and Kaminski, R. (1988) 'Play skills development and instruction for young children with handicaps.' In S.L. Odom and M.B. Karnes (eds) *Early Intervention for Infants and Children with Handicaps: An Empirical Base.* Baltimore, MD: Paul H. Brookes.

Frith, U. (1993) 'Autism.' *Scientific American* June, 108–114.

Gabriels, R.L. (2002) 'Art therapy with children who have autism and their families.' In C. Malchiodi (ed) *The Clinical Handbook of Art Therapy.* New York: Guilford.

Gabriels, R.L., Hill, D.E., Pierce, R., Rogers, S.J. and Wehner, B. (2001) 'Predictors of treatment outcome in children with autism.' *Autism: An International Journal of Research and Practice 5,* 4, 407–429.

Garretson, H.B., Fein, D. and Waterhouse, L. (1990) 'Sustained attention in children with autism.' *Journal of Autism and Developmental Disorders 20,* 1, 101–114.

Greenspan, S. (1992) 'Reconsidering the diagnosis and treatment of very young children with autistic spectrum or pervasive developmental disorder.' *Zero to Three National Center for Clinical Infant Programs 13,* 2, 1–9.

Greenspan, S.I. and Wieder, S. (1998) *The Child with Special Needs: Encouraging Intellectual and Emotional Growth.* A Merloyd Lawrence Book. Reading, MA: Addison-Wesley.

Gutstein, S.E. (2000) *Autism Aspergers: Solving the Relationship Puzzle. A New Developmental Program that Opens the Door to Lifelong Social and Emotional Growth.* Arlington, TX: Future Horizons.

Hanft, B.E. and Feinberg, E. (1997) 'Toward the development of a framework for determining the frequency and intensity of early intervention services.' *Inf Young Children 10,* 1, 27–37.

Harris, S.L. and Handleman, J.S. (2000) 'Age and IQ at intake as predictors of placement for young children with autism: a four- to six-year follow-up.' *Journal of Autism and Developmental Disorders 30,* 2, 137–141.

Hecimovic, A., Powell, T.H. and Christensen, L. (1999) 'Supporting families in meeting their needs.' In D.B. Zager (ed) *Autism: Identification, Education, and Treatment,* 2nd edn. Mahwah, NJ: Erlbaum.

Janzen, J.E. (1999) *Autism: Facts and Strategies for Parents.* San Antonio, TX: Therapy Skill Builders.

Johnson-Martin, N.M., Jens, K.G., Attermeier, S.M. and Hacker, B.J. (1995) *Assessment Log and Developmental Progress Charts for The Carolina Curriculum (CCISN and CCPSN, 12 months to 3 years)*. Baltimore, MD: Paul H. Brookes.

Kanner, L. (1949) 'Problems of nosology and psychodynamics of early infantile autism.' *American Journal of Orthopsychiatry 19*, 416–426.

Kazdin, A.E. (2001) 'Bridging the enormous gaps of theory with therapy, research, and practice.' *Journal of Clinical Child Psychology 30*, 1, 59–66.

Kendall, P.C. and Bacon, S.F. (1988) 'Cognitive behavior therapy.' In D.B. Fishman, F. Rotgers and C.M. Franks (eds) *Paradigms in Behavior Therapy: Present and Promise.* New York: Springer.

Kitchener, K.S. (1988) 'Dual role relationships: what makes them so problematic?' *Journal of Counseling and Development 67*, 217–221.

Koegel, L.K. (2000) 'Interventions to facilitate communication in autism.' *Journal of Autism and Developmental Disorders 30*, 5, 383–391.

Koegel, R.L., Dyer, K. and Bell, L.K. (1987) 'The influence of child preferred activities on autistic children's social behavior.' *Journal of Applied Behavior Analysis 20*, 243–252.

Koegel, R.L., O'Dell, M.C. and Koegel, L.K. (1987) 'A natural language teaching paradigm for nonverbal autistic children.' *Journal of Autism and Developmental Disorders 17*, 187–200.

Krasner, L. (1988) 'Paradigm lost: on a historical/sociological/economic perspective.' In D.B. Fishman, F. Rotgers and C.M. Franks (eds) *Paradigms in Behavior Therapy: Present and Promise.* New York: Springer.

Lerner, J. (1985) *Learning Disabilities: Theories, Diagnosis, and Teaching Strategies*, 4th edn. Boston, MA: Houghton Mifflin.

Lezak, M.D. (1995) *Neuropsychological Assessment*, 3rd edn. New York: Oxford University Press.

Liss, M., Fein, D., Allen, D., Dunn, M., Feinstein, C., Morris, R., Waterhouse, L. and Rapin, I. (2001) 'Executive functioning in high-functioning children with autism.' *Journal of Child Psychology and Psychiatry 42*, 261–270.

Lord, C. and Schopler, E. (1989) 'Stability of assessment results of autistic and non-autistic language-impaired children from preschool years to early school age.' *Journal Child Psychology and Psychiatry 30*, 4, 575–590.

Lovaas, O.I. (1981) *Teaching Developmentally Disabled Children: The ME Book.* Baltimore, MD: University Park Press.

Lovaas, O.I. (1987) 'Behavioral treatment and normal educational and intellectual functioning in young autistic children.' *Journal of Consulting and Clinical Psychology 55*, 1, 3–9.

Lovaas, O.I., Koegel, R.L. and Schreibman, L. (1979) 'Stimulus over selectivity in autism: a review of research.' *Psychological Bulletin 86*, 1236–1254.

Lovaas, O.I. and Smith, T. (1989) 'A comprehensive behavioral theory of autistic children: paradigm for research and treatment.' *Behavior Therapy and Experimental Psychiatry 20*, 17–29.

Luiselli, J.K., Cannon, B.O., Ellis, J.T. and Sisson, R.W. (2000) 'Home-based behavioral intervention for young children with autism/pervasive developmental disorder.' *Autism: The International Journal of Research and Practice 4*, 4, 427–437.

McEachin, J.J., Smith, T. and Lovaas, O.I. (1993) 'Long-term outcome for children with autism who received early intensive behavioral treatment.' *American Journal on Mental Retardation 97*, 359–372.

Marcus, L.M., Garfinkle, A. and Wolery, M. (2001) 'Issues in early diagnosis and intervention with young children with autism.' In E. Schopler, N. Yirmiya, C. Shulman and L.M. Marcus (eds) *The Research Basis for Autism Intervention.* New York: Kluwer Academic/Plenum.

Matson, J.L., Benavidez, D.A., Compton, L.S., Paclawakyj, T. and Baglio, C. (1996) 'Behavioral treatment of autistic persons: a review of research from 1980 to the present.' *Research in Developmental Disabilities 17*, 433–465.

Maurice, C., Green, G. and Luce, S.C. (eds) (1996) *Behavioral Intervention for Young Children with Autism: A Manual for Parents and Professionals.* Austin, TX: PRO-ED.

Mesibov, G.B. (1991) 'Autism.' In R. Dulbecco (ed) *Encyclopedia of Human Biology.* San Diego, CA: Academic Press.

Mesibov, G.B. (1996) 'Division TEACCH: a collaborative model program for service delivery, training, and research for people with autism and related communication handicaps.' In M.C. Roberts (ed) *Model Programs in Child and Family Mental Health.* Hillsdale, NJ: Erlbaum.

Mesibov, G.B. (2000) *The Scope and Breadth of the TEACCH Approach to Educating Students with Autism.* Presented at the Twenty-First Annual TEACCH Conference, Chapel Hill, NC, May.

Murray-Slutsky, C. (2000) 'Behavioral issues: intervention strategies.' In C. Murray-Slutsky and B.A. Paris (eds) *Exploring the Spectrum of Autism and Pervasive Developmental Disorders: Intervention Strategies.* San Antonio, TX: Therapy Skill Builders.

Murray-Slutsky, C. and Paris, B.A. (eds) (2000) *Exploring the Spectrum of Autism and Pervasive Developmental Disorders: Intervention Strategies.* San Antonio, TX: Therapy Skill Builders.

Nordin, V. and Gillberg, C. (1998) 'The long-term course of autistic disorders: update on follow-up studies.' *Acta Psychiatrica Scandinavica 97*, 2, 99–108.

O'Neill, R.E., Horner, R.H., Albin, R.W., Storey, K. and Sprague, J.R. (1990) *Functional Analysis of Problem Behavior: A Practical Assessment Guide.* Sycamore, IL: Sycamore.

Ozonoff, S. (1997) 'Neuropsychological assessment and treatment strategies.' Presented at the Eighteenth Annual TEACCH Conference, Chapel Hill, NC, May.

Ozonoff, S. and Cathcart, K. (1998) 'Effectiveness of a home program intervention for young children with autism.' *Journal of Autism and Developmental Disorders 28*, 1, 25–32.

Piaget, J. (1970) *The Science of Education of the Psychology of the Child.* New York: Grossman.

Prizant, B. and Wetherby, A. (1998) 'Understanding the continuum of discrete-trial traditional behavioral to social-pragmatic developmental approaches in communication enhancement for young children with autism/PDD.' *Seminars in Speech and Language 19*, 329–354.

Quill, K.A. (2000) *Do–Watch–Listen–Say: Social and Communication Intervention for Children with Autism.* Baltimore, MD: Paul H. Brookes.

Reese, P.E., Howard, J. and Reese, T.W. (1966) *Human Operant Behavior: Analysis and Application*, 2nd edn. Dubuque, Iowa: Wm C. Brown.

Rieber, R.W. and Carton, A.S. (eds) (1993) *The Collected Works of L.S. Vygotsky: Volume 2 – The Fundamentals of Defectology (Abnormal Psychology and Learning Disabilities).* New York: Plenum.

Rimm, D.C. and Masters, J.C. (1979) *Behavior Therapy: Techniques and Empirical Findings*, 2nd edn. New York: Academic Press.

Rogers, S.J. (1998) 'Empirically supported comprehensive treatments for young children with autism.' *Journal of Clinical Child Psychology 27*, 2, 168–179.

Rogers, S.J. (ed) (2000) 'The Denver model: a comprehensive, integrated approach to young children with autism and their families (treatment manual).' Unpublished manuscript, University of Colorado Health Sciences Center.

Rogers, S.J., Hall, T., Osaki, D., Reaven, J. and Herbison, J. (2000) 'The Denver model: a comprehensive, integrated educational approach to young children with autism and their families.' In S. Harris and J. Handleman (eds) *Preschool Education Programs for Children with Autism*, 2nd edn. Austin, TX: PRO-ED.

Rollins, P.R., Wambaco, I., Dowell, D., Mathews, L. and Reese, P.B. (1998) 'An intervention technique for children with autistic spectrum disorder: joint attentional routines.' *Journal of Communication Disorders 31*, 181–193.

Scheuffgen, K., Happé, F., Anderson, M. and Frith, U. (2000) 'High "intelligence" low "IQ"? Speed of processing and measured IQ in children with autism.' *Development and Psychopathology 12*, 1, 83–90.

Schopler, E. (2001) ' Treatment for autism from science to pseudo-science or anti-science.' In E. Schopler, N. Yirmiya, C. Shulman and L.M. Marcus (eds) *The Research Basis for Autism Intervention.* New York: Kluwer Academic/Plenum.

Schopler, E., Lansing, M., Waters, L. and Davis, J.H. (1983) *Individualized Assessment and Treatment for Autistic and Developmentally Disabled Children: Volume III – Teaching Activities for Autistic Children.* Baltimore, MD: University Park Press.

Schopler, E., Mesibov, G.B. and Hearsey, K. (1995) 'Structured teaching in the TEACCH system.' In E. Schopler and G.B. Mesibov (eds) *Learning and Cognition in Autism.* New York: Plenum.

Schopler, E., Reichler, R.J. and Lansing, M. (1980) *Individualized Assessment and Treatment for Autistic and Developmentally Disabled Children: Volume II – Teaching Strategies for Parents and Professionals.* Baltimore, MD: University Park Press.

Schreibman, L. (2000) 'Intensive behavioral/psychoeducational treatments for autism: research needs and future directions.' *Journal of Autism and Developmental Disorders 30*, 5, 373–377.

Schreibman, L. and Anderson, A. (2001) 'Focus on integration: the future of the behavioral treatment of autism.' *Behavior Therapy 32*, 619–632.

Sheinkopf, J.S. and Siegel, B. (1998) 'Home-based behavioral treatment of young children with autism.' *Journal of Autism and Developmental Disorders 28*, 15–23.

Siegel, B. (1999) 'Autistic learning disabilities and individualizing treatment for autistic spectrum disorders.' *Inf Young Children 12*, 2, 27–36.

Skinner, B.F. (1953) *Science and Human Behavior.* New York: Macmillan.

Stahmer, A.C. (1999) 'Using pivotal response training to facilitate appropriate play in children with autistic spectrum disorders.' *Child Language Teaching and Therapy 15*, 1, 29–40.

Stevens, M.C., Fein, D.A., Dunn, M., Allen, D., Waterhouse, L.H., Feinstein, C. and Rapin, I. (2000) 'Subgroups of children with autism by cluster analysis: a longitudinal examination.' *Journal of the American Academy of Child and Adolescent Psychiatry 39*, 3, 346–352.

Stone, W.L., Ousley, O.Y. and Littleford, C.D. (1997a) 'Motor imitation in young children with autism: what is the object?' *Journal of Abnormal Psychology 25*, 6, 475–485.

Stone, W.L., Ousley, O.Y., Yoder, P.J., Hogan, K.L. and Hepburn, S.L. (1997b) 'Nonverbal communication in two- and three-year-old children with autism.' *Journal of Autism and Developmental Disorders 27*, 6, 677–696.

Szatmari, P., Bryson, S.E., Streiner, D.L., Wilson, F., Archer, L. and Ryerse, C. (2000) 'Two-year outcome of preschool children with autism or Asperger's syndrome.' *American Journal of Psychiatry 157*, 1980–1987.

Todd, J.T. and Morris, E.K. (1992) 'Case histories in the great power of steady misrepresentation.' *American Psychologist 47*, 11, 1441–1453.

Trevarthen, C., Aitken, K., Papoudi, D. and Roberts, J. (1998) *Children with Autism: Diagnosis and Interventions to Meet their Needs*, 2nd edn. London: Jessica Kingsley.

Wadsworth, B.J. (1978) *Piaget for the Classroom Teacher*. New York: Longman.

Whaley, K.T. and Shaw, E. (eds) (1999) *National Early Childhood Technical Assistance System (NECTAS) Resource Collection on Autism Spectrum Disorders*. Chapel Hill, NC: NECTAS.

Whitaker-Haun, R. and Haun, S. (1997) 'Music and the autistic child: making a connection.' *Early Childhood Connections* Spring, 28–29.

Williams, E., Costall, A. and Reddy, V. (1999) 'Children with autism experience problems with both objects and people.' *Journal of Autism and Developmental Disorders 29*, 5, 367–378.

Williams, E., Reddy, V. and Costall, A. (2001) 'Taking a closer look at functional play in children with autism.' *Journal of Autism and Developmental Disorders 31*, 1, 67–77.

Wolery, M., Bailey, D.B. and Sugai, G.M. (1988) *Effective Teaching Principles and Procedures of Applied Behavior Analysis with Exceptional Students*. Boston, MA: Allyn and Bacon.

Zinober, B. and Martlew, M. (1985) 'The development of communicative gestures.' In M.D. Barrett (ed) *Children's Single-Word Speech*. New York: Wiley.

CHAPTER 6

Making Communication Meaningful
Cracking the Language Interaction Code

Adriana L. Schuler and E. Cheryl Fletcher

> *The child shall have the right to freedom of expression; this right shall include freedom to seek, receive and impart information and ideas of all kinds, regardless of frontiers, either orally, in writing or in print, in the form of art, or through any other media of the child's choice.* (United Nations Convention on the Rights of the Child, Article 13, 1989)

Helping children with autism to become better communicators presents a unique challenge, because generally these children do not truly understand the idea of communication. Moreover, their reliance on highly unconventional means to express a narrow range of communicative functions speaks to the pervasiveness of the communicative handicaps experienced by people with autism and their families. The persistence of a restricted repertoire of communicative means and functions with little room for communicative repairs (i.e. the ability to restate and reformulate the misunderstood message) illustrates the core features of the autism syndrome. The stunning diversification of the communicative repertoires of typically developing children around 20 months of age when they discover the powers of symbols presents a stark contrast.

Following a brief explanation of the terms communication, speech, and language, the chapter begins with an overview of the communication challenges commonly encountered by children with autism and their families. To provide the reader with a better understanding of the highly diverse communicative behaviors that may be encountered across the spectrum, a three-dimensional classification framework is presented. In addition, an interview format to be used with parents and other caregivers is featured.

Subsequently, recommendations for intervention are given in regard to the most challenging features of the autism spectrum. The individualized use of complementary methods is advocated to support gradual transitions into more advanced symbolic forms of representation. The need for functionality is underscored, emphasizing the importance of visual, non-transient communication systems, including picture symbols and written words. Finally, the critical role of the communication partner in scaffolding interactions and in the overall program design is emphasized.

Defining communication, speech, and language

It is easy to be fooled by an often uncanny ability to memorize and reproduce rote-memorized speech. It is our students with autism who have taught us most eloquently that while communication, speech, and language are related terms, they are not synonymous. These terms have overlapping, but not identical meanings. Speech output does not necessarily imply communication, and, even less so, language (Fay and Schuler 1980).

Communication

This term refers to the range of signals conveyed through our verbal and nonverbal behaviors, the impact of those behaviors on the behavior of others, and the information exchanged in the process. Infants start out with nonverbal signals, which provide the foundations for the later acquisition of verbal communication. While early communications seem beyond conscious control, the intentional control of nonverbal and, later, verbal behaviors increases dramatically during the first two years of life. The most competent communicators use a wide variety of verbal as well as nonverbal communicative means for a number of different reasons or functions that extend well beyond the concrete requests with which children with autism generally start out.

Speech

The term 'speech' refers merely to the act of vocalizing, the act of producing sound through the vibrations of our vocal cords. One may find a child with autism who seems mute most of the time, but who may vocalize when excited, frustrated or agitated, but yet be unaware of the fact that he or she is producing sounds. The body is acting on its own, often unintentionally. Children who communicate at a pre-intentional level often seem to be unaware of the fact that they can produce sound, or, even if they do make sounds, they are unaware of the potential control over other people that speech affords.

Language

Language is used to refer to a formalized system of communication, which allows for the communication of an infinite number of decontextualized meanings. Contrary to natural gestures, the meaning of words cannot be guessed from contexts, particularly not abstract meanings, such as those that refer to experiences and/or thoughts that are removed in time and space. Language allows for the communication of more abstract meanings because it incorporates symbolic reference and grammatical organization. While the term 'verbal' is often thought to refer to vocal output or speech, the term 'language' is used in a broader sense, making reference to a system of meanings. Therefore, it is not restricted to speech, but includes spoken as well as written words, signs, icons, photographs, drawings and a range of more or less formalized augmentative and/or alternative means of communication.

Features of communication in autism

Children with autism lack social understanding (see Garfin and Lord 1986) and have trouble grasping the nature of communication and the social use of speech. Therefore, they are prone to repeat literally the speech of others rather than internalize it and use it in conventional ways. When examining the communication patterns of individuals with autism, it is particularly important to make the distinction between non-intentional and intentional communicative behaviors. Much of the communicative repertoire of individuals with autism is expressed at a pre-intentional level without much reciprocity, even when they appear to be using a great deal of speech. This basic lack of understanding of the idea of communication is reflected in highly restricted communicative repertoires. Not only is communication used for limited communicative functions or purposes, but also it is highly stereotypic in that the same means, such as a rote memorized phrase, may be repeated ad nauseam with the exact same wording and intonation and without the benefit of additional gestures (Wetherby, Prizant and Schuler 2000).

Lack of communicative functions: objects versus people

Closer examination of the functions or purposes of communication reveal similarly restricted communicative repertoires, often characterized by a lack of social referencing and perspective taking. Communicative efforts, especially in early stages of communication and language development, are heavily skewed towards behavior regulation functions, such as requesting an object or protesting an event, as opposed to functions which are more social in nature, such as commenting, describing or sharing emotions. Most communicative efforts are object and routine centered, and seldom fulfill social needs, such as much of the chit chat that typically developing children engage in as a means of regulating social interactions. As documented by Wetherby and Prutting (1984) in a comparison of the communicative repertoires of children with autism with their developmentally matched peers, instrumental language functions, such as requests for tangibles are much more common than more social language functions, such as commenting and sharing. These findings matched those of Leo Kanner (1943), in the early 1940s, who claimed communication to be centered around objects rather than people.

Lack of communicative means: paucity of nonverbal communication

The limited grasp of communicative intent is also reflected in an overall paucity of nonverbal communication. A lack of nonverbal and paralinguistic behaviors, such as gestures, facial expression, intonation, and body orientation, which normally serve to augment communicative effectiveness, is commonly observed. Reliance on a narrow range of communicative means, which are, moreover, often highly context dependent, leaves little room for the type of negotiation and clarification that normally serves to take the edge off behavior escalations. Therefore, interactions with children with autism are often complicated by their challenging communicative behaviors. Many of the challenging behaviors exhibited by individuals with autism are better understood as unconventional attempts to communicate in the face of serious communicative limitations. For instance, troubling behaviors such as aggression and self-injury may be used to secure attention, to escape from a task or situation, to protest against changes of schedule and routine, or to regulate social interactions so that they become more predictable.

Pitfalls of pragmatics

The trouble children with autism experience with both the means as well as the functions of communication makes the pragmatics of communication particularly challenging. The subtleties of typical communicative exchanges, where both intentional as well as pre-intentional means of communication are mixed, are tough to comprehend. For instance, a speaker may delicately drop the topic of a conversation when her partner starts to blush at the introduction of a particular topic of conversation. To complicate matters, that same partner might want to conceal his embarrassment by intentionally focusing attention elsewhere. This simultaneous use of multiple levels of communicative signaling presents the core feature of human communication. As may be further demonstrated by their problems with humor and irony, it's this feature that eludes people with autism. The fact that many individuals with autism prefer the written over the spoken word may at least be partially explained by the diminished need for negotiations with the listeners, which typically require the coordination of multiple inputs and levels of signaling.

Selected assessment frameworks and strategies

The prevalence of communication differences and the complexities involved make the involvement of a speech and language pathologist (SLP) most desirable. In fact, the SLP is often the first professional approached when parents are trying to understand what is wrong with their child. When it comes to the design of an intervention program within the zone of proximal development (ZPD) the input of a SLP is invaluable. The term 'zone of proximal development' was introduced by Vygotsky (1962) in the mid-1930s to refer to the distance between what someone can do independently as opposed to with assistance of the people around them. To optimize language development of a particular child, it is important that the surrounding adults and peers speak within the proximal zone. The skewed language profiles commonly encountered in autism make it difficult for communication partners to find the right calibration and register. Consequently, speech presented to children with autism is often too complex or too simple, limiting opportunities for communicative growth. To truly gauge levels of development across the speech, language, and communication domains parents as well as practitioners need a proper framework and/or classification system to evaluate and target growth and fine tune the needed supports.

Classifying speech and language behaviors

Figure 6.1 presents a visual summary of the different types of communication, speech, and language behaviors typically encountered in children with autism as a function of the extent to which the children produce any *speech*, including any *immediate* or *delayed* forms of *echolalia* (i.e. the literal repetition of the speech of others with only a very limited appreciation of its conventional meaning) and the extent to which their vocalizations display evidence of communicative intent. The three columns serve to distinguish between children who are primarily mute and those who use immediate or delayed forms of echolalia. The first column describes three different levels of vocalization as a function of the degree of communicative intent displayed. The second column pertains to *immediate* forms of echolalia and the third column refers to *delayed* forms of echolalia.

Vocalizations

The term 'vocalization' refers to a continuum of sound production and word approximations with varying levels of communicative intent.

NON-FOCUSED VOCALIZATIONS

Different from the reciprocal babbling of typically developing infants, non-focused vocalizations seem unrelated to social context and are not accompanied by conventional gestures (e.g. hand leading and reaching). The vocalizations seem more driven by internal states, such as agitation, distress, or excitement. Rather than being motivated by the anticipation of a particular outcome, these vocalizations seem to be the non-intentional side product of internal variables.

FOCUSED VOCALIZATIONS

The term 'focused vocalizations' is used in reference to those vocalizations that seem more context sensitive, more discriminative, and generally less stereotypic. In other words, a larger variety of sounds is produced in a more flexible fashion. While communicative intent may not be evident, the vocalizations are often accompanied by emerging albeit non-conventional gestures.

FUNCTIONAL VOCALIZATIONS

When the vocalizations are produced in clear anticipation of certain outcomes, as may be evidenced by the obvious frustration experienced when

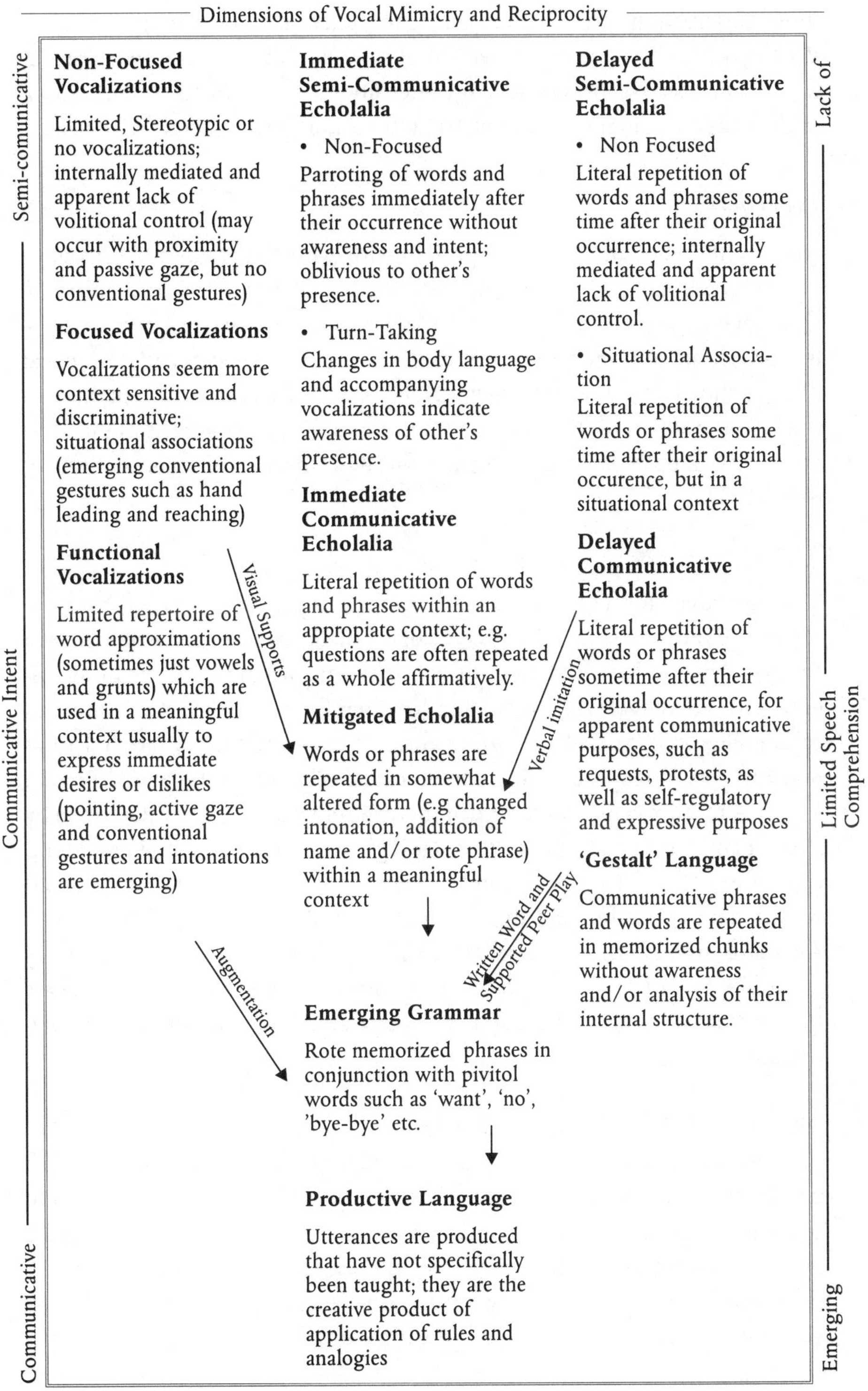

Dimensions of Vocal Mimicry and Reciprocity

Non-Focused Vocalizations

Limited, Stereotypic or no vocalizations; internally mediated and apparent lack of volitional control (may occur with proximity and passive gaze, but no conventional gestures)

Focused Vocalizations

Vocalizations seem more context sensitive and discriminative; situational associations (emerging conventional gestures such as hand leading and reaching)

Functional Vocalizations

Limited repertoire of word approximations (sometimes just vowels and grunts) which are used in a meaningful context usually to express immediate desires or dislikes (pointing, active gaze and conventional gestures and intonations are emerging)

Immediate Semi-Communicative Echolalia

• Non-Focused
Parroting of words and phrases immediately after their occurrence without awareness and intent; oblivious to other's presence.

• Turn-Taking
Changes in body language and accompanying vocalizations indicate awareness of other's presence.

Immediate Communicative Echolalia

Literal repetition of words and phrases within an appropiate context; e.g. questions are often repeated as a whole affirmatively.

Mitigated Echolalia

Words or phrases are repeated in somewhat altered form (e.g changed intonation, addition of name and/or rote phrase) within a meaningful context

Emerging Grammar

Rote memorized phrases in conjunction with pivitol words such as 'want', 'no', 'bye-bye' etc.

Productive Language

Utterances are produced that have not specifically been taught; they are the creative product of application of rules and analogies

Delayed Semi-Communicative Echolalia

• Non Focused
Literal repetition of words and phrases some time after their original occurrence; internally mediated and apparent lack of volitional control.

• Situational Association
Literal repetition of words or phrases some time after their original occurence, but in a situational context

Delayed Communicative Echolalia

Literal repetition of words or phrases sometime after their original occurrence, for apparent communicative purposes, such as requests, protests, as well as self-regulatory and expressive purposes

'Gestalt' Language

Communicative phrases and words are repeated in memorized chunks without awareness and/or analysis of their internal structure.

Visual Supports

Verbal imitation

Written Word and Supported Peer Play

Augmentation

Semi-comunicative

Communicative

Communicative Intent

Lack of

Limited Speech Comprehension

Emerging

Figure 6.1 Charting Speech and Language Behaviors

those anticipations are violated, the term 'functional vocalizations' is used. When efforts do not result in desired outcomes, children may try to 'repair' the communicative breakdown by intensifying their efforts, often adding other means of communication such as intonation, gestures, and active gaze.

Echolalia

Not all children with autism will present with echolalia or go through a stage of being echolalic. However, just as with the neurotypical population *all* children with autism who become verbal either display delayed or immediate forms of imitation. Immediate forms of echoing occur when children repeat phrases shortly after hearing them. Delayed echolalia refers to repetition at some later point, with the delayed repetition of TV commercials as the most common example. The following sections describe a continuum of forms of echolalia.

IMMEDIATE SEMI-COMMUNICATIVE ECHOLALIA

This immediate form of echoing refers to those types of repetitions that seem relatively void of meaning. In this type of echolalia, children seem oblivious to the presence of others, and their speech lacks concurrent action and body orientation, eye contact with others, and/or other forms of nonverbal communication. The most socially oblivious form of such echoing is referred to as non-focused, immediate semi-communicative echolalia (Schuler and Prizant 1985). A more socially aware type of this echoing was originally described by Prizant and Duchan (1981) as 'turn-taking'. This immediate semi-communicative form of echolalia may be indicative of an emerging awareness of a conversational partnership and the differentiation of speaker and listener roles. An illustration of this type of echolalia is when Jimmy says, 'Jimmy say good-bye to daddy', when prompted to do so. This is more socially aware because the child waits for the adult to stop talking before starting his echoing routine.

IMMEDIATE COMMUNICATIVE ECHOLALIA

This immediate form of echoing occurs when phrases are repeated to fulfill particular communicative functions, and shows a better grasp of the meaning of communication despite the fact that the grammatical structure of language is not yet understood. For example, a child asked, 'Do you want a cookie?' may repeat this question in an affirmative manner, as indicated by the accompanying body motions, gestures, or intonation patterns. It is encouraging when this type of immediate repetition occurs for reasons other than requesting, such as when a child repeats a directive when carrying out the corresponding action.

DELAYED SEMI-COMMUNICATIVE ECHOLALIA

When a child produces memorized phrases or words without an appropriate context some time after the occurrence of the model utterance, this is called delayed semi-communicative echolalia, as captured in the third column. Again, a differentiation is being made between relative non-focused, socially more oblivious forms of repetition and those that at least show some contextual discrimination. Common examples of this type of non-focused delayed echolalia are the indiscriminate repetitions of whole or parts of commercial advertisements often produced with the same animation and/or theatrical effects. For instance, Johnny would repeat the following phrase preserving the identical intonation, while flapping his arms and jumping around excitedly: 'Barney was brought to you by the makers of Juicy Juice ©, 100 per cent real fruit juice, and by the J. Arthur Vining Foundation ©, the corporation for public broadcasting and by contributions to your PBS stations from viewers like you.'

Increasingly discriminate examples of semi-communicative echolalia occur when the repeated words or phrases are uttered in a similar situational context. The most classic example of this type of echolalia is when a child repeats phrases typically uttered by adults when that child is upset or agitated. Under those circumstances the child may say things such as, 'Stop hitting yourself, everything will be OK, you calm down now.' This child is merely associating the situational context (also called 'situation association': Schuler and Prizant 1985) with the memorized phrase rather than using the phrase as a self-calming device. More situation association is demonstrated by Mark, who was observed to walk to the computer while muttering to himself 'Click on the sound' apparently repeating the instructions from his last computer activity, perhaps in anticipation of what was to come. Such anticipation and situational differentiation is encouraging and may well pave the road for more intentional and more clearly communicative uses of echoing.

DELAYED COMMUNICATIVE ECHOLALIA

This type of echoing refers to the use of rote, stereotyped phrases to express a limited set of meanings. Besides the obvious requesting functions, this type of echoing has often been observed in the context of discontent and protest. For instance, Daniel would say 'No videos' or 'Go to Dr Bellamy's house' as an attempt to escape. Again, it is most encouraging when echoing is used to express related functions. For example, Sarah learned to use the phrase 'You, sit down now' as a way to regulate her own behavior after initial rote repetition.

MITIGATED ECHOLALIA

This term refers to the less literal repetition of words and phrases. Slight alterations are introduced, including changes in intonation and addition or deletion of pivotal words (e.g. please, no, more, or want). For instance, when Timmy is told, 'Time for Timmy to go to the potty', he may respond by saying, 'No, time for Timmy to go to potty' or 'Timmy go potty later'. At a more basic level, a child may change a question intonation into an affirmative mode of speaking when literally repeating a question, such as 'You want to go outside?'

GESTALT LANGUAGE

This term refers to the continued reliance on rote phrases or even whole paragraphs that are produced communicatively, albeit often unconventionally (Prizant 1983). For example, Isaac repeatedly used the phrase, 'I lost the file, I have to reboot', when he apparently had forgotten what he wanted to say. The literal repetition of memorized language forms may persist, and caretakers need to be tuned into a child's interests and experiences to help interpret and dissect the unprocessed gestalt forms which otherwise may seem odd.

EMERGING GRAMMAR

Both gestalt language and mitigated forms of echolalia are indicative of emerging grammatical abilities, as illustrated by the child who, dismayed on finding that it was still foggy, told his mother, 'The sun is broken, fix it'. Although heavily relying on gestalt language, this child is displaying the kind of rule-governed verbal behavior generally seen as the hallmark of generative language.

Even when children have worked out the basic rules of syntax, pragmatics continue to be rather elusive and deserve to be a prime focus of intervention. Problems are seen in the overly literal use of language and limited comprehension of written text, despite often remarkable decoding skills. For example, children have been observed reading aloud foreign titles on magazines or books with little awareness of the fact that they cannot understand what they are reading.

Role of the speech and language pathologist

The role of speech and language pathologists in the assessment and treatment of the person with autism is a highly significant one and involves the following:

- assessing and describing the level of the child's communication skills as opposed to what the child is able to produce when prompted
- explaining to caregivers the nature of their child's communication difficulties
- developing intervention strategies to increase the child's communication effectiveness
- adapting their own communication style with techniques such as waiting and decreasing the amount of speech output
- educating caregivers and other treatment providers about intervention strategies to facilitate the child's communication
- participating in multidisciplinary teams when possible
- coordinating home–school speech and language treatment programs.

In summary, the speech and language pathologist's role is to educate parents and other treatment providers on how to adapt their communication style and the environment so that the child with autism may become a successful communicator. In order to do so the speech language pathologist needs to work together with the family or other caregivers to obtain an accurate picture of the child's communicative behaviors in everyday contexts. The following interview format was developed specifically as a tool to help obtain this information for the most severely impacted children.

Assesssing communicative means and functions through a semi-structured interview

While a comprehensive discussion of assessment issues is beyond the scope of this chapter (see also Koegel, Koegel and Smith 1997), what follows is a brief description of an assessment tool that has proven to be particularly helpful in those cases when the combination of language and behavior challenges makes it virtually impossible to use more conventional assessment tools.

Communication interview

The communication interview was originally developed by Schuler (1981) and has since been expanded and field-tested (Schuler *et al.* 1989). It has been further adapted and refined to be included in this chapter (Table 6.1). The primary aim of this interview is to investigate which communicative behaviors or *means* are used for which communicative purposes or *functions*. This information is most readily obtained through a systematic, semi-structured interview, which invites closer collaboration between parents, caregivers and professionals. Unlike standardized assessment instruments, this interview may be used repeatedly over short periods of time to show changes in a child's communication skills.

As portrayed in Table 6.1, the communication interview examines five basic communication functions or contexts which typically emerge first in the repertoire of children with autism, including requests for affection and inter-action, requests for adult action, and requests for desired items (e.g. objects or food), along with protests and comments. If additional higher-level functions have emerged, the interviewer is encouraged to expand upon the existing framework by adding additional questions and contexts.

Before starting out, the interviewer should make the interviewee familiar with the range of communication *means* at the top of the protocol sheets and the *functions* (vertical columns). It should be made clear to the interviewee that not all of these behaviors may be communicative, and that it may not always be easy to distinguish between communicative and non-communicative forms of behaviors such as crying or self-injury. It is important that the interviewer coaches the interviewee in evaluating the communicative functions of the behaviors observed.

Before proceeding any further, the interviewer may need to provide further explanations of some of the communicative means examined. For instance, the terms 'passive gaze' as opposed to 'active gaze' usually require clarification. This is most easily accomplished through examples. Passive gaze often occurs when the child stands in proximity to a person or object and just stares. Active gaze, on the other hand, occurs when the child shifts his or her gaze back and forth between the desired object and the person to whom the request is being directed. Children who use active gaze demonstrate greater understanding of the relationship between their actions and the actions of

Table 6.1 Communication Interview

Communication Interview

Name: _____

DOB: _____

Date completed: _____

Interviewee: _____

Completed by: _____

Comments

Behavior	\[Comments\]	1. REQUESTS FOR AFFECTION AND INTERACTION: WHAT IF CHILD WANTS	ADULT TO SIT NEAR	PEER TO SIT NEAR	NON-HANDICAPPED PEER TO SIT NEAR	ADULT TO LOOK AT HIM	ADULT TO TICKLE CHILD	ADULT TO CUDDLE/EMBRACE CHILD	TO SIT ON ADULTS LAP	OTHER:	2. REQUESTS FOR ADULT ACTION: WHAT IF CHILD WANTS	HELP WITH DRESSING	TO BE READ A BOOK	TO PLAY BALL/ GAME	TO GO OUTSIDE, TO STORE	OTHER:
CRYING																
AGGRESSION																
TANTRUMS/SELF-INJURY																
PASSIVE GAZE																
PROXIMITY																
PULLING OTHER'S HANDS (HANDLEADING)																
TOUCHING/MOVING OTHER'S FACE OR BODY																
GRABS/REACHES																
ENACTMENT																
REMOVES SELF/WALKS AWAY																
VOCALIZATION/NOISE																
OTHER																
ACTIVE GAZE																
GIVES OBJECT																
GESTURES/POINTING																
FACIAL EXPRESSION																
SHAKES HEAD 'NO'/NODS HEAD 'YES'																
INTONATION																
OTHER																
INAPPROPRIATE ECHOLAIA																
APPROPRIATE ECHOLAIA																
PICTURES & OTHER VISUAL SYMBOLS																
ONE WORD SPEECH																
ONE WORD SIGN																
COMPLEX SPEECH																
COMPLEX SIGN																
WRITTEN WORDS																

Summary

Main Means:

Main Functions:

Other Observations:

Behaviour	3. REQUESTS FOR OBJECTS, FOOD OR THINGS: WHAT IF CHILD WANTS						4. PROTEST: WHAT IF						5. DECLARATION/COMMENT: WHAT IF CHILD WANTS		
	AN OBJECT OUT OF REACH	A DOOR/CONTAINER OPENED	A FAVORITE FOOD	MUSIC/RADIO/TV	KEYS/TOY/BOOK	OTHER:	COMMON ROUTINE IS DROPPED	FAVORITE TOY/FOOD IS TAKEN AWAY	TAKEN FOR RIDE WITHOUT DESIRE	ADULT TERMINATES INTERACTION	REQUIRED TO DO SOMETHING BUT DOESN'T WANT TO	OTHER:	TO SHOW YOU SOMETHING	YOU TO LOOK AT SOMETHING	OTHER:
CRYING															
AGGRESSION															
TANTRUMS/SELF-INJURY															
PASSIVE GAZE															
PROXIMITY															
PULLING OTHER'S HANDS (HANDLEADING)															
TOUCHING/MOVING OTHER'S FACE OR BODY															
GRABS/REACHES															
ENACTMENT															
REMOVES SELF/WALKS AWAY															
VOCALIZATION/NOISE															
OTHER															
ACTIVE GAZE															
GIVES OBJECT															
GESTURES/POINTING															
FACIAL EXPRESSION															
SHAKES HEAD 'NO'/NODS HEAD 'YES'															
INTONATION															
OTHER															
INAPPROPRIATE ECHOLAIA															
APPROPRIATE ECHOLAIA															
PICTURES & OTHER VISUAL SYMBOLS															
ONE WORD SPEECH															
ONE WORD SIGN															
COMPLEX SPEECH															
COMPLEX SIGN															
WRITTEN WORDS															

others, suggesting a greater level of intentionality. Active gaze may also be accompanied by gestures such as reaching or pointing and perhaps body orientation. The term 'enactment' refers to a ritualized sequence of behaviors in which a child engages in anticipation of an expected outcome. For example, a child might seat him- or herself in a stroller as an indication of a desire to go outside or take the car keys to indicate a desire to go for a ride. These behaviors are clearly pre-symbolic, but suggest some basic under-standing of cause and effect.

In order to sample existing, different communicative functions, the inter-viewee is asked questions about the child's responses to specific everyday communicative *contexts*. The interviewee is asked what the child might be likely to do in the sketched contexts. The behaviors reported for a particular communication function are marked in the appropriate column.

When the interview is completed, the results may be summarized on the interview protocol sheet. The responses obtained speak to the overall level of interactiveness. Suitable communication objectives are identified through inspection of the profile obtained. Appropriate communicative means may be expanded to cross new contexts and functions, while undesirable communicative means may be replaced by more mutually satisfying ones.

By participating in the interview process, the interviewees typically become more aware of their interaction and communication patterns. It is believed that such gains in meta-communicative knowledge are very important for them to become more effective facilitators of the communicative development of their children. For instance, the interview process helps the interviewees realize that many of the behaviors they had previously thought of as inappropriate are in fact communicative acts.

Intervention issues: promoting meaningful communication and comprehension

To improve the communicative skills of children with autism it is critically important to realize that we are not merely dealing with cases of slow or incomplete development. Exposure to everyday instances of spontaneous language use has for many children not led to an understanding of what communication is all about. They differ from children with other forms of language delay in two important ways. First, they display very little initiative, as may be evidenced by the fact that they do not use grunts and body language to compensate for their lack of speech. The fact that those who speak are prone to repeat the speech of others literally may be further testimony to the lack of communicative intent. Second, speech or no speech, almost all of the children on the spectrum are challenged when it comes to the processing of speech and related auditory input (Wetherby *et al.* 2000). Following an initial discussion of the challenges surrounding the establishment of communicative intent, the implications of auditory processing differences and related differences in thinking and learning will be presented. The final discussion of this section centers around a table that presents major intervention objectives and the accompanying activities.

Communicative intent

As discussed earlier in this chapter, it is important to distinguish between non-intentional and intentional communicative behaviors in planning intervention. Much of the communicative repertoire of individuals with autism remains largely pre-intentional even when they appear to be using a great deal of speech.

BUILDING ANTICIPATION

It is the anticipation that comes with the repetition of a particular sequence of events that provides the motivation to engage in some type of communicative behavior when the anticipated sequence is violated. Because of this reality the repetition of daily rituals, routines and ceremonies, such as 'circle time', should be an important part of any attempt to teach communication skills, as the recycling of routine sequences provides the foundation for the more explicit communicative behaviors. The violation of a particular set of anticipations may 'seduce' an otherwise not communicative child into a communicative act (Wetherby, Prizant and Schuler 2000; Sussman 2000). For example, a child who wants to continue a terminated tickling game might approach the tickling partner, lift his or her arm in anticipation, take that partner's hand and attempt to put that same hand back in the favorite tickling position. At a more advanced stage this same child may say or sign 'tickle' or use some type of picture or other visual symbol. As so insightfully described in Bruner's (1975) by now classic paper on the ontogeny of human communication, the above example may serve to illustrate how early communication behaviors tend to be very physical, thriving on the anticipation of familiar routines.

FUNCTIONALITY

In teaching children with autism to communicate through the use of speech, signs, gestures, or some type of picture system and/or written words, it is most important to start with those forms of language that have the greatest and most immediate impact. Every communicative behavior solicited from the child should be met by tangible and reinforcing consequences. For instance, a thirsty child who is being taught to say or sign 'water', 'juice' or 'drink' or use a picture symbol needs to receive the requested item immediately. The consequences of this kind of language are directly relevant to that child, and also natural rather than contrived, which enhances the chances of spontaneous use as well as generalization. It is critical that the child learns to experience the power of language in whatever form, as a means of effecting his or her environment and getting his or her needs met. This is why it is so important not to focus solely on speech. The use of natural gestures needs to be taught and other more formalized forms of augmentation introduced. Whenever appropriate they should be presented in conjunction with written language symbols.

SOCIAL SUBTLETIES

Other more socially referenced language functions may not provide for such salient and relevant consequences. It is much more difficult to teach a child to say 'juice' when looking at a picture of a glass of orange juice, or say 'the boy is jumping' when looking at picture of children playing soccer. In everyday speech such utterances are followed by more social and subtle consequences, such as nods or smiles, which the child with autism may neither notice nor understand. In a carefully structured teaching situation a child can be taught to produce these types of more social utterances by providing more tangible consequences, but such consequences would be contrived. As discussed by Koegel (2000), more naturalistic teaching paradigms have been found to be more effective in the long run.

Speech and auditory processing

A second major challenge in teaching language to children with autism pertains to the integrity of speech production and auditory processing mechanisms. Commonly children with autism are reported to not respond to speech directed to them, or to respond inconsistently, causing many parents to question their children's hearing early in life. As discussed by Ratey (2001), clinical observations have led professionals to speculate on biological differences that might explain troubles with, for example, the type of rapid processing that is a critical feature of speech comprehension. The following statement, uttered by an adolescent with autism, speaks clearly to the kinds of challenges experienced, 'Slow down. I can't listen that fast. My brain is only a pre-Pentium.'

VISUOSPATIAL ADVANTAGE

Commonly reported problems in attending to and attaching meaning to spoken language may indeed be the result of more basic processing differences. While many children with autism may be capable of memorizing whole pieces of dialogue, their comprehension of speech tends to be minimal, as is their comprehension of nonverbal communicative signals. In contrast, these children are often astute observers of visual details and seem to be more competent when it comes to processing visual gestalts (Grandin 1995; Schuler 1995). Generally speaking, individuals with autism perform considerably better when presented with non-transient rather than transient stimulus input. Non-transient stimuli (e.g. pictures, drawings, writing) refer to information that remains visible or present over time. Transient stimuli refer to information input that fades over time (e.g. speech, gesture, facial expression) and requires integrity of temporal processing. Lastly, as originally observed by Kanner (1943) and further investigated by Papy, Papy and Schuler (1995), children with autism seem to find it easier to make abstractions and inferences about object properties and spatial orientation than about the impact of their own and others' actions.

VISUALIZING GRAMMAR

For children with autism to transition into a more symbolic mode of mind, a more dynamic interaction-based level of representation needs to be added to a more static set of meanings, such as those used to label objects and their physical properties. The common persistence of echolalia and 'gestalt language' (as discussed above) speaks to the fact that children with autism find it difficult to detect how phrases can be segmented into smaller meaningful pieces, including single words and individual speech sounds. The internal structure of sentences seems to elude them. They need to learn how they can create their own utterances from scratch rather than rely on the use of prefabricated units. This requires that larger memorized utterances are segmented into smaller meaningful units, and that single words and phrases are combined in new creative ways. The use of written words and other visual communication systems has been found to be most useful, as they help to visualize the organizational structure. For this purpose it is important to capitalize upon the power of written words, as many children with autism learn to recognize written words on their own (so-called hyperlexia) without the benefit of specific instruction. With careful instructional guidance written words may be used as stepping-stones to spoken language.

Table 6.2 Developing symbolic language: A road map		
	Challenges/Objectives	Activities
Making Speech Meaningful	**Consistent Responding to Speech** Lack of consistent responses to the spoken work leads many parents to believe their child may be deaf. Many children with autism respond inconsistently or not at all to the speech of others. In these cases an 'auditory wake-up call' may be needed.	• Training to respond to name • Training child to look at speaker when addressed
	Personal Cause and Effect Understanding Autistic children's common reliance on pre-intentional communication may speak to their limited understanding of the impact of their own and other people's actions. They seem to lack an understanding of means–end relations and human causality. They may need to be taught specifically to anticipate highly dramatized routines.	• Create anticipation through highly salient routines and ceremonies: use exaggerated affect if needed • Strengthen sense of personal power through participation in carefully structured choice making routines (teach pointing, if necessary)
	Associating Actions with Speech Children with autism often excel in object naming and labelling but have a lack of understanding of object use. They have difficulty associating their own and other people's actions with spoken words. They need a more enactive mode of representation if they are to develop a more symbolic mode of thinking.	• Establish simple motor responses to single spoken words or phrases (e.g. sit, jump) • Establish more complex responses to combinations of words and phrases (e.g. jump and turn versus jump)

Promoting True Language		
	Challenge of Segmentation	
	Children with autism have difficulty detecting how phrases can be segmented into smaller meaningful pieces, including single words and individual speech sounds. They often continue to rely on 'gestalt forms' as the internal structure of sentences seems to elude them.	• Visualizing grammar through the use of written words and visual symbols • Present systematic variations in grammatic patterns • Within play context present systematic variations on themes, closely matching child's actions with contingent speech
	Language beyond Requests	
	Requests for concrete objects and protests against routine violations are typically the first dimensions of communication to be learned by children with autism. The challenge is to expand their communicative repotoire to include more socially and cognitively referenced language functions such as self-regulation and commenting.	• Promote variety of activities and contexts that invite the participation in a widee functional diversification of communicative behaviors. • Model a variety of communicative functions Promote reciprocity and extend numbers of interactional turns by providing opportunities for joint attention, joint action such as in 'circle time' and Integrated Play Groups.
	Integrating Nonverbal with Verbal Communication	
	Even after aquiring impressive language skills, persons with autism often retain unusual delivery style characterized by monotonous or sterotypic intonation patterns and poor nonverbal communication.	• Avoid single focus on speech production out of context. • Teach gestures and nonverbal forms of communication • Establishing pragmatic foundations through role play, participation in Integrated Play Groups and explicit instruction in theatre and dance.

Cracking the language interaction mode

The combination of differences in learning and thinking discussed above along with the limited understanding of people, their feelings, their intentions and their states of mind taxes the acquisition of symbolic language so much that many children remain at a pre-symbolic level of operation. After all, language involves the mapping of social as well as object knowledge and utilizes a speech-based transient mode of communication. Children with autism are challenged not only by the code used to represent meanings, but also by the language content involved. In helping children with autism crack the language code we typically face a number of major challenges, depending on the levels of functioning encountered. Table 6.2 summarizes these different types of challenges and related objectives as a function of levels of representation and overall language development. The second column of Table 6.2 lists a number of activities that may be used to meet the larger objectives.

MAKING SPEECH MEANINGFUL

For children who are largely pre-intentional and who have very little speech, the primary goal is to attend to and attach meaning to speech. By learning to make connections between the causes and effects of their own actions, children begin to appreciate the power of speech as a tool to meet their needs. For children who do have speech, but whose communication is largely pre-intentional, the primary goal is to guide them into the use of a more symbolic form of 'true language'. When dealing with children who are largely nonverbal and pre-intentional the reality that needs to be faced is that speech may not always be a viable primary communication option.

ALTERNATIVES TO SPEECH

Assessment findings as described earlier in this chapter may indicate that natural gestures need to be established first, and/or a more formalized non-speech communication system may need to be introduced. Yet this does not mean that speech should not be worked on. While working on speech augmentation and/or natural gestures, efforts can be made to increase rates of vocalization and/or the establishment of vocal imitation.

At the most basic level children need to learn to respond consistently to their name and begin to assign meaning to speech. If necessary an 'auditory wake-up call' may need to be orchestrated, specifically teaching the child to respond to his or her name and take notice of people in the daily environment. Later on they need to be taught not only to use speech for purposes of labeling, but also to make reference to their own and other people's actions, inviting a more enactive mode of representation, which sets the stage for a more symbolic mode of thinking.

PROMOTING TRUE LANGUAGE

A primary goal in dealing with children who display communicative intent, but whose speech is still rote and pre-symbolic, is to teach how words are combined in grammatical ways and how language is used symbolically. For this purpose it is most important that language input is carefully monitored within the proximal zone of development (described earlier in this chapter). In addition, multiple contexts and experiences need to be targeted to avoid overly literal meanings generated by single experiences in single contexts. This need to move into more symbolic modes of language may speak further to the importance of peer relations and symbolic play. As further discussed below, supported participation in dramatic peer play has been found to enhance the transition from stereotypic, largely echolalic speech, to creative language use.

LANGUAGE BEYOND REQUESTS

A greater understanding of objects and space as compared with people is also reflected in the fact that requests for concrete objects and protests against routine violations are typically the first functions of communication to be learned by most children with autism. The challenge is to expand their communicative repertoire to include more social and cognitively referenced language functions, such as self-regulation and social commenting (Hadwin *et al.* 1997). A prime challenge in dealing with more social forms of reference is that people are always changing their appearance and location. As discussed earlier in this section, the establishment of joint attention, action and affect requires the careful selection of suitable contexts and interaction styles (for more in-depth discussion, see next section).

PEER-SUPPORTED PLAY

To help children appreciate a larger number of reasons to communicate social contexts that invite joint attention, joint affect and joint action need to be targeted, as they are the critical ingredients of more socially referenced forms of communication. Interventions that feature peer-supported play interactions (Schuler and Wolfberg 2000; Wolfberg 1995, 1999; Wolfberg and Schuler 1993; Zercher *et al.* 2001) are promising because they seem to increase rates of joint attention and invite more symbolic language use. Moreover, use of play as a medium of intervention offers opportunities to balance the best of drill and practice with more naturalistic teaching paradigms. Where incidental teaching may not offer sufficient opportunities for the practice needed to reach mastery, play offers more opportunities for systematic practice. The careful selection of motivating play scripts allows a targeted scenario, such as being checked out at the cash register, to be repeated over and over, and the participating children to switch roles. In fact, just like typically developing children, they will continue playing a theme over and over until they know it by heart.

INTEGRATING VERBAL AND NONVERBAL COMMUNICATION

A final goal pertains to the monotonous and/or stereotypic intonation patterns and the parallel paucity of concomitant nonverbal communication that seems so characteristic of even the most competent communicators. While some of these peculiarities in vocal delivery may be a reflection of the autistic theory of mind or lack of it, they may also be a reflection of prevailing training strategies. The extreme emphasis that is commonly placed upon speech and vocal output may not be productive in the long run. Based on recent qualitative research of longer term outcomes much benefit may be derived from explicit instruction in theater, dance, and related role play (Muller, Burton and Schuler 2001).

Need to mix and match

The various challenges as described in Table 6.2 and discussed previously may be helpful in the selection of treatment approaches and strategies. Complementary strategies and program components may be derived from different treatment approaches and theoretical models to match best the needs of individual children. For instance, the usefulness of the discrete-trial training (DTT) model, as described by Lovaas (1987) and popularized by Maurice (1993), has been documented in teaching children to respond consistently to their name and improve their overall awareness and interest in speech. The same paradigm, however, may be limiting when it comes to more dynamic and symbolic dimensions of language. Social-communication approaches, such as those described by Quill (1995, 2000), Wetherby, Schuler and Prizant (1997), and Sussman (2000), may be more compatible with the cultural nature of language acquisition. The TEACCH model (Schopler, Mesibov and Hearsey 1995) has been helpful in reducing anxiety through the provision of visual structure and the elimination of excessive verbalization. These strategies also improve children's comprehension of their daily living environment. A major contribution of the Floor-Time model (Greenspan and Wieder 1998) is that it addresses the quality of the social relationship in general. With regard to language, this child-centered approach, is more inviting of turn-taking and longer cycles of interaction (see Chapter 5 for a more detailed description of these treatment models).

Context and interaction style as mediators of competence

Since children with autism may initially be incapable of establishing a joint focus of attention, the give and take of everyday conversations presents a challenge. The back and forth flow of reciprocal communication is not easily established. Therefore, the burden of change should not be placed on the most disabled communication partner. Since communication requires interaction, the prime responsibility for more successful communication lies with the more competent partner.

NEED FOR ACCOMMODATIONS

Without specific accommodations, communication will remain a one-way enterprise. In order to arrive eventually at more reciprocity the adult needs, at least initially, to accommodate the interests and initiatives of the child involved, even if they take unconventional forms. Because such accommodations need to be customized, close observation and ongoing evaluation of the child's current levels of understanding and competence are critical. Such observations should pinpoint the situational contexts, interaction styles, modes of communication, and related supports that invite the greatest levels of communicative initiatives and competence within the zone of proximal development (Vygotsky 1962).

NEED FOR FACILITATION

When working with a child who is as communicatively challenged as a child with autism, communication partners are maximally taxed. Rather than focusing on the child's deficiencies, partners must select those registers and styles of communication, which optimize children's participation. Besides monitoring and modulating their style of communication and mode of inter-action, communication partners might also want to exaggerate their intonation and facial expression or playfully intrude upon the child to facilitate communication (Greenspan and Wieder 1998; Sussman 2000). The goal of these techniques is to create environments that are responsive even to minimal communicative initiations from the child and shape those initiatives into more robust, persistent, and conventionalized signals.

FORM, USE, AND CONTENT

Finally, communication partners need to engage in ongoing evaluation of their attempts to facilitate communication. Specifically, they evaluate the dimensions of form, use, and content of their communication style.

Form refers to the complexity of the utterances presented. Ideally, language forms are presented that approximate or are within the child's proximal zone. Use of back and forth repetition of each other's speech is very important here, but carefully planned systematic variations (e.g. 'Jimmy's apple' or 'big apple') on a targeted form (e.g. 'yummy apple') need to be presented, rather than more literal repetitions of the same utterance. This makes the verbal interaction last over several turns. Similarly, children should not be asked to repeat long utterances beyond their comprehension, such as 'I want a slice of green apple, please' when 'More apple please' would suffice.

Use refers to the reasons for which people communicate and in which context. Practitioners and parents need to examine the pragmatics of their own utterances as well as of the children they interact with. Bombarding the child with long lists of stereotyped commands is not likely to provide the child with an experience of communicative power. More empowering communicative equivalents may be taught when undesirable behavior serves an important communicative function.

Content refers to the meanings that are conveyed and the levels of abstractions involved. Therefore, the child's level of cognitive understanding needs to be examined. For instance, it may not be productive to teach a child labels for a series of pictures if that child is not able to match real-life objects with their pictorial representations. Similarly, it does not make sense to have a child without object permanence request objects out of sight or activities out of context. Communication needs to be established at a more concrete level. For example, more meaningful and concrete requests are taught by having the child request the continuation of fun activities that were deliberately terminated. To provide the child with a sense of success requires the partner to tailor carefully the type of prompting and contextual support needed. First and foremost, the communication partner needs to know how to get the child's attention without drowning him or her in meaningless speech, how to take turns by imitating the child, when to wait and hold out for a response, when not to talk, and not to dominate the interaction when facing limited competence. To say it in fewer words: animate, imitate, participate, and wait!

Conclusion

In summary, it needs to be recognized that autism is a complex disorder and that there is no one universal approach to assessment and treatment that will be effective for all children with autism. Rather, approaches need to be tailored for each individual child and each family. In our experience the most effective approaches are those that draw from various theoretical models and applied research, and are continuously fine-tuned based on the ongoing evaluation of data collected. Meaningful communication and comprehension should always be prime considerations.

References

Bruner, J. (1975) 'From communication to language: a psychological perspective.' *Cognition 3*, 255–289.

Fay, W.H. and Schuler, A.L. (1980) 'Emerging language in autistic children.' In R.L. Schiefelbusch (ed) *Language Intervention Series*. Baltimore, MD: University Park Press.

Garfin, D. and Lord, C. (1986) 'Communication as a social problem in autism.' In E. Schopler and G. Mesibov (eds) *Social Behavior in Autism*. New York: Plenum.

Grandin, T. (1995) *Thinking in Pictures and Other Reports of my Life with Autism*. New York: Double Day.

Greenspan, S.I. and Wieder, S. (1998) 'Developmental patterns and outcomes in infants and children with disorders in relating and communication: a chart review of 200 cases of children with autistic spectrum diagnoses.' *Journal of Developmental and Learning Disorders 1*, 1, 87–141.

Hadwin, J., Baron-Cohen, S., Howlin, P. and Hill, K. (1997) 'Does teaching theory of mind have an effect on the ability to develop conversation in children with autism?' *Journal of Autism and Developmental Disorders 27*, 519–539.

Kanner, L. (1943) 'Autistic disturbances of affective contact.' *Nervous Child 2*, 217–250.

Koegel, L.K. (2000) 'Interventions to facilitate communication in autism.' *Journal of Autism and Developmental Disorders 30*, 233–240.

Koegel, L.K., Koegel, R.L. and Smith, A. (1997) 'Variables related to differences in standardized test outcomes for children with autism.' *Journal of Autism and Developmental Disorders 27*, 383–391.

Maurice, C. (1993) *Let me Hear Your Voice*. New York: Fawcett Columbine.

Mueller, E., Burton, B. and Schuler, A.A. (2001) 'A qualitative analysis of those contexts that build social inclusion and understanding in individuals with Asperger's Syndrome.' Paper presented to the tenth scientific meeting of the International Society for Research in Child and Adolescent Psychopathology. Vancouver, June 28–30 2001.

Lovaas, O.I. (1987) 'Behavioral treatment and normal educational and intellectual functioning in young autistic children.' *Journal of Consulting and Clinical Psychology 55*, 3–9.

Quill, K. (1995) *Teaching the Autistic Child: Strategies to Promote Social and Communicative Competence*. Albany, NY: Delmar.

Quill, K. (2000) *Do–Watch–Listen–Say*. New York: Paul H. Brookes.

Papy, F., Papy, G. and Schuler, A.L, 'La pensée hors language; à la recontre d'adolescents autistes.' In B. Gilelo, *Series de Psychopathology*. Paris: Editions Bayard

Prizant, B.M. (1983) 'Language acquisition and communicative behaviour in autism: towards an understanding of the whole of it.' *Journal of Speech and Hearing Disorders 48*, 296–307.

Prizant, B.M and Duchan, J.F (1981) 'The functions of immediate echolalia in autistic children.' *Journal of Speech and Hearing Disorders 46*, 241–249.

Prizant, B.M., Schuler, A.L. and Wetherby, A. 'Facilitating communication; pre-language approaches.' In F. Volkmar and R. Paul (eds), *Handbook of Autism and Disorders of Atypical Development*. New York: Wiley.

Ratey, J.J. (2001) *A User's Guide to the Brain*. New York: Pentium.

Schopler, E., Mesibov, G.B. and Hearsey, K. (1995) 'Structured teaching in the TEACCH system.' In E. Schopler and G.B. Mesibov (eds) *Learning and Cognition in Autism*. London: Plenum.

Schuler, A.L. (1981) 'The relationship between disruptive behavior and communicative deficiencies.' Paper presented to the Annual Meeting of the American Speech and Hearing Association, Los Angeles, CA, November.

Schuler, A.L. (1995) 'Thinking in autism: differences in learning and development.' In K. Quill (ed) *Teaching Children with Autism: Methods to Enhance Communication and Socialization*. Albany, NY: Delmar.

Schuler, A.L., Peck, C.A., Willard, C. and Theimer, K. (1989) 'Assessment of communicative means and functions through interview: assessing the communicative capabilities of individuals with limited language.' *Seminars in Speech and Language 10*, 51–61.

Schuler, A.L. and Prizant, B.M. (1985) 'Echolalia.' In E. Schopler and G. Mesibov (eds) *Communication Problems in Autism*. New York: Plenum.

Schuler, A.L., Wetherby, A.M. and Prizant, B.M. (1997) 'Enhancing language and communication: prelanguage approaches.' In D. Cohen and R. Volkmar (eds) *Handbook of Autism and Developmental Disorders*, 2nd edn. New York: Wiley.

Schuler, A.L. and Wolfberg, P.J. (2000) 'Promoting peer socialization and play: the art of scaffolding.' In A.M. Wetherby and B.M. Prizant (eds) *Communication and Language Issues in Autism and Pervasive Developmental Disorders: A Transactional Developmental Perspective*. Baltimore, MD: Paul H. Brookes.

Sussman, F. (2000) *More than Words*. Toronto: Hanen Centre.

United Nations Convention on the Rights of the Child (1989) www.umicef.org

Vygotsky, L.S. ([1934] 1962) *Thought and Language*. Cambridge, MA: MIT Press.

Wetherby, A.M., Prizant, B.M. and Schuler, A.L. (2000) 'Understanding the nature of language and communication disorders.' In A.M. Wetherby and B.M. Prizant (eds) *Communication and Language Issues in Autism and Pervasive Developmental Disorders: A Transactional Developmental Perspective*. Baltimore, MD: Paul H. Brookes.

Wetherby, A.M. and Prutting, C. (1984) 'Profiles of communicative and cognitive-social abilities in autistic children.' *Journal of Speech and Hearing Research 27*, 364–377.

Wetherby, A.M., Schuler, A.L. and Prizant, B.M. (1997) 'Enhancing communication and language development: theoretical foundations.' In D. Cohen and R. Volkmar (eds) *Handbook of Autism and Developmental Disorders*, 2nd edn. New York: Wiley.

Wolfberg, P.J. (1995) 'Enhancing children's play.' In K.A. Quill (ed) *Teaching Children with Autism: Strategies to Enhance Communication and Socialization*. New York: Delmar.

Wolfberg, P.J. (1999) *Play and Imagination in Children with Autism*. New York: Teachers College Press.

Wolfberg, P.J. and Schuler, A.L. (1993) 'Integrated play groups: a model for promoting the social and cognitive dimensions of play in children with autism.' *Journal of Autism and Developmental Disorders 23*, 467–489.

Zercher, C., Hunt, P., Schuler, A. and Webster, J. (2001) 'Increasing joint attention, play and language through peer supported play.' *Autism: The International Journal of Research and Practice 5*, 4, 374–398

CHAPTER 7

Occupational Therapy Intervention and Autism

*Tracy Murnan Stackhouse, Nancy Seccombe Graham
and Jill Sargent Laschober*

*The objective of therapy...is to improve the sensory processing so that...the child
will form simple adaptive responses as a means of helping him learn to organize his
behavior. When therapy does make a difference, the child's life is changed
considerably. (Ayres 1979, p. 130)*

In this chapter, we explore current issues in pediatric occupational therapy
practice as it relates to children with autism. Occupational therapy (OT) is a
related practice in educational, medical, and community settings. Occupational therapy is based on the belief that humans are occupational beings able
to maximize their health and quality of life when engaged in meaningful
activity (American Occupational Therapy Association (AOTA) 2000).
Throughout the life cycle, biological, psychological, social or environmental
factors may interrupt the adaptive occupational process and create dysfunction. Utilizing a variety of theoretical methods, OT empowers individuals to
overcome dysfunction, make choices regarding occupational engagement,
and optimize function and quality of life over the lifespan. According to
Keilhofner (1995), a leading OT theorist,

> The core of occupational therapy practice...is in the patient's participa-
> tion in occupations, or activities, which have been carefully selected to
> influence health status... [Occupational therapists] are interested in
> whether the person has a meaningful place in the social system as well as
> whether or not they can move about and participate in that social system.
> (Keilhofner 1995, p.11)

The overriding notion of occupation is the common theme across the methods any particular OT might choose to aid individuals to engage in the activities that provide meaning to their lives.

Role of the occupational therapist

The typical occupational therapy role in the life of a child with autism ranges from consultation with family members, school personnel, group homes, and community agencies to direct intervention with the child aimed at improvement of occupational performance in skill areas as well as remediation of underlying performance component deficits. The practice is characterized, but not limited to, expertise in sensory and motor functioning especially with regard to how these basic neural functions impact occupational outcomes such as motor coordination, tool use, play, and independence in daily living skills.

Overview of occupational therapy issues in autism

Occupational therapists utilize a variety of frames of reference to accomplish the goals of their intervention (Kramer and Hinojosa 1993). However, it is beyond the scope of this chapter to review all of the theoretical approaches an OT may utilize. This chapter will focus on foundational sensory processing and motor performance areas and how these relate to developmental outcomes in play, school performance, and adaptive skill areas.

Sensory and motor processing or difficulties therein are not included in the specific criteria used to diagnose autism (see Chapters 1 and 2 for diagnostic criteria). Thus far, the literature presents a set of mixed findings concerning both sensory and motor processing. In order tounderstand better the findings and how they might help to guide treatment, a brief review of the relevant research findings is provided.

Motor issues in autism

A specific motor impairment has never been indicated in autism. Some findings suggest a proficiency in fine motor manipulation skills (Rapin 1997). However, other literature indicates that individuals who fall on the spectrum may demonstrate delays and difficulties in motor development (e.g. Baranek 1999; Dawson and Adams 1984; DeMeyer *et al.* 1972; Minshew, Goldstein and Seigel 1997). Delayed gross and fine motor development is reported

(Cornish and McManus 1996; Leary and Hill 1996; Manjiviona and Prior 1995; Mauk 1993). Suggestions of general incoordination, unusual gait and reaching patterns, and poor neuromotor foundations including low muscle tone (Greenspan 1992) and kinesthetic processing deficits (Bennetto 2000) are also reported.

Sensory issues in autism

Primary sensory deficits are not reported in autism, with the exception of some autistic-like behaviors seen in children and adults with blindness. However, sensory-processing difficulties have long been suggested as present or even causal in autism. These include first-hand accounts from adults with autism who describe distortions in visual, auditory, and touch modalities. Seeing air particles, hearing a familiar voice each time as a shotgun blast rather than a voice, feeling touch as pain, being overwhelmed by background noises are just some of their experiential descriptions (Grandin 1995; Grandin and Scariano 1986; Williams 1992). In addition, a variety of sensory-based difficulties have been documented. These include unusual vestibular and tactile processing (Ayres and Tickle 1980; Ornitz 1989), as well as abnormal auditory responsivity (Kientz and Dunn 1997; Ornitz and Ritvo 1968; Rojas *et al.* 2001). To date, there is no absolute indication of disruption in sensory processes. However, parental report of a greater number of sensory symptoms in children with autism as compared with normally developing and developmentally delayed children, though not in comparison with children with fragile X syndrome, deaf-blindness, or specific sensory modulation problems (Lord 1995; McIntosh *et al.* 1999), is a compelling finding that lingers in the issues of autism that are not well understood. As the questions and methodology for addressing the sensory-processing issues are refined, there appears to be a suggestion that this is an important line for continued investigation. See Rogers and Stackhouse (2002) for a comprehensive review of the sensory research findings in autism.

Sensory integration (SI) theory

Based on anecdotal evidence and clinical findings shared in the pediatric therapy community through informal workshops, OT has a strong tradition of providing therapy to address sensory and motor difficulties seen in children with autism. The most formalized theory used to create a framework for this intervention is sensory integration based on the work of Dr A. Jean Ayres

(1972), an occupational therapist, scientist, and theoretician. Ayres originally presented her theory of SI for use with school-age children with a specific pattern of disruption in sensory processing that resulted in difficulties with occupational performance including learning. In the midst of her focus on children with 'hidden deficits', Ayres suggested a link between her theoretical findings and the intervention they suggested and the difficulties seen in autism.

Classical sensory integration theory is conceptualized as a theory of brain–behavior relationships (Parham and Mailloux 1996). Ayres (1972) defined sensory integration as the organization of sensory input in the brain for emitting adaptive responses. 'Sensory integration provides a broad developmental perspective about how the brain develops the capacity to perceive, learn, and organize behavior' (Case-Smith, Pratt and Allen 1996, p.42). SI incorporates information from the neurosciences into its theory base to describe how a child's organization of sensory stimuli leads to purposeful actions such as play. Ayres was careful to emphasize that her theory was based on how sensations and the responses to them are what cause the brain to develop (Case-Smith et al. 1996, p.135). This critical feature of adaptive response is vital to understanding how SI is a frame within the broader scope of OT. Within this framework, sensory processing is viewed categorically and always in reference to adaptive response.

Two broad categories are used to cluster the basic sensory processes with respect both to nervous system processing and their impact on action and behavior. Sensory modulation and sensory discrimination are the terms used for these categories. These categories are in keeping with the SI framework as well as with standard neuroscience, as noted in the classic text, *Principles of Neural Science* by Kandel, Schwartz and Jessell (1999, p.339): 'sensory systems are not only our means for perceiving the external world, but are also essential for maintaining arousal, forming our body image, and regulating movement'. Both modulation and discrimination sensory functions will be described in terms of overall theory and implications for treatment. Incorporated in this review are case examples used to illustrate the value an OT perspective brings for specific difficulties in adaptive life-skill development.

Sensory modulation

Sensation gives information about the importance and relevance of the information. Classically this was thought of as the protective or survival information system. This is best described when thinking of sensation encountered that is harmful: we go away from it in order to 'survive'. However, we all go toward sensation as well. We seek a hug, a smell, or a feel to enhance our mood and level of comfort.

Sensory sensitivity is an abbreviated way of referring to the process of sensory stimuli becoming sensory information for use in the nervous system. Sensory systems extract four basic attributes from the stimulus – modality (quality), intensity, duration, and location – that are combined in sensation. These attributes combine to produce adequate sensory stimulus for detection. This is known as the sensory threshold phenomenon. When detectable criteria are reached, the signal is fired and processed according to its modality, and type of information it is bringing to the nervous system (Kandel *et al.* 1999). Behaviorally observable responses to sensory input are a by-product of sensory sensitivity interacting with basic arousal mechanisms. In order to understand the inferences made about behavioral responses, a theoretically driven model of this aspect of sensory processing is necessary. Such a model is emerging in the OT literature using the term 'sensory modulation'.

Sensory modulation is defined as the intake of sensory information via typical sensory mechanisms such that the value, direction, and grading of sensory responsivity is in proportion to the input and its context (Stackhouse and Wilbarger 1997). Difficulties in this area include sensory seeking and avoidance behavior, sensory defensiveness, and problems with self-regulation, which is the capacity to maintain an alert and aroused state appropriate for the conditions and demands of the environment. There is an inverse 'U' relationship between arousal level and optimum function. The best functioning occurs in the middle gray range, known as the 'optimal state' or 'just right' level of arousal. On either the up or down side of this range, function is limited by the state of over- or under-arousal. With disordered sensory modulation, 'the child is much more likely to react poorly to the environment: some are hard to engage, others are over eager to please. Some withdraw and others act hyperactive' (Ayres 1979, p.62). Such responsivity is the output of diminished adaptability in basic arousal mechanisms coupled with poorly modulated sensory reactivity. For example, a child may have difficulty screening out background noises in the classroom with subsequent difficulties in attending to relevant and important information. Additionally, maintaining an appropriate alertness is another component of a sensory modulation disorder. Some children appear 'unavailable' or passive in their play and interactions because they do not appropriately utilize sensory information to orient and direct their attention towards their active environments. It should be noted that for children who do not have a primary difficulty in social-emotional functions, sorting out the potential overlap between sensory and emotionally based difficulties lies in identifying clear sensory-based symptoms. For children with autism, who have a social-emotional overlay, symptom delineation is even more critical. The following review of sensory modulation issues is an attempt to make explicit the sensory basis of these concerns in order to facilitate deeper understanding.

Sensory defensiveness is defined as a tendency to react negatively or with alarm to sensory input that is generally considered harmless or non-irritating. 'Common symptoms may include over sensitivity to light or unexpected touch, sudden movement or over reaction to unstable surfaces, high frequency noises, excesses of noise or visual stimuli and certain smells' (Wilbarger and Wilbarger 1991, p.3). Over-sensitivity or over-gathering of sensation in any or all of the sensory systems creates such over-stimulation that persons with sensory defensiveness are typified by avoidant responses to sensory input, and can easily cycle into fear, fight or flight, and freeze responses because of the autonomic nervous system connections to this part of sensory processing.

Defensiveness in the tactile system makes physical and social contact difficult to tolerate. Learning social rules, boundaries, and interaction is easily impacted by this disorder, resulting in difficulties in pragmatic skill and early play development (Oetter, Richter and Frick 1993). Hypersensitivity in the oral tactile system makes oral experiences (e.g. talking, feeding, and physical contact) difficult to manage. Marshalla (1994) reported that children have tactile difficulties with production of specific sounds, such as fricatives, due to the unpleasant feel of the sound in the mouth. When these patterns are avoided secondary to hypersensitivity, they have a detrimental effect on skill development. Affolter (1991) reported that children with difficulties in tactile, kinesthetic input have a disordered sequence of their language development, with some children producing longer sentences before the normal sequence of one and two word phrases. Affolter's observations support different developmental sequences of language performance among sensory disordered children.

Over-sensitivity in movement systems may result in difficulties tolerating normal movement experiences or avoidance of movement; children who are afraid to swing, climb, and typically explore early childhood environments exemplify this. Within the occupational therapy field, this phenomenon is referred to as gravitational insecurity and is related to temperamental shyness and anxiety (Koomar 1996). The inhibited exploration of the environment that results from movement hypersensitivity affects the quality of early perceptual experiences impacting the early perceptual-conceptual knowledge necessary for language development.

Hypersensitivity in the auditory system is another feature of sensory defensiveness. Background noise is particularly difficult to filter out. Inability to do this leads to distractibility, and listening (especially in academic or social settings) can become a difficult task. In severe cases, avoidance of what most people consider normal levels of environmental noise is demonstrated. These children have been observed to cover their ears, hunch their shoulders, or make their own 'white noise' in an attempt to dampen these noxious stimuli. Many children may also physically hide to avoid this bombardment.

Auditory attention and discrimination are well defined as prerequisites to phonological and language development (Dodd 1995). The child who presents with auditory hypersensitivity will often avoid the aversive stimuli of typical social environments where competing and distracting background noise is hard to control. If these children are unable to avoid these environments, attention to relevant stimuli becomes difficult to maintain. In these situations, it becomes difficult to screen out essential from non-essential auditory information. The defensive sensory process affects the concentration needed to attend to language and develop communication.

Auditory defensiveness may mask developing language and phonological skills and make them unavailable for use until the hypersensitivity is treated. Patricia Wilbarger (personal communication, December 5 2001) reported the unfolding of previously hidden language development in the weeks following intensive intervention for sensory defensiveness. The auditory and visual systems serve as our primary anticipatory systems, meaning that we see or hear what is going on around us and adjust physical and social responses prior to engaging in interactions. Children who demonstrate visual hypersensitivity will decrease the amount of scanning and tracking they do in their environment. This in turn affects how efficiently they are able to anticipate and plan their repertoire of social and motor responses.

Defensiveness in auditory or visual systems decreases our effectiveness as social participants. The most overt expression of visual defensiveness is gaze aversion. Most simply, decreased eye contact signals that a person is visually overwhelmed. Belser and Sudhalter (1995) studied the relation between gaze avoidance and social anxiety. In a study of children with fragile X syndrome (FXS) who had significant sensory processing disorders, they demonstrated that less deviant language occurs when the stress of social interaction through eye contact is diminished. They compared children with FXS to children with Down syndrome and children with attention deficit and hyperactivity disorder (ADHD). They found that FXS children who demonstrated physiological hyper-arousal issues showed deviant language including perseveration and tangential speech. The other groups did not have the hyper-arousal variable and did not demonstrate these deviant language patterns. Belser and Sudhalter are currently investigating similar phenomena in children with autism, as the similarities in behavioral phenotype are striking, as are anecdotal reports of social-behavioral management of this issue.

Self-regulation relates to having trouble managing sensory input and how the resultant varying responses (e.g. over- or under-responsiveness) to sensory input affect arousal levels. Overactivity or protective shutting down typifies over-arousal, and withdrawn behavior is demonstrated when sensory overload occurs. Under-arousal is typified by delayed, slow or passive response to the environment. These responses are the most common and simple to understand. There are several other clusters of self-regulatory problems associated with sensory modulation disorders that the interested reader can investigate further (Anzalone and Williamson 2000; Miller-Kuhaneck 2001).

Language in children with difficulties managing arousal states can look deviant. Children who easily move into an over-aroused state may show poor topic maintenance (Belser and Sudhalter 1995), inattention, impulsivity, lack of inhibition with speech (i.e. talking incessantly with little attention to content), poor organization of language, poor grading in the output of vocal quality, and perseveration. Additionally, if these children become so over-whelmed that they cannot cope, they shut down. This is usually seen first in significantly decreased verbalizations, poor eye contact, and reduced interactions with people and objects in the environment.

On the converse side of the arousal spectrum is under-arousal. Some people think of this in its extreme as a lack of registering what is going on around them. Usually these children appear as being passive participants in their environment. They are slow to respond, especially to isolated or single channel sensory input. They tend to respond better if given combined cues, such as touch and auditory coupled with visual. This under-arousal is reflected in the quality of their play experience, which is then reflected in their language. They are usually slow to acquire receptive and expressive language abilities as their play interactions lack the richness needed to explore and develop schemas. Limited vocabulary development, poor social skill development, and slow processing and response time typify their language abilities.

For families of young children with autism, OT participation in the intervention team brings a perspective on developmental concerns that often proves useful in a deeper understanding of the complex nature of this serious neurodevelopmental disorder. The OT can use the lens of SI theory to interpret puzzling and challenging behaviors that cannot always be explained by the core deficits of autism, but appear frequently as associated features (i.e. sleep problems, intense tantruming, aggression, resistance to daily living tasks, sensitivity to noise).

The following case examples illustrate the utility an SI approach offers by providing a bridge to intervention for some features of autism that do not fit neatly into more traditional frameworks based on core deficits and cognitive-behavioral approaches. The cases offer a view of two main categories of modulation disorders: sensory defensiveness and poor self-regulation.

Sensory defensiveness case example: Hannah

Hannah, a 3-year-old girl recently diagnosed with autism, was described by her parents as a fussy child with frequent and intense temper tantrums. She never slept through the night and often awakened crying, as if in pain. She disliked music and most children's television shows, covering her ears and crying when her parents attempted to expose her to these activities. She disliked any grooming procedure, especially having her face washed. She avoided playground equipment and disliked any form of roughhousing (active physical play) with her father. Whenever activities were forced upon her, she immediately became distressed, attacking her parents and destroying furniture. One day, by chance, the streetlight across from Hannah's house was broken. That was the first time Hannah ever slept through the night. The following morning, she escaped from the house, ran to the light post and hugged it. After the light was fixed, she stopped sleeping through the night again. Hannah had been able to hear the buzz from the street light, which she found to be a painful noise.

Sensory regulation case example: Robby

Robby, a 9-year-old boy with a diagnosis of autism, was always in trouble at school and at home. He had three younger school-aged siblings, both of his parents worked, and morning routines were described as chaotic. For example, Robby consistently challenged his mother's patience, as he appeared to ignore all requests to get out of bed and move quickly through the morning routine. He frequently fell asleep on the bus ride to school and was very difficult to arouse once he arrived. Gradually as the day progressed, he seemed finally to wake up for short periods of time and was able to complete work independently. However, at lunchtime, Robby's behavior changed dramatically. Initially, he sat and ate his lunch in the crowded and noisy cafeteria, but within a short period of time he was unable to sit quietly in his chair. He made loud noises, leapt into the air, and then attempted to flee from the room. Robby rarely ate more than little bites of his sandwich. At recess, he often attempted to play chase with his peers; however, he was frequently sent to the principal's office for unintentionally hurting another child during chase games. When he returned to class, he was expected to sit quietly and read at his desk. Although Robby enjoyed reading at other times, he was unable to sit and focus during independent reading time. He moved about the room, distracting peers, which resulted in further reprimands. Robby struggled to match an appropriate arousal level to the task demands throughout his day, with the exception of a brief period of time in the morning. As a result, he annoyed his peers, was often in trouble at home and at school, and completed very little schoolwork.

In contrast to the disorganization from sensory modulation disruption, children may act disorganized because they feel that way inside, more physically than emotionally. These children are often described as not knowing where their bodies are in space. They have deficient 'maps' of their bodies and how to use them. They have trouble planning, organizing, and sequencing their actions. This problem is called dyspraxia.

Sensory discrimination is a major category of sensory processing. The sensory integrative disorders outlined by Ayres (1989) were mostly clustered in this area. The hallmark of the sensory discrimination system is as an information-gathering network for the nervous system, and through this it is our learning system. There is an interaction between sensory modulation and discrimination functions, as the modulation system sets the tone for learning while the discrimination system takes in the details that contribute to the knowledge.

Sensory discrimination includes patterns of functioning that are emergent processes based in discrete sensory processing. This includes, but is not limited to, the large clusters of functions identified by Ayres (1989) such as praxis, bilateral motor coordination/integration and sequencing, visual and tactile space and form perception, eye–hand coordination and auditory-language processing. Discriminative sensory input is that input that usually leads to conscious perception or to impact motor control (Kandel *et al.* 1999). Each sensory system has the role of providing information to our brains to give us the qualities that inform or help us learn and know what it is we are encountering. This is discriminative information. In our touch systems, discriminative information tells us the details about which finger is which and about the feeling and intention of a gentle caress.

Praxis can be defined broadly as a motor planning process. Occupational therapists have elaborated praxis to encompass sensory integrative functions within the nervous system. Speech and language pathologists have their own interpretation of dyspraxia, focused on the oral/verbal areas. It is important to note that these differences in semantics can be confusing at times . Gaining insight into each other professionals' expertise only adds to our knowledge base and in turn strengthens our clinical and team skills. According to occupational therapy SI theory, praxis is an emergent process that is categorized into phases. Ayres (1989) identified each phase:

1. Ideation, or the ability of the brain to conceive of an action: what to do.

2. Planning, or the ability to organize the plan for action: how to do it.

3. Execution, or the ability to carry out a sequence of action: just do it!

Praxis is the process used in all skill development. Difficulties with praxis result in dyspraxia; this can be seen across oral, verbal, gross and fine motor domains. Ayres (1972, 1989) devoted much of her research efforts toward developing evaluation tools helpful in delineating subtypes of dyspraxia and their neurosensory processing correlates.

The distinction between motor coordination, motor planning, and motor skill development is often clarified when observing a child who has intact motor coordination but has limited or uneven motor skill development associated with praxis problems. The following case study describes such a child.

Limited play case example: Jared

Jared is a 3-year-old boy diagnosed with autism, whose restricted range of interest was demonstrated by his limited repertoire of play interests: he loved water play and balls. Jared lined up and twirled balls but had not learned to throw a ball. When someone threw a ball to him he averted his gaze and wiggled his fingers in front of his face. Except for balls, Jared did not like to touch things and rarely handled objects. As a baby he crawled very little and held his palms off the floor which allowed him to experience very little of the proprioception and deep pressure generated by weight-bearing through his hands.

In this case example, sensory defensiveness may have limited Jared's sensory exploratory play. He also presents with limited motor schemas. Both of these limit his kinesthetic experience and compromise his body awareness. It is not surprising that he had trouble generating ideas and action plans for play. His interest in balls and water could be used to engage him in activities that might provide a richer variety and intensity of proprioceptive and deep touch pressure to his hands. In addition, an appreciation of the learning style of children with autism would influence the methods chosen to help him acquire conventional ball play skills.

Relation of sensory processing to core deficits in autism

OT intervention is aimed at facilitating development in basic sensory and motor functions, and improving praxis, as well as the practice and refinement of strategies and skills, all with the goal of occupational outcomes.

The end result of an act of praxis is skilled motor behavior. In this way, skill is considered the ability to match the demands of the task to capacity via a strategy or method. Skill is a complex of chained actions aimed at a result, not a single response to stimuli. For skill to occur, capacity, time, and effort are linked from the context to the goal or outcome suggested by the situation. Almost every skilled performance involves the chain of central mechanisms from sensory mechanisms to the action system. Central mechanisms can be viewed broadly in three categories: perceptions of object, event, and demand; choice of responses to them; and execution of coordinated action giving expression to the choice. These parallel the motor planning process suggested by Ayres. It is important to map onto this framework the specific difficulties and strengths children with autism present in order to devise appropriate intervention plans.

While non-motor *per se*, social skills ascribe to the same basic central mechanisms. Social-cognitive skills include:

- the perception of others' needs and desires and of the effect one's own actions have on others
- decisions about how to react to the communication and actions of others to achieve the desired interaction

- actions from modulating touch, proximity of body, voice quality, etc. used to meet the goal.

As such, the methods used for remediation of sensory or motor functions have application that extends into social and perhaps communication domains. This is fitting with the overall role of the occupational therapist in addressing the foundations for the important occupations of each individual.

Postural mechanisms

Sensory modulation and discrimination are parallel, distinct processes. The information for each can be traced through different brain centers. Sensory integrative theory has evolved to cluster around these two major branches in sensory-processing phenomena. At the interface of these functions are basic postural mechanisms.

Postural control is a product of parallel redundant sensory processing in the vestibular, proprioceptive, and visual systems. It contributes to both sensory discrimination and sensory modulation functions. The development of a stable base from which to move is a critical element of coordinated motor skill and movement. With well-developed postural control, the child is able to move about and explore the environment, the beginnings of the rich input necessary to develop higher-order cognition, especially language and social-cognitive concepts. It is not surprising, therefore, that stability-mobility patterns play a significant role in the smooth expression of related motor activities (e.g. ocular motor control, eye–hand development, articulation, upper trunk control for hand use, suck–swallow–breathe synchrony (Oetter *et al.* 1993).

Postural support is also the foundation for 'centering' and self-regulation. Many arousal mechanisms operate bidirectionally with input from the vagus nerve. Disruptions in muscle tone and immature breath support are red flags for assessment and potential treatment in this area. These theoretical claims are important for autism, as postural control difficulties have been documented (Kohen-Raz, Volkmar and Cohen 1992).

The following case example describes an occupational therapist's intervention regarding the issue of postural support.

Postural support case example: Sam

Sam is a 6-year-old boy diagnosed with autism who was referred to occupational therapy due to his poor fine motor and visual motor skill performance and poor work completion. The occupational therapist observed Sam at school and noted that he rarely used his non-dominant hand to support any fine motor task performance, because he consistently used this hand to support himself in his chair. Sam's affect was flat with minimal vocalizations to his teaching assistant. His breathing was shallow with occasional deeper audible inhalations. Breath-holding during handwriting and typing tasks was also observed. Sam was verbally cued throughout his day to 'wake up and do your work'. His best attending time was when his teacher read aloud; he sat and listened quietly (although he lay on the floor versus sitting like the other children). Limited independent work completion was observed. During transitions Sam walked through the hallway leaning against the wall whenever possible.

Sam's occupational therapist hypothesized that he presented with the following:

- tonic low arousal, which did not match the task demands for most activities at school
- postural strength and control difficulties, as evidenced by his persistent need to stabilize himself in his chair, seek support when walking through the halls, and lay on the floor during floor-sitting activities
- postural weaknesses and poor arousal levels impacted by his poor respiratory control.

Aspects of an OT intervention plan for Sam would include:

- educating school personnel to identify indicators of low arousal and provide Sam with a school schedule that incorporated physical activities designed to support a higher level of arousal
- adjusting the height of Sam's chair and desk to ensure optimal positioning for trunk stability, thus freeing both hands for tasks
- providing direct individual therapy intervention to improve postural strength and respiratory control.

Occupational therapy interventions

Interventions based in sensory processing theory are very powerful, and often a component of a child's OT intervention. Within OT, the changes in a child come not from the application of any specific technique or method but from the adaptive responses occurring during the therapeutic process. Adaptive responses range from scratching when you feel an itch, to learning to refine a golf swing, to assertively dealing with a difficult or intimidating situation. They can happen automatically, with rehearsed patterns, such as driving a car on a familiar route, or can require split-second precision such as veering around a child who runs out in front of the vehicle. Adaptive responses develop using internal and external feed forward and feedback loops of sensation and thought, as in learning to drive a standard transmission for the first time. Challenging adaptive responses at the 'just right' level is fundemental to SI intervention.

Many education and intervention programs for children with autism include multisensory learning experiences with an emphasis on visual structure. This is because visual learning is strength in autism (Mesibov, Schopler and Hearsey 1994), and in general a multisensory approach is thought to enhance learning. From an OT perspective, this is viewed as influencing the discriminative or learning sensory systems. However, having the right amount of stimuli without overload creates the ambience of learning and does just as much to enhance learning as opportunities for rich exploration. Sensory experience sets our nervous system's capacity to attend and influences memory functions as well. With an appropriate amount of sensory input, the nervous system is organized and enhanced to motivate us to explore, interact, and learn. This drive toward exploration is directed at the environment, the task at hand, and the interaction occurring given the task and environment. Occupational therapy intervention differs from perceptual motor training. Intervention is not comprised of working through a sequence of skills to be acquired and tricks to teach them, nor do the best treatment sessions follow a preplanned list of activities to be practiced. Rather, treatment evolves in a play context where the therapist manipulates variables in the sensory environment, activity, structure, and interaction to elicit more sophisticated postural responses, improved sensory modulation, and acts of praxis (Stackhouse and Wilbarger 1997). These elements are at the core of best practices in sensory integration.

Therapists familiar with sensory integration treatment who are beginning to work with children who have autism are sometimes surprised to find that the remediation of underlying sensory processing and motor components often does not result in spontaneous acquisition of new motor skills. A burst in acquisition of untaught motor skills is not uncommon in sensory integration treatment of children with non-autism spectrum disorders. By contrast, in autism, remediation of deficits in skill components (i.e. equilibrium responses or vestibular modulation) may make a child more available for motor learning, but motor 'teaching' is necessary to realize that new potential for skill.

While this chapter has focused on a review of current concepts in sensory and motor aspects of OT interventions, and the experienced OT is careful to integrate this knowledge into their overall clinical reasoning, treatment is much more comprehensive than this. Children with autism have complex needs that are developmental, and therefore changing, as well as being situated in a family. These concerns should always be a part of an OT treatment plan.

Because most children with autism present with strengths in visual learning, providing structure and routine with visual cues is fundamental to successful intervention for most of these children.

Getting ready for school case example: Joan

This case example illustrates the combination of sensory integration, role development, and visual structure methodologies to support a child in natural and inclusive settings. Table 7.1 summarizes examples of OT assessment and interventions for a 12-year-old middle school girl with autism, who is having difficulties getting ready for school and continues to have difficulty participating through the early part of her school day.

Conclusion

Among the cornerstones of best practices in autism are three principles that have been central in guiding the development of the discipline of occupational therapy:

- the commitment to discovering and nurturing an individual's strengths
- the organization of intervention around preferred activities and interests of the individual

- the commitment to maximizing health and quality of life by creating accessible, adapted environments that support meaningful participation in the occupations most valued by the individual.

Across all areas of practice, occupational therapists share in common principles of treatment based on the premise that engagement in purposeful activity valued by the individual enhances life. From its conception in 1898 as a service for adults with mental health challenges, through its adaptation and expansion to meet the needs of returning World War I and II veterans with unprecedented needs for rehabilitation services, to its expansion to incorporate new information in the neurosciences and the pioneering work of Ayres (1972, 1979), occupational therapists have aimed high: at its best occupational therapy seeks to empower individuals coping with disability to identify their desired occupational roles and help them create activities that will develop the skills they need to succeed in those roles.

Occupational therapists are now challenged again to themselves grow and adapt in order to join colleagues across disciplines in offering meaningful and effective services for individuals with autism.

Table 7.1 Functional manifestion of sensory integration disruptions and intervention rationale

Observations	Interpretation	Intervention principle	Strategies
Waking routine • Does not wake to alarm • Younger sister must shake her to wake her • Once awake, Joan does not get out of bed without repeated coaxing • Wanders around bedroom, sometimes gets back in bed • Relies on verbal redirection from sister to start dressing	• Joan's sensory modulation is oriented toward low arousal states, especially early in the day when the level of sensory input is low. By late morning, amassed sensory input raises arousal level and participation is more spontaneous. • Praxis deficits make it difficult for Joan to initiate her routine. She does not have a well-established routine of what to do first upon rising.	• Build more proprioceptive and non-noxious tactile input into morning routine • Rearrange bedroom to provide more physical structure cues for independent initiation and sequencing of activities	• Add treadmill exercise to morning routine: cue to treadmill by moving alarm clock from sister's bedside table to shelf beside treadmill • Use Joan's special interest in charts and maps to create a motivating wall chart on which Joan will record each day's mileage • Cue Joan from treadmill to next task with cartoon coach drawing on lower corner of chart, saying 'To the shower'
Shower routine • Spends excessive time in the shower • Washes hair several times, using every product in the shower • Omits some tasks	• Stays in shower to help her wake up • Difficulties with sequencing and organization	• Use physical structure to support understanding of the task • Use visual cues to support sequencing of tasks	• Place Joan's products in a plastic shower basket labeled with her name. Using marker label products with numbers to cue first, second, third, and last tasks.

Dressing routines • Cannot decide what to wear • Waits for sister to show her what to put on • May forget to wear some garments • Puts clothes on in wrong sequence; may put underwear on over outerwear	• Disruptions in arousal impact ability to persist with task • Praxis deficits result in difficulty putting garments on in logical order • Limited ability to choose appropriate clothing due to inability to anticipate day's events and limited observation of peers	• Decrease reliance on cues from sister by developing visual supports for dressing sequence and making choices	• Provide photographs of complete outfits • At the beginning of the week, have Joan and her mother select 5–7 photos appropriate for the season • Post 5–7 photos of appropriate outfits on bullet board beside closet • Have Joan's sister print cues on lower border of photos, e.g. 'Good for a party'
Breakfast routines • Sits at built-in eating area • Lies down • Does not finish meal • Eats slowly	• Food choices and seating area provide minimal alerting sensations	• Provide seating that generates increased movement, postural challenge, and proprioceptive input • Expand breakfast food repertoire to include foods that provide alerting sensation	• Allow Joan to eat at kitchen counter on tall stool with turning seat and foot rails • Teach Joan to make breakfast smoothies in the blender

School behavior • Inconsistent participation in classes at school: better in afternoon Morning class observations: • Lies on desk • Completes little work • Wanders around room • Doesn't respond to teachers' questions • Doesn't ask for help	• Sensory modulation challenges contribute to variability in arousal level. Joan needs a greater intensity, duration, and frequency of sensory input, primarily movement, to remain alert and readily engaged. • After her late morning swimming class, when she has finally received sufficient sensory input, her attention is good and she is more responsive to teachers and peers and more organized with her materials	• Modify schedule and use part of study hall time for a school job that will incorporate alerting proprioceptive input • Develop visual supports for independent completion of work job	• Have Joan travel to six classrooms on the second floor, collect library books and carry them to the first floor library • To limit reliance on teachers to cue and redirect • Provide clipboard with checklist to remind Joan of the rooms she needs to visit • Outline the room number on the wall outside the designated classrooms with a band of blue electrician's tape • To help Joan avoid becoming distracted and wandering the school, Joan and her teacher make predictions each day of the exact time Joan will return to class. Joan writes the predictions on the board and checks to see who was closest.

References

Affolter, F. (1991) *Perception, Interaction and Language.* New York: Springer Verlag.

American Occupational Therapy Association (AOTA) (2000) *American Occupational Therapy Association Official Documents.* Rockville, MD: AOTA.

Anzalone, M. and Williamson, G.G. (2000) 'Sensory processing and motor performance in autism spectrum disorders.' In A.M. Wetherby and B.M. Prizant (eds) *Autism Spectrum Disorders.* Baltimore, MD: Paul H. Brookes.

Ayres, A.J. (1972) *Sensory Integration and Learning Disorders.* Los Angeles: Western Psychological Services.

Ayres, A.J. (1979) *Sensory Integration and the Child.* Los Angeles: Western Psychological Services.

Ayres, A.J. (1989) *Sensory Integration and Praxis Tests.* Los Angeles: Western Psychological Services.

Ayres, A.J. and Tickle, L. (1980) 'Hyper-responsivity to touch and vestibular stimuli as a predictor of positive response to sensory integration procedures in autistic children.' *American Journal of Occupational Therapy 34,* 375–381.

Baranek, G.T. (1999) 'Autism during infancy: a retrospective video analysis of sensory-motor and social behaviors at 9–12 months of age.' *Journal of Autism and Developmental Disorders 29,* 213–224.

Belser, R.C. and Sudhalter, V. (1995) 'Arousal difficulties in males with fragile X syndrome: a preliminary report.' *Developmental Brain Dysfunction 8,* 4–6, 270–279.

Case-Smith, J., Pratt, P.N. and Allen, A.S. (eds) (1996) *Occupational Therapy for Children,* 3rd edn. St. Louis, MO: Mosby.

Cornish, K.M. and McManus, I.C. (1996) 'Hand preference and hand skill in children with autism.' *Journal of Autism and Developmental Disorders 26,* 597–610.

Dawson, G. and Adams, A. (1984) 'Imitation and social responsiveness in autistic children.' *Journal of Abnormal Child Psychology 12,* 2, 209–225.

DeMeyer, M.K., Alpern, G.D., Barton, S. (1972) 'Imitation in autistic, early schizophrenic, and nonpsychotic subnormal children.' *Journal of Autism and Childhood Schizophrenia 2,* 264–287.

Dodd, B. (1995) *Differential Diagnosis and Treatment of Children with Speech Disorder.* San Diego, CA: Singular.

Grandin, T. (1995) 'The learning style of people with autism: an autobiography.' In K.A. Quill (ed) *Teaching Children with Autism: Strategies to Enhance Communication and Socialization.* Albany, NY: Delmar.

Grandin, T. and Scariano, M.M. (1986) *Emergence: Labeled Autistic.* Novato, CA: Arena.

Greenspan, S. (1992) 'Reconsidering the diagnosis and treatment of very young children with autistic spectrum or pervasive developmental disorder.' *Zero to Three Bulletin 13,* 2, 1–9.

Kandel, E.R., Schwartz, J.H. and Jessell, T.M. (1999) *Principles of Neural Science,* 4th edn. Norwalk, CT: Appleton and Lange.

Keilhofner, G. (1995) *A Model of Human Occupation, Theory, and Application,* 2nd edn. Baltimore, MD: Williams and Wilkins.

Kientz, M.A. and Dunn, W. (1997) 'A comparison of the performance of children with and without autism on the sensory profile.' *American Journal of Occupational Therapy 51*, 530–537.

Kohen-Raz, R., Volkmar, F.R. and Cohen, D.J. (1992) 'Postural control in children with autism.' *Journal of Autism and Developmental Disorders 22*, 419–432.

Koomar, J. (1996) 'The relation of gravitational insecurity to behavioral inhibition.' Unpublished doctoral dissertation, Boston University, MA.

Kramer, P. and Hinojosa, J. (eds) (1993) *Frames of Reference for Pediatric Occupational Therapy.* Baltimore: Lippincott Williams and Wilkins.

Leary, M.R. and Hill, D.A. (1996) 'Moving on: autism and movement disturbance.' *Mental Retardation 34*, 39–59.

Lord, C. (1995) 'Follow-up of two year olds referred for possible autism.' *Journal of Child Psychology and Psychiatry and Allied Disciplines 36*, 1365–1382.

McIntosh, D.N., Miller, L.J., Shyu, V. and Hagerman, R.J. (1999) 'Sensory modulation disruption, electrodermal responses and functional behaviors.' *Developmental Medicine and Child Neurology 41*, 608–615.

Manjiviona, J. and Prior, M. (1995) 'Comparison of Asperger syndrome and high functioning autistic children on a test of motor impairment.' *Journal of Autism and Developmental Disorders 25*, 23–40.

Marshalla, P. (1994) *Oral Motor Techniques in Articulation Therapy.* Seattle, WA: Innovative Concepts.

Mauk, J.E. (1993) 'Autism and developmental disorders.' *Pediatric Clinics of North America 40*, 567–578.

Mesibov, G., Schopler, E. and Hearsey, K.S. (1994) 'Structured teaching.' In E. Schopler and G. Mesibov (eds) *Behavioral Issues in Autism.* New York: Plenum.

Miller-Kuhaneck, H. (ed) (2001) *Autism: A Comprehensive Occupational Therapy Approach.* Rockville, MD: AOTA.

Minshew, N., Goldstein, G. and Seigel, D.J. (1997) 'Neuropsychological functioning in autism: profile of a complex information processing disorder.' *Journal of the International Neuropsychological Society 3*, 303–316.

Oetter, P., Richter, E. and Frick, S. (1993) *MORE: Integrating the Mouth with Sensory and Postural Functions.* Hugo, MN: PDP Press.

Ornitz, E. (1989) 'Autism at the interface between sensory processing and information processing.' In G. Dawson (ed) *Autism: Nature, Diagnosis and Treatment.* New York: Guilford.

Ornitz, E. and Ritvo, E. (1968) 'Perceptual inconstancy in early infantile autism.' *Archives of General Psychiatry 18*, 76–97.

Parham, L.D. and Mailloux, Z. (1996) 'Sensory integration.' In J. Case-Smith, P.N. Pratt and A.S. Allen (eds) *Occupational Therapy for Children*, 3rd edn. St Louis, MO: Mosby.

Rapin, I. (1997) 'Autism.' *New England Journal of Medicine 337*, 97–104.

Rogers, S.J. and Bennetto, L. (2000) 'Intersubjectivity in autism: The roles of imitation and executive function.' In M. Amy, E. Wetherby, M. Barry, E. Prizant, *Autism Spectrum Disorders: A Transactional Developmental Perspective.* Baltimore, MD: Paul H. Brookes Publishing Co. p. 79–107.

Rogers, S. and Stackhouse, T. (2002) 'Sensory processing in autism: a review of the literature' (in preparation).

Rojas, D.C, Benkers, T.L., Rogers, S.J., Teale, P.D, Reite, M.L., Hagerman, R.J. (2001) 'Auditory evoked magnetic fields in adults with fragile X Syndrome.' *Neuroreport*, August 8, 12 (11), 2573–6.

Stackhouse, T.M. and Wilbarger, J.L. (1997) 'STEPSI: a clinical reasoning model for sensory modulation disorders.' Symposium presented at American Occupational Therapy Annual Meeting, Baltimore, MD, April.

Wilbarger, P. and Wilbarger, J. (1991) *Sensory Defensiveness in Children 2–12: An Intervention Guide for Parents and Other Caretakers*. Santa Barbara, CA: Avanti Educational Programs.

Williams, D. (1992) *Nobody Nowhere*. New York: Times Books.

CHAPTER 8

Quality Indicators of Best Practices
A Guide for Educators

Teresa D. Bunsen

I am the decisive element in the classroom. It is my personal approach that creates the climate. It is my daily mood that makes the weather. As the teacher I possess tremendous power to make a child's life miserable or joyous. I can be a tool of torture or an instrument of inspiration. I can humiliate or humor, hurt or heal. In all situations it is my response that decides whether a crisis will be escalated or de-escalated, and a child humanized or de-humanized. (Ginott 1972, p.467)

The professional education literature regarding intervention in the area of autism has tended to congregate around rather narrow areas of interest (e.g. strategies for socialization, communication, or environment). However, recent studies (e.g. Lord *et al.* 2001) indicate that no single education or treatment area exists in a vacuum with regard to its influence on a child with autism. The questions faced by educators and families are: 'What needs to be included in an educational environment?' and 'How does collaboration occur between home and school educational programs?' This chapter advocates for the assimilation of all aspects of support and their intra-relationships, as well as reviewing the impact of each of these aspects on the development of strong and stable educational programs. Included in this chapter are descriptions of how communication, academic, social, and environmental supports can be used within a multi-methodology classroom for children with autism. These practices are applicable across the age span when appropriate modifications are made to meet the individualized needs of the student and the grade level setting. The techniques could easily be modified for home settings; however, this chapter will focus on the creation of optimal school learning environments for children with autism. The elementary grade level has been chosen as an example environment to present these components, as it is often the first environment in which school structures are imposed on children's intervention programs.

Rationale for developing multi-methodology educational programs

The field of autism has become a top priority in school districts around the United States. The prevalence of this disorder appears to be rising (Chakrabarti and Fombonne 2001), and districts have reported a dramatic increase in the number of children needing services (Simpson and Zionts 2000). Designing educational settings for children with autism can be perplexing and challenging to special educators and related service providers. Difficulties unique to this population include impairments in social relatedness and social communication, as well as restricted and repetitive interests and behaviors (*DSM-IV*: APA 1994). (See Chapter 2 for further diagnostic information.) These behaviors permeate both home and school settings. Therefore, gaining a clearer understanding of this disorder is imperative for the development and implementation of effective educational practices, including the use of structures and supports in classrooms.

Samples of current programming

There are several specific curriculums that have addressed the issue of educational programming for children with autism. A sample of those that have influenced the development of the field include LEAP, ABA and TEACCH.

LEARNING EXPERIENCES ALTERNATIVE PROGRAM (LEAP)

The LEAP program reflects a behavioral and developmental approach within an inclusive preschool classroom. Skills are taught utilizing peer modeling, direct instruction, and applied behavioral analysis techniques (i.e. prompting, fading, and both artificial and natural reinforcement) (Strain and Cordisco 1994). (See Chapter 9 for further discussion of the treatment outcome research of this peer model.)

APPLIED BEHAVIORAL ANALYSIS (ABA)

Applied behavioral analysis, as described by Maurice, Green and Luce (1996) and used in the UCLA Young Autism Project (Smith and Lovaas 1997), is an intervention utilizing a variety of behavioral teaching techniques, such as prompting, fading, and both artificial and natural reinforcement. (See Chapter 5 for further details about this approach and behavioral teaching techniques.) It is characterized by the intensive nature of the program averaging 40 hours or more a week of one-to-one behavioral treatment. ABA includes a specific curriculum defined by a sequence of skills that must be mastered before progressing.

TREATMENT AND EDUCATION OF AUTISTIC AND RELATED COMMUNICATION HANDICAPPED CHILDREN (TEACCH)

The TEACCH program (Schopler 2000) was founded in 1972. The goal of the TEACCH program is to provide a continuity of interventions for individuals from preschool to school age to adulthood. It utilizes a combination of structured teaching techniques from behavioral and cognitive intervention philosophies. The program seeks to organize the learning environment for the purpose of minimizing behavior difficulties. (See Chapter 5 for more information about this approach.)

The LEAP, ABA, and TEACCH curricula are by no means all-inclusive of the research available in historical educational programming for children with autism. However, these three programs are commonly found in the literature. Each program advocates a specifically designed curriculum to be used with this population.

Child-centered programming

Educators are moving toward collaborative, multidisciplinary child-centered programming. The collaborative approach involves continual preparation, sharing of knowledge across disciplines, and ensuring that all professionals are working toward the same goals and benchmarks (Howard *et al.* 2001). The team must include active parental involvement and support (Hart 1993). By effectively overlapping approaches and environments to address the multiple needs of these children, the team collaboration is strengthened. One goal of the collaborative approach is to design an individual education program (IEP) that addresses each child's unique needs, not a predetermined program. (See Chapter 11 for further discussion of IEPs.) The availability of services cannot drive the IEP development (Bateman and Linden 1998; Yell and Drasgow 2000). Research supports that intensive, comprehensive year-round intervention programs are effective for improving the outcomes of children who have developmental disorders in general (Lord *et al.* 2001). Research has also demonstrated that multi-methods of instruction that are individually designed to meet a child's needs are legally defensible (Horton 2000). Thus, by providing opportunities in multiple settings that support success and generalize learning and interactions, the child's education becomes individualized.

Educational supports

Educational supports are defined as the use of supplementary aids and services that enable a child with disabilities to benefit from special education. Supplementary aids and services 'are provided in regular education classes or other education-related settings to enable children with disabilities to be educated with nondisabled children to the maximum extent appropriate' (Individuals with Disabilities Education Act 1997, 20 USC § 1401, 29). Supports may be included in the areas of:

- communication (e.g. computer programs such as Boardmaker ©, Print-It ©, Write-It ©: Mayer-Johnson 2000a, b, c)
- academics (e.g. visual cues and visual task analyzing)
- social interaction (e.g. structured play groups, logical themes for interaction times)
- environment (e.g. individualized and group calendars, home-school notebooks, clear boundaries, additional staff) (Bunsen, Balcerak and Hernandez 2000).

It is becoming increasingly possible to view education beyond the perceived limits of placement issues to one of a fluid policy with an emphasis on levels of support.

There are formal and informal resources of support. Informal support refers to people who provide services such as emotional support and practical assistance in a classroom. Examples of these would include parent and community volunteers (e.g. foster grandparents, retired community members, or business partnership volunteers). The best supports are those that are natural and are embedded within social relationships (e.g. classmates, friends: Snell and Brown 2000). Formal supports are services that are prearranged and paid for. These would include additional paraprofessional staff for particular activities or respite care workers.

Concept of best practice

Bunsen and Butz (2000) composed a list of Quality Indicators of Best Practices (see Appendix 8.1) from a review of literature and compilation of program components advocated for children with autism (e.g. Donnelly 2000; Maurice *et al.* 1996; Prizant 1998; Trevarthen *et al.* 1996). As one reviews this list of Quality Indicators of Best Practices in Appendix 8.1, it is hoped that educators can find commonalties across disciplines and across what is thought to be 'good solid teaching practices for all children'. Additionally, Appendix 8.1 provides detailed examples of how each of the indicators would manifest itself in an educational environment, and was composed from teachers, parents, administrators, and related service providers from around the United States who participated in a series of methods workshops focusing on children with autism (Bunsen 2001; Bunsen *et al.* 2000).

The following avenues are proposed as a start-off point for educators and related service providers to consider in the design and implementation of programs for children and youth with autism.

1. Family involvement.

2. Multidisciplinary team approach to evaluation, assessment, and intervention, including collaboration among professionals serving the children within the classroom environment and in the school setting.

3. Data-driven systems for skill acquisition as well as behaviors, including ongoing assessment activities.

4. Structured environment and predictable routines. Appropriate and activity-based intervention that addresses students' individualized programming needs. Active engagement of children throughout the day across all activities.

5. Rich staff to child ratio (e.g. less than or equal to three students to every adult). Instructional groupings that include individual, small, and large groups. Integration opportunities for students to address social, language, and play skills.

6. Transition component in place. Use of proactive positive behavioral supports.

7. Administrative support and availability of resources.

Guidelines for creating a school-based program

Actions and avenues of accomplishment

As an educator begins to create an environment for children with autism, there is a methodical course of action to follow. The following guidelines are described in the form of *actions* and *avenues for accomplishment* and provide issues for educators to consider when developing effective learning environments.

ACTION: REFLECT ON PHILOSOPHICAL BELIEF SYSTEM

Avenues for accomplishment include:

1. Reflecting on how children learn, not only their academic but also their social-emotional skills.

2. Researching the published curricula or techniques that are advocated by the philosophers in each of the paradigms.

3. Refining the skill of articulating the philosophy and the research behind it. Give thought to how the other paradigms would manifest themselves in teaching styles. The programs and interventions must be flexible enough to be implemented in classrooms where a different philosophical thought exists.

4. Reflecting on how to design interventions and to react to behaviors or incident in a classroom.

ACTION: INVESTIGATE THE CLASSROOM ENVIRONMENT

Avenues for accomplishment include:

1. Reviewing individual education programs.

2. Taking inventory of materials and order necessary materials.

3. Introducing the child to the general education staff.

4. Meeting and discussing the program philosophy with paraprofessionals and with the related services providers.

5. Designing classroom space and density, such as the shape of the circle time area, and considering where structured play could be facilitated.

ACTION: DOCUMENT PROGRAM AND CURRICULA

Avenues for accomplishment include:

1. Researching the curricula to be used for the targeted grade levels and documenting the reasons for choosing the curricula (i.e. reading, math and affective curricula). Of note, techniques and methodologies should be research based.

2. Profiling students' learning styles and accounting for them in the design of the educational setting (Horton 2000).

ACTION: OBSERVE AND EVALUATE STUDENTS' SKILLS

Avenues for accomplishment include:

1. Becoming thoroughly familiar with the student's IEP (Olson and Platt 1992).

2. Observing and evaluating students' skills during the first three weeks of school. Samples of standardized assessments include the Vineland Adaptive Behavior Scales (Sparrow, Balla and Cicchetti 1984), Woodcock Johnson-III (Woodcock and Johnson 2000), Test of Nonverbal Intelligence (TONI-3: Brown, Sherbenou and Johnson 1997), Leiter – R (Roid and Miller 1997), Brigance Diagnostic Inventory of Early Development (Brigance 1981), Peabody Individual Achievement Test – Revised (Markwardt 1998), and in the area of autism include the Autism Screening Instrument for Education Planning – Second Edition (ASIEP-2: Krug, Arick and Almond 1996), the Psychoeducational Profile – Revised (PEP-R: Schopler *et al.* 1990) and the Adolescent and Adult Psychoeducational Profile (AAPEP: Mesibov *et al.* 1990) (see Chapter 3 for further information on formal assessments). Informal assessments include the Student Benchmark Matrix (Jackson and Leone 1999), Interaction Diagram (Figure 1) (Bunsen 2001), Motivation Assessment (Durand and Crimmins 1992), reinforcement surveys (Mason *et al.* 1989), play checklists (Quill 2000; Wolfberg and Schuler 1993), affective checklist (McGinnis and Goldstein 2000), and strength-based assessments (e.g. Behavioral and Emotional Rating Scale: Epstein and Sharma 1998).

ACTION: IMPLEMENT INDIVIDUALIZED PROGRAMS

Avenues for accomplishment include:

1. Utilizing the Quality Indicators of Best Practices outlined in the previous section (Bunsen and Butz 2000).

2. Building a profile of the unique strengths, needs, and learning styles of students during the implementation phase.

ACTION: DOCUMENT STUDENTS' SUCCESSES

Avenues for accomplishment include:

1. Documenting student's success on a daily basis utilizing a variety of data-gathering tools and methods. All data should have a direct connection to the student's IEP goals.

2. Using frequency, duration, or latency data on daily documentation forms and quarterly progress notes (O'Neill *et al.* 1997); also including anecdotal data through home–school notebooks (Simpson and Zionts 2000).

Need for a data-driven system

DATA OPPORTUNITIES

Documenting the effects of comprehensive educational programs is not typical in most classrooms. However, this must change in order for educational environments for children with autism to sustain their validity for families and school districts. Data can be generated through the use of communicative, academic, social, and environmental supports within a multi-methodology classroom. Planning for data collection can begin at the IEP meeting. Table 8.1 provides an example of a student goals/objectives matrix to plot where the student's IEP objectives will be addressed and where documentation will be collected. Parent input is imperative in planning for the possibilities for multiple sites to generalize the objectives for their child.

Table 8.1 IEP goals/objectives matrix

Student's Name:				Date:			
Team Members:							

IEP goals/objectives matrix

	Opening circle in first grade class	Reading group	Math group	Recess	Science	Lunch	Story time
IEP objectives [student] will...							
Greet adults upon entering each environment	X	X	X	X	X	X	X
Utilize 'wh' questions (what and where)	X	X	X	X	X	X	X
Ask for help by raising his/her hand	X	X	X		X	X	X
Take turns while playing a game with classmates and adults		X	X	X			
Ask a classmate to play				X		X	

DOCUMENTING THE EFFECTS OF COMMUNICATION SUPPORTS

Communication supports are concrete signals or cues that provide maximal opportunities for students to understand the environment and help prompt students to interact with others. The purpose of communication supports includes:

1. developing functional means of communication by expanding the student's types of communicative intents and purposes

2. increasing the student's complexity of receptive and expressive language skills

3. expanding the student's ability to engage with others socially, conversationally, and in play (Bunsen *et al.* 2000).

Finally, the effectiveness of communication supports can be documented through the use of an interaction diagram (e.g. Figure 8.1 below) during play, functional activities (e.g. snack/lunchtime or on a field trip) or group activities with more competent peers.

DOCUMENTING THE EFFECTS OF ACADEMIC SUPPORTS

Academic supports can be defined as concrete cues that assist a child in understanding the educational requirements in each setting. These can include, but are not limited to, visual representations of stories for reading groups, the use of computer programs to assist in story writing, or a paraprofessional to read the directions and questions to a child with a low reading level. Academic supports include activities such as reframing word problems, utilizing visual presentations to teach abstract concepts (e.g. time) and testing test-taking skills. The need for academic supports increases greatly as a child enters third grade and the climate in academic learning changes. The third grade brings such changes as state testing, introduction of word problems in math, reading to learn instead of learning to read, and testing of reading comprehension skills.

The quarterly progress report establishes the need for mid-quarter team meetings, and provides an opportunity for special education and related service personnel to support the general education teacher. This assistance may be in the form of better understanding techniques or strategies for the child to meet his or her goals. The data to authenticate the quarterly progress report are generated from daily documentation. Utilizing an after-school meeting between teacher and paraprofessionals allows for daily data to be reviewed, as well as anecdotal notes on any unusual behaviors that might have happened during the day.

DOCUMENTING THE EFFECTS OF SOCIAL SUPPORTS

Social supports are defined as cues that prompt a child to interact at meaningful times and understand the naturally occurring social cues from others. Social supports include interaction patterns and the opportunities that students have for intermingling with more competent peers. As facilitators of social interaction, educators must document the interaction patterns that occur (Block, Bunsen and Gabriels 2000). The interaction diagram (see Figure 8.1) provides staff with the avenue to observe and document the interaction patterns and opportunities of a group of children. It may be used with diverse group sizes and in various locations. The sample in Figure 8.1 was taken during a 10-minute segment of lunchtime. As one can see, staff dominated the interactions within this group. All of the children in the sample were diagnosed with autism. Based on the results of the interaction diagram, educators can develop more effective, research-based social interaction interventions (e.g. peer-supportive models).

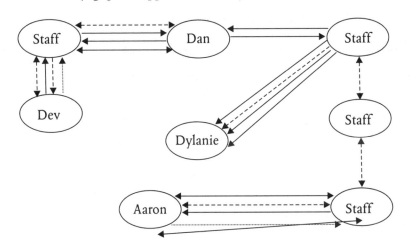

Action	Representation
Nonverbal interaction (e.g. eye glance, facial expression, pointing)	.... dotted arrow
Initiated interaction (e.g. called their name, touched them for attention)	- - - - - slashed arrow
Returned verbal interaction from initiation	————solid line arrow

Figure 8.1 Interaction diagram

DOCUMENTING THE EFFECTS OF ENVIRONMENTAL SUPPORTS

Environmental supports are physical arrangements that communicate space density, group sizes, clear boundaries, access to materials, organization of materials, classroom themes, and behavior expectations to students. There are currently many visual strategies programs on the market for educators to purchase and emulate in their classrooms (e.g. Bryan and Gast 2000;

Hodgdon 1995). When an environmental support is created, an educator must once again be able to articulate the purpose for the structure. Using the basic elements of creative learning environment of climate, space, and time (Isenberg and Jalongo 2001), supports are embedded to ensure that the environment remains child-centered and responsive to interactive behaviors such as play. This can then help an educator to design an appropriate corresponding data collection system to monitor the effectiveness of the support provided. Table 8.2 provides a sample of how environmental structures can be cataloged and possibly worded for use as IEP benchmarks/objectives.

Table 8.2 Examples of environmental supports

Environmental support	Purpose for student
Names on chairs or in circle time	Increase name and photo recognition, modeling
Words on tape for lining up	Increase word recognition
Move individual chairs to each activity	Increase smooth transitions
Individual schedules	Name recognition, 'What's the next activity', smooth transitions, matching
Names on tables	Name recognition
Basket system with photos and activity words	Matching
Basket schedule	Individual work basket time, individual independent schedules
Daily work folders per week for paraprofessionals	Independent activity, data/artifact collection
Individual math/reading/language/arts envelopes per week for paraprofessional	Daily activities listed, data collection (introduced/mastered/and initialed)
Headphones	Block noise and continue working
Social stories notebooks	Reminders of social norms
Social stories (Gray 1994)	Increase initiation
Timer	Concept of time, structure waiting, boundaries for free time
Write-It© computer program (Mayer-Johnson 2000c)	Participation in journal activity

Source: Adapted from Bunsen, Balcerak and Hernandez 2000

When designing environmental supports or choosing one of the many published programs on schedule presentation (e.g. TEACCH 1992 or Janzen 1996), it is important to keep in mind that these programs support the establishment of the surroundings but do not replace the active teaching and learning that must occur within the educational environment.

Conclusion

This chapter has sought to answer 'What is the best educational environment?' for children with autism. Blending it all together, the answer lies in the design of a multi-methodology classroom utilizing communicative, academic, social, and environmental supports. It is best not to answer the question with the name of a published program, but by whether or not the classroom and the student's educational programs incorporate all of the quality indicators. Marzano (1992) proposed the following interesting questions for all teachers to ask themselves.

1.   What will I do to help students feel accepted by the teacher and peers?

2.   What will I do to help students perceive the classroom as a comfortable, safe, and orderly place?

3.   What will I do to help students perceive tasks as valuable?

4.   What will I do to help students believe they can perform the tasks?

5.   What will I do to help students understand and be clear about tasks?

When these questions have been answered, the educational setting is ready to support active learners. Education is moving toward collaborative, multidisciplinary child-centered programming. This approach involves the sharing of knowledge and skills across disciplines and environments (e.g. home and school). By effectively overlapping approaches and environments, the multiple needs of these children can be met.

Acknowledgements

I am indebted to my friends and colleagues in the autism field for sharing their expertise and editorial suggestions: in particular Jan Harley, and the Alaska, Texas and Nevada teachers and parents who particpated in the strategy sessions.

APPENDIX 8.1

Quality Indicators of Best Practices

A. Family involvement

1. Provide journals that go back/forth between home/school.

2. Design family letters/planner/agendas for current assignments, upcoming events, due dates of assignments, or special occasions, to encourage conversations at home.

3. Encourage active parental involvement in such activities as IEP meetings, writing goals, identifying benchmarks, and sharing their observations.

4. Make a phone call to parents before all scheduled meetings and preview of progress.

5. Organize parent nights, Moms' Tea, sibling parties, Bring a Family Member Day; share a meal with administrative staff.

6. Conduct parent and teacher conferences twice a year, make home visits, make phone calls, and send email message updates to parents.

7. Trade videotapes with the family to view child in different situations and affective reactions.

8. Request parents to volunteer with outings in the classroom, supervise after-school socials or community service projects.

9. Follow-up with referrals sent home by the nurse's office for needed medications and make phone calls to parents.

B. Transdisciplinary team approach to evaluation assessment and intervention

1. Provide a safe place (e.g. nurse's office) for the child to calm him or herself.

2. Utilize nurses on the IEP for any unusual medical needs, recent medication changes, or a better understanding of what the medication may be doing for the child.

3. Conduct intervention meetings for students demonstrating a need for modifications in the regular classroom.

4. Require entire team including paraprofessionals to attend all three-year re-evaluations and IEP meetings.

5. Include observations from *all* persons who work with the child; include joint observations across settings.

6. Utilize a journal by specialists to document daily activities, progress, and future needs in individual therapies; utilize a generalization map (see Table 8.1: IEP goals/objectives matrix) to insure objectives are addressed in multiple arenas.

7. Provide parents with time to compose their thoughts before the IEP meeting. Send home observation requests and ask that the form be brought to the meeting.

8. Have the student attend IEP meetings and give input on goals and objectives.

9. Share professional schedules.

10. Conduct year-round school programming.

C. Collaboration among professionals serving children within the classroom environment and in the school setting

1. Conduct mid-quarter team meetings to assist the general educator in meeting the child's academic goals.

2. Define goals, benchmarks, and successful teaching methods.

3. Provide professional observations to insure generalization across settings, e.g. when one teacher is successful allow cooperating teacher observation time.

4. Establish meetings for teacher and paraprofessionals for documentation.

5. Update nurses with pertinent information on goals and benchmarks.

6. Create and update notebooks on characteristics of disabilities for a professional library.

7. Provide building level in-service training on quality indicators.

8. Share lesson plans between all professionals.

9. Identify student's escalation and de-escalation cycle and the most successful intervention techniques.

10. Utilize co-therapy sessions.

D. Data-driven systems for skill acquisition and behaviors: includes ongoing assessment activities

1. Use monthly and yearly calendars.

2. Interview family and previous teachers for Present Levels Of Performance (PLOP).

3. Schedule regular videotape opportunities targeting affective skills.

4. Provide weekly data checks of progress in the regular education classroom. Target work completed to mastery and make any needed modifications.

5. Utilize student matrix, generalization maps, interaction diagrams, and progress reports.

6. Utilize a daily computer log for nurses' visitation time and reason.

7. Use activity worksheets based on goals and benchmarks.

8. Utilize pre- and post-testing at each quarter or unit.

E. Structured environment and predictable routines

1. Provide monthly calendars.

2. Consistently write assignments in the same location, for child to observe and copy, for example, daily routine and individual schedules in the room or in the student's binder. These must include scheduled free time, special activities, medications, etc.

3. Utilize transitional signals (e.g. timer, music, lights) to prepare for the next event.

4. Provide clear boundaries (e.g. place for large/small group activities, individual work, snack/free time).

5. Teach planned flexibility by utilizing a visual representation of change; review and predict anticipated behaviors (i.e. activity clocks).

6. Promote generalization by utilizing identical symbols in all environments (i.e. education, related services, home).

7. Choose a general education setting that uses similar structure and philosophy to the special teacher's.

8. Utilize social stories or story scripts.

9. Adhere to the routine.

F. Develop appropriate and activity-based intervention that addresses student individualized programming needs

1. Provide specific jobs for group projects, assign roles, and define what to do and what the child is accountable for.

2. Use games and physical movement to get all children involved in the activity.

3. Set up problem-solving opportunities (e.g. leave something out and ask 'What should we do?').

4. Use age-appropriate activities that are known school-wide, for example, have entire staff refrain from hugging students; use a handshake or high five instead.

5. Encourage staff to generalize activities across the curriculum, for example, use a dot sentence strip in the nurse's office for, 'I need my pill, please.' Use the same activity when picking up attendance sheets, 'I need the attendance, please.'

6. Utilize an affective curriculum (i.e. skill streaming).

7. Utilize activities that mirror the general education curriculum, but are age and ability appropriate (e.g. use a simple chapter book when classmates are reading from chapter books).

G. Active engagement of children throughout the day across all activities

1. Utilize an inclusion model where all students with disabilities are placed into the general classroom for part or all of their day.

2. Incorporate multiple modalities, multisensory, and manipulative driven techniques.

3. Utilize greetings and farewells across various settings.

4. Provide strategies and ideas for specialists (i.e. music, art, physical education (PE), library) to promote active engagement within their specific arenas (e.g. play drums or tap sticks together to keep the beat during music, hold a puppet or have their own book during story time in the library).

5. Provide adult support for unstructured times (e.g. recess and lunch to facilitate involvement with the activity or other students).

6. Utilize choice boards for free-time activities.

7. Instruct all staff on the expected behavior within the area of the school and community setting.

8. Develop similar and equal expectations of the child, for example wait time to process questions and consistent responses among all teachers.

9. Teach a questioning script or strategy to the student. Observe how teachers address questions within individual settings.

10. Provide an adult to meet the student in the morning to review completed or incomplete homework or projects in progress and then discuss what is going to occur that day. After school the adult should check with the student regarding what homework needs to be completed.

11. Encourage the peer partnerships, peer tutoring, and cooperative learning dyads and triads.

H. Rich staff to child ratio

1. Divide entire student body among all adults in the building (maintenance and support staff included) to work with small groups of students.

2. Negotiate meaningful caseloads for special education staff.

3. Develop a team collaborative philosophy in the classroom.

4. Team-teach with the counselor or nurse so they can integrate into the classrooms, and observe and work with students in a different capacity.

5. Develop a rotation system for working with students so that staff can maintain a fresh perspective regarding individual challenges.

6. Encourage therapists to perform tasks in the classroom.

7. Develop multiple volunteer systems including foster grandparents, older students, peer aides, etc.

I. Instructional groupings that include individual, small and large groups

1. Utilize physical arrangements to guide group involvement: hula-hoops, desks facing each other, rugs, kidney tables, tape on floor for personal space, photos for lining up, vary circle time arrangements, play themes, prompts, etc.

2. Utilize cooperative learning groups and projects with a variety of involvement roles.

3. Utilize a waiting room at the nurse's office where the child knows to come in, sit down, and wait to be called on.

4. Utilize small groups for class projects and classroom work.

5. Participate in school-wide assemblies.

J. Integrate opportunities for students to develop social, language, and play skills

1. Utilize electives to reinforce language (e.g. requesting skills, problem-solving, etc.).

2. Schedule community outings that integrate language and reading (e.g. reading signs, labels, menus, recipes, etc.).

3. Integrate 'Wh' questions within daily meetings with nurses, counseling staff, front office staff, librarians, etc.

4. Collaborate with kindergarten teachers to integrate during play, circle time, outside play, snack time, and show and tell; teach 'Circle of Friends' etc.

5. Establish buddy classes with art, reading, music, PE, etc.

6. Establish a competent peer playgroup that shares interests, energy levels, and interaction styles.

7. Utilize icebreaker activities, interest surveys, interaction diagrams, etc.

8. Introduce skills to peer partners so they can facilitate a reluctant peer in play and guide and assist them.

9.   Utilize school-wide activities where students learn and play together, build relationships, and experience intramural programs.

10.   Facilitate a student observation of peers and allow time to discuss observed behaviors.

K. Transition component in place

1.   Establish a routine of teaching skills across settings so change is not a surprise.

2.   Review and predict daily transitions.

3.   Encourage parents to take their child out into the community and become involved in activities outside the home.

4.   Utilize a pod setting that is monitored by the core teaching staff.

5.   Establish small group to large group transitions where students can become comfortable working in a larger group.

6.   Utilize transitional auditory and visual cues (e.g. timer, music, lights) to prepare for the next event.

7.   Establish a chart of preparation activities (e.g. organization, relaxation skills).

8.   Utilize social stories (Gray 1994).

9.   Identify positive behavioral supports currently in place in the new setting.

10.   Preview an environment via videotape or field trip.

11.   Take field trips to the receiving schools or utilize open houses for incoming students.

12.   Schedule visitations for receiving teachers.

13.   Schedule meeting for the nurses to transition the medical needs.

14.   Facilitate a parent transition program to tour the new school, meet teachers, staff, and principal, etc.

15.   Establish teaching skills with the future in mind (e.g. the operation of a combination lock in preparation for middle school).

16.   Create a timeline with parents for school to career transitions and target needed skills.

L. Generalization should be built into the instructional activities and classroom routine

1. Utilize the generalization map or a concept-planning guide (Janzen 1996).

2. Create a portfolio to represent mastery generalized in four different locations.

3. Provide a variety of materials addressing same subject matter (e.g. red crayons, buttons, apples, socks).

4. Develop a rotation system where different people work with students throughout the day.

5. Utilize homework packets to reinforce carryover of classroom instruction.

6. Utilize a common curriculum theme or topic throughout academic and nonacademic activities.

M. Use of proactive positive behavioral supports

1. Utilize proactive discipline, for example, teachers and students problem solve together, teachers accompany students to the office.

2. Establish peaceable schools: teach conflict resolution and an anti-bullying campaign.

3. Identify student's escalation and de-escalation cycle and successful intervention techniques.

4. Utilize a consistent routine and student engagement so when an activity is completed, they know what to do next. If not, they are taught, 'I am finished with this task, what would you like me to do next?'

5. Teach students how to replace inappropriate behaviors with appropriate behaviors across multiple settings.

6. Utilize a Motivation Assessment (Durand and Crimmins 1992), a visual cues chart for life space intervention (Bunsen 2001), and a reinforcement or interest survey (Mason *et al.* 1989).

7. Utilize positive language in behavior goals to identify behaviors to be reinforced.

8. Review with staff the communicative intent of behaviors.

9. Utilize a consistent behavior plan across school, home and community.

10. Establish a means of supporting staff in difficult behavior episodes.

N. Administrative support and availability of resources

1. Share and advertise program's success.

2. Model confidentiality.

3. Provide a confidentiality and FERPA (Family Educational Rights and Privacy Act) inservice to school-wide staff.

4. Educate administration to build understanding of your program to increase support.

5. Discuss philosophical beliefs with principal.

6. Invite administrators to all meetings or activities.

7. Invite community specialists, principal, the director of special education, or business partners into classroom.

8. Have specialists available for questions on transitioning their methods from the clinical setting to the classroom and home.

9. Encourage 'touch base' meetings with the classroom teachers.

10. Utilize volunteers and provide documentation: date, time, person present, responsibility, etc.

11. Advocate for funds to attend special education conferences.

12. Advocate for the inclusion of special education topics in professional development days and to bring in professionals with expertise in special education.

13. Invite specialists, mentors, paraprofessionals, and school staff (e.g. janitors, kitchen staff) to help problem solve and generate solutions.

14. Be familiar with the central special education office and staff, state resource guides, internet sites, local agencies, parent advocate groups, and general education curriculum and daily demands.

15. Write grants.

16. Develop a brochure detailing available resources (e.g. support groups, community services, federal agencies, respite/day care services, pediatricians, internet sites, etc.).

17. Share information with the central office for children relocating.

18. Reinforce colleagues: notes, postcards, pictures, notes from students, etc.

References

American Psychiatric Association (1994) *Diagnostic and Statistical Manual of Mental Disorders (DSM–IV)*, 4th edn. Washington, DC: APA.

Bateman, B. and Linden, M.A. (1998) *Better IEPs: How to Develop Legally and Educationally Useful Programs*, 3rd edn. Longmont, CO: Sopris West.

Block, A., Bunsen, T. and Gabriels, R. (2000) 'Facilitating the play of preschoolers with autism and their friends.' Paper presented at the Second Annual Reaching for Potential: Strategies and Methodologies for Children and Youth with Autism Spectrum Disorders Conference, Denver, Co, February.

Brigance, A.H. (1981) *Brigance Diagnostic Inventory of Early Development*. North Billerica, MA: Curriculum Associates.

Brown, L., Sherbenou, R.J. and Johnson, S.K. (1997) *Test of Nonverbal Intelligence*, 3rd edn. Austin, TX: PRO-ED.

Bryan, L. and Gast, D. (2000) 'Teaching on task and on-schedule behaviors to high-functioning children with autism via picture activity schedules.' *Journal of Autism and Developmental Disorders 30*, 6, 553–567.

Bunsen, T.D. (2001) 'Behavioral supports for children with autism.' Paper presented at the Statewide Special Education Conference, Anchorage, AK, February.

Bunsen, T., Balcerak, E. and Hernandez, L. (2000) 'CASE: communicative, academic, social, environmental model in an eclectic classroom for autism spectrum disorders.' Paper presented at the second Annual Reaching for Potential: Strategies and Methodologies for Children and Youth with Autistic Spectrum Disorders Conference, Denver, CO, February.

Bunsen, T.D. and Butz, J.A. (2000) 'Creating environments which work for young children with autism.' Paper presented at the Annual CEC Convention, Vancouver, BC, April.

Chakrabarti, S. and Fombonne, E. (2001) 'Pervasive developmental disorders in preschool children.' *Journal of the American Medical Association 285*, 24, 3093–3099.

Donnelly, J. (2000) *Designing Effective Autism Programs: Serving Students with Autism, A Legal Perspective*. Burnsville, MN: Oakstone Legal and Business.

Durand, M.V. and Crimmins, D.B. (1992) *Motivational Assessment Scale (MAS) Administrative Guide*. Topeka, KS: Monaco and Associates.

Epstein, M.H. and Sharma, J.M. (1998) *Behavioral and Emotional Rating Scale: A Strength-Based Approach to Assessment*. Austin, TX: PRO-ED.

Ginott, H. (1972) *Teacher and Child: A Book for Parents and Teachers*. New York: Macmillan.

Gray, C. (1994) *The New Social Story Book: Jenison Public Schools*. Arlington, TX: Future Horizons.

Hart, C. (1993) *A Parent's Guide to Autism*. New York: Pocket Books.

Hodgdon, L. (1995) *Visual Strategies for Improving Communication: Volume 1 – Practical Supports for School and Home*. Troy, MI: Quirk Roberts.

Horton, J. (2000) *Facing Legal Challenges by Students with Autism: Serving Students with Autism, A Legal Perspective.* Burnsville, MN: Oakstone Legal and Business.

Howard, V., Williams, B., Port, P. and Lepper, C. (2001) *Very Young Children with Special Needs: A Formative Approach for the 21st Century*, 2nd edn. Upper Saddle River, NJ: Merrill.

Individuals with Disabilities Education Act (1997) Pub. L. No. 105–117, 105th Cong., 1st sess.

Isenberg, J. and Jalongo, M. (2001) *Creative Expression and Play in Early Childhood*, 3rd edn. Upper Saddle River, NJ: Merrill.

Jackson, L. and Leone, M. (1999) *Building Positive Behavioral Supports.* Colorado Springs, CO: PEAK Parent Center.

Janzen, J.E. (1996) *Understanding the Nature of Autism: A Practical Guide.* San Antonio, TX: Therapy Skill Builders.

Krug, D., Arick, J. and Almond, P. (1996) *ASIEP-2: Autism Screening Instrument for Education Planning.* Austin, TX: PRO-ED.

Lord, C., Bristol-Power, M., Cafiero, J.M., Filipek, P.A., Gallagher, J.J., Harris, S.L., Leslie, A.M., McGee, G.G., McGee, J., Odom, S.L., Rogers, S.J., Volkmar, F.R. and Wetherby, A. (2001) *Educating Children with Autism.* Commission on Behavioral and Social Sciences and Education. Washington, DC: National Academy of Sciences.

McGinnis, E. and Goldstein, A. (2000) *Skillstreaming the Elementary School Child.* Austin, TX: PRO-ED.

Markwardt, F.C. (1998) *Peabody Individual Achievement Test – Revised.* Circle Pines, MN: American Guidance Service.

Marzano, R. (1992) *A Different Kind of Classroom: Teaching with Dimensions of Learning.* Alexandria, VA: Association for Supervision and Curriculum Development.

Mason, S.A., McGee, G.G., Farmer-Dougan, V. and Risley, T.R. (1989) 'A practical strategy for ongoing reinforcer assessment.' *Journal of Applied Behavior Analysis 22,* 171–179.

Maurice, C., Green, G. and Luce, S.C. (eds) (1996) *Behavioral Intervention for Young Children with Autism: A Manual for Parents and Professionals.* Austin, TX: PRO-ED.

Mayer-Johnson Co. (2000a) *Boardmaker.* Solana Beach, CA: Mayer-Johnson Co.

Mayer-Johnson Co. (2000b) *Print-It.* Solana Beach, CA: Mayer-Johnson Co.

Mayer-Johnson Co. (2000c) *Write-It.* Solana Beach, CA: Mayer-Johnson Co.

Mesibov, G., Schopler, E., Schaffer, B. and Landrus, R. (1990) *Adolescent and Adult Psychoeducational Profile.* Austin, TX: PRO-ED.

Olson, J. and Platt, J. (1992) *Teaching Children and Adolescents with Special Needs.* New York: Merrill.

O'Neill, R.E., Horner, R.H., Albin, R.W., Sprague, J.R., Storey, K. and Newton, J.S. (1997) *Functional Assessment and Program Development for Problem Behavior*, 2nd edn. Pacific Grove, CA: Brooks/Cole.

Prizant, B. (1998) 'Enhancing communicative and socioemotional competence in young children with autism and pervasive developmental disorder.' Paper presented to the Autism Workshop, Phoenix, AZ, March.

Quill, K.A. (2000) *Do–Watch–Listen–Say: Social and Communication Intervention for Children with Autism.* Baltimore, MD: Paul H. Brookes.

Roid, G. and Miller, L. (1997) *LEITER International Performance Scale – Revised.* Chicago: Stoelting.

Schopler, E. (2000) 'TEACCH services for preschool children.' In S.L. Harris and J.S. Handleman (eds) *Preschool Education Programs for Children with Autism*, 2nd edn. Austin, TX: PRO-ED.

Schopler, E., Reichler, R.J., Bashford, A., Lansing, M.D. and Marcus, L.M. (1990) *Psychoeducational Profile – Revised*. Austin, TX: PRO-ED.

Simpson, R. and Zionts, P. (2000) *Autism: Information and Resources for Parents, Families, and Professionals*. Austin, TX: PRO-ED.

Smith, T. and Lovaas, I. (1997) 'UCLA young autism project: a reply to Gresham and MacMillan.' *Behavioral Disorders 22*, 202–218.

Snell, M. and Brown, F. (2000) 'Development and implementation of educational programs.' In M. Snell and F. Brown (eds) *Instruction of Students with Severe Disabilities*, 5th edn. Upper Saddle River, NJ: Merrill.

Sparrow, S.S., Balla, D.A. and Cicchetti, D.V. (1984) *Vineland Adaptive Behavior Scales*. Circle Pines, MN: American Guidance Service.

Strain, P. and Cordisco, L. (1994) 'LEAP preschool.' In S.L. Harris and J.S. Handleman (eds) *Preschool Education Programs for Children with Autism*. Austin, TX: PRO-ED.

TEACCH (1992) *Independent Tasks: Work Activities for Students with Autism and Other Visual Learners*. Chapel Hill, NC: TEACCH, University of North Carolina.

Trevarthen, C., Aitken, K., Despina, P. and Robarts, J. (1996) *Children with Autism: Diagnosis and Interventions to Meet their Needs*. London: Jessica Kingsley.

Wolfberg, P. and Schuler, A. (1993) 'Integrated playgroups: a model promoting the social and cognitive dimensions of play in children with autism.' *Journal of Autism and Developmental Disorders 23*, 3. 467–489.

Woodcock, R.W. and Johnson, M.B. (2000) *Woodcock-Johnson Psycho-educational Battery – III*. Chicago: Riverside.

Yell, M. and Drasgow, E. (2000) 'Litigating a free appropriate public education: the Lovaas hearing and cases.' *Journal of Special Education 33*, 4, 205–214.

Part III
Family and Community Interventions

CHAPTER 9

Sib To Sib – Making Connections

A Psychoeducational Sibling Support Group

Lauren H. Kerstein and Robin L. Gabriels

> *...having a handicapped brother or sister does not necessarily result in problematic sibling relationships, and [this factor] directs the attention of research toward studying the conditions under which positive sibling relationships can develop.* (McHale, Sloan and Simeonsson 1986, p.412)

Professionals are faced with numerous challenges when working with children who have autism and their families. Within these challenges lies a risk of overlooking the sibling relationship. Providing children with the skills and opportunities to spark an interest in engaging and teaching their sibling with autism may increase a mutual feeling of connectedness and enjoyment in the activities they experience together. This chapter presents a brief summary of the research regarding sibling relationships when one of the siblings has autism, and a review of teaching and support models designed for both peers and siblings to interact with children who have autism. Finally, a clinical model for developing a group that includes both sibling support and methods for fostering sibling interactions will be discussed.

Overview of sibling research

Growing up together can be difficult even for 'typical' siblings. Aggressiveness, quarrels, strong feelings of affection, and intense emotional ties are some of the many dynamics in sibling relationships regardless of whether one of the siblings has special needs (Bank and Kahn 1982).

There are a number of studies that examine the effects of having a child with special needs in the family, but only a few of these studies specifically address siblings in which one sibling has autism. Of the few, most of the studies are retrospective in nature or interviewed the parents, but not the sibling. Regardless, it is important to examine these studies, as they contribute to our better understanding of the sibling issues involved when there is a child with autism in the family. The research reviewed suggests directions for interventions and falls into four categories: sibling stress, peer teaching interventions, sibling teaching interventions, and sibling support interventions.

Sibling stress: comparative findings

The research regarding sibling stress is varied. In some studies, siblings report stress, but the level of stress is not always clinically significant. DeMyer (1979) conducted a comparative investigation of children who have a sibling diagnosed with autism and of children who have typically developing siblings. Findings indicated that there were no significant differences in sibling stress between the two groups, although 30 per cent of the children who had a sibling with autism reported worries and anxieties associated with the special needs. This same group of siblings also reported feelings of neglect and having problems with toileting, teasing, and jealousy.

Roeyers and Mycke (1995) conducted a project in which they examined children between the ages of 8 and 15 years. The children had siblings diagnosed with mental retardation, autism, or both, or had siblings who were developing typically. This study attempted to identify factors that impacted the sibling relationships of these children. Results indicated that all children had a positive view of their sibling relationship. However, children with a sibling diagnosed with autism reported experiencing stressors including more embarrassment in the presence of their peers and difficulty dealing with the reactions of their peers to their siblings with autism. Conversely, they reported better acceptance of their siblings with autism relative to children with typically developing siblings. This study also found that the amount and frequency of stressors and children's affective reactions to these stressors played a significant role in the sibling relationship.

McHale et al. (1986) examined sibling relationships in which one sibling was diagnosed with either autism or mental retardation or had no special needs. This study specifically examined the effects of cultural differences, parent personality, age at diagnosis, self-concept, and gender on sibling relationships. The study results did not find significant differences in the func-tioning of siblings with or without siblings with disabilities. They also found that children generally had positive things to say about their siblings whether or not the sibling had a disability. They found that while most of the children had positive things to say, there were some children who had very negative things to say about their relationship, again regardless of whether the sibling had a disability or not. However, children with siblings who had autism tended to be more negative overall in describing their relationship than the other children in the study. For example, the children spoke of worries about the future of the sibling with special needs, perceived parent favoritism toward the sibling with special needs, and felt rejected by parents. It appeared that the children described a more positive relationship when they believed their parents to respond positively to the sibling with special needs, and when they understood the 'handicapping condition'.

Bågenholm and Gillberg (1991) expanded upon the McHale *et al.* (1986) study in an attempt to identify whether the siblings of children with special needs exhibited more behavior problems. Similar to the McHale *et al.* (1986) study, their results indicated that children were all fairly positive about the relationships with their siblings regardless of disability status. However, again children with siblings who had autism were more negative overall in describing their relationships than the other children in the study.

Researchers have examined depression, social adjustment, competence, behavioral adjustment, adjustment and performance at home and school, and self-concept in siblings of a child diagnosed with autism in comparison with children who have siblings developing typically or with other diagnoses, such as Down syndrome (Dyson and Fewell 1989; Gold 1993; Mates 1990; Rodrigue, Geffken and Morgan 1993). These studies revealed no significant differences in depression between the groups of the children with siblings diagnosed with autism and the children with siblings developing typically or diagnosed with Down syndrome. The studies did, however, discuss behavioral, adjustment, performance, and self-concept concerns. All of the difficulties identified in the studies were viewed as individually based and influenced by many other familial and environmental factors, such as parents' discussion of autism, parental support, peer support, marital satisfaction, and age of the child. In summary, it appears that all of the studies (Bågenholm and Gillberg 1991; DeMyer 1979; Dyson and Fewell 1989; Gold 1993; McHale *et al.* 1986; Mates 1990; Rodrigue *et al.* 1993; Roeyers and Mycke 1995) found that children with siblings who had autism or typically developing siblings tended to be positive in describing their relationships. These studies also described reasons to be concerned about behavior, adjustment, performance, self-concept, and relational issues in some children who have siblings with autism.

A review of the research also reveals that specific and concrete information assists in strengthening children's relationships with their siblings who have autism. This information also seemed to play a role in decreasing the siblings' stress (Harris 1994). Roeyers and Mycke (1995) found that children had a relatively good understanding of autism. This is contrary to other studies (e.g. Bågenholm and Gillberg 1991; DeMyer 1979; Dyson and Fewell 1989; Gold 1993; McHale *et al.* 1986; Mates 1990; Rodrigue *et al.* 1993) that found that children tended to receive minimal information regarding the diagnosis of autism. Roeyers and Mycke (1995) attributed this to the fact that the families of their children were members of a parent association in which they received information about autism. The relationship between children's understanding of and receipt of information regarding autism seemed to be directly related to the quality of the sibling relationship (Bågenholm and Gillberg 1991; Glasberg 1999; Harris 1994; Roeyers and Mycke 1995). This is an important factor to note in the development of intervention programs for children and their siblings with autism.

Given the mixed findings in the research regarding sibling stress and social-emotional well-being along with the consistent findings that knowledge about autism assists siblings, it is important to determine the need and content of intervention programs. A variety of models have been created and utilized to assist children with autism with building skills in social and academic arenas. Simultaneously, professionals working in this field have recognized the need to support siblings and other family members through groups and other therapeutic interventions. The following are some examples of such intervention strategies to consider when developing intervention programs for siblings of children with autism (Bågenholm and Gillberg 1991).

1. Provide children with simple explanations to give to others when describing their sibling with special needs. This will help decrease feelings of embarrassment and discomfort when asked by peers about their sibling with autism.

2. Address children's concerns such as their belief that they can share feelings only with someone outside the home.

3. Explore children's statements about having to do much more around the house than their sibling with special needs.

4. Address children's concerns regarding being interrupted by their sibling with autism, or having their belongings broken by their sibling.

5. Discuss children's issues regarding the future of their sibling with autism.

6. Intervene when children report feelings of loneliness.

Peer teaching interventions

Peer teaching interventions instruct typically developing peers to work with and teach skills to children with autism. The LEAP program (Goldstein and Wickstrom 1986; Strain 1985) demonstrated that typical peers (as young as 36 months) can be taught to promote social and communicative interactions with children who have autism. Similar findings have been found in other programs (e.g. Handlan and Bloom 1993). Research has demonstrated that peer teaching is more successful when children with autism have mastered the skills required for an activity before engaging with their peers around similar activities (Handlan and Bloom 1993). Research has also found that peer inter-actions increase when peers are:

- sensitized to the feelings of frustrations experienced by children with disabilities (Handlan and Bloom 1993)
- helped to recognize and understand unexplained or undesirable behaviors (Downing and Eichinger 1996)
- taught how to decrease these frustrations and undesirable behaviors in order to reduce fear and to increase positive relationships (Handlan and Bloom 1993)
- given techniques to intervene appropriately with aggression instead of striking back or further isolating the child with autism (Downing and Eichinger 1996)
- encouraged to utilize creative problem-solving techniques (Downing and Eichinger 1996)
- taught behavioral modeling and coaching techniques, including verbal reinforcement and prompting (Handlan and Bloom 1993).

There have been many promising results of the LEAP program including the finding that elementary school-aged children can be taught to utilize behavior management and tutoring strategies with children who have special needs (Kohler and Strain 1990). The positive nature of the results with peers as teachers is quite encouraging for the use of siblings as teachers. Maintaining peer-mediated intervention is challenging when the interactions are motivated externally (Odom and Strain 1984). Therefore, it seems logical that siblings might make good lifelong teachers, as siblings may have more intrinsic motivation than classroom peers to continue helping their siblings with autism (Celiberti and Harris 1993).

Sibling teaching interventions

Celiberti and Harris (1993) examined the efficacy of teaching children how to encourage play with their siblings who have autism using behavior modification skills. The authors discussed the possibility that children want to engage in interactions with their sibling who has autism, but discontinue their attempts because they may become discouraged due to the lack of responsiveness and reciprocity along with the behavior problems of their siblings with autism. Celiberti and Harris (1993) designed a program in which they taught children the skills they might need to engage their sibling with autism. They found that typically developing siblings could be taught behavioral teaching techniques (e.g. prompting and praising) and that these skills generalized over time. It is important to note that the children who participated in this study reported increased comfort in interacting with their sibling with autism and ascribed this to having participated in the training. Reports from the families indicated that the activities in which the children participated with their sibling with autism became broader as a function of training, and extended to interactions when toys were not present, such as during dinnertime or outdoor activities (Celiberti and Harris 1993; Harris 1994). Thus, the results of this study indicated that sibling intervention can be effective in enhancing and expanding sibling interactions.

Schreibman, O'Neill and Koegel (1983) examined the effectiveness of teaching behavior modification techniques to children and the effects of these techniques on children's ability to teach their siblings with autism a variety of developmental skills. Although children were able to provide relatively clear instructions prior to the study, they exhibited trouble using effective prompts and consequences, and did not know how to conduct clear discrete trials (Schreibman et al. 1983). Study results demonstrated that children were better able to teach their siblings with autism to respond correctly to tasks after being taught to use behavioral teaching techniques such as shaping, chaining, and contingent reinforcement. (See Chapter 5 for a description of these techniques.) They further found that children's use of these behavioral techniques generalized across settings.

El-Ghoroury and Romanczyk (1999) investigated the differences in interactions between mothers, fathers, and siblings of children with autism. This study found that siblings with autism made more vocal-verbal social initiations toward siblings than toward parents, although these initiations were limited in number. As part of this study, the children were taught to engage their siblings with autism using various play techniques that encouraged more social responsiveness from their sibling. Overall, findings suggested that it may be beneficial for siblings to be involved with the process of teaching their sibling with autism developmental life skills.

Sibling support interventions

As suggested by Bågenholm and Gillberg (1991), sibling support groups might be useful for children who have a sibling with autism. These groups can give children an opportunity to discuss and better understand the behaviors of their siblings with autism. Support of this nature appears to influence positively the relationship between siblings and gives children the knowledge they need in order to engage in conversation with others about their sibling who has autism. A resource for professionals is Meyer and Vadasy's (1994) book, *Sibshops: Workshops for Siblings of Children with Special Needs*, which outlines a variety of interventions, activities, and topics to consider in conducting sibling groups with children aged 8 to 13 years.

Psychoeducational sibling support group model

Group overview

The focus will now shift to a description of a psychoeducational support group developed by the authors of this chapter, called *Sib to Sib: Making Connections*. This group was designed to provide sibling support and, at the same time, teach children how to engage positively their sibling who has autism. The goals of this group include:

- providing opportunities for support and feedback from others about how to cope with having a sibling who has autism
- instructing children about effective use of behavioral techniques to engage and teach their sibling with autism

- encouraging the generalization of learned interaction techniques to the family environment.

The group has been piloted with children ranging in age from 7 to 12 years and for their siblings with autism (age range: 5 to 9 years). At the start of the group, the siblings with autism all had attending skills, but were limited in their use of language. Although this model has been used exclusively with boys thus far, it presumably would be useful for girls as well as for children who have siblings with other neurodevelopmental disorders.

Group structure

Prior to commencing the group, individual family interviews are conducted to determine siblings' ages and levels of developmental functioning in order to create groups that are complementary in sibling ability levels. This is an important consideration because children with autism vary greatly in their levels of impairment and this factor can influence the group's success. As part of this initial interview, parents are also asked about their perceptions of their children's current sibling relationship. The group structure involves three components:

- sibling support
- sibling interaction time
- final multifamily group.

The groups alternate weekly between children meeting alone for support one week and joint meetings with all siblings together for psychoeducational interaction activities. The final session is a multifamily group meeting to review and celebrate sibling progress. After piloting this model for six to eight sessions, the feedback from the children was that a longer model in the range of eight to twelve weeks would be a more helpful length of time in which to work through issues and improve sibling interactions.

Sibling support
STRUCTURE AND ACTIVITIES

As previously mentioned, the sibling support meetings occur every other week. During this time, siblings receive support from others, gain increased knowledge about autism, and problem-solve better ways to cope and engage with their sibling who has autism. These objectives are accomplished through a combination of art and music activities, group discussion, and observation of their sibling interactions via videotape. The following is a list of example activities and discussion topics.

1. Have group members create a mural or write a song together about autism to describe what it is.

2. Encourage group members to draw or discuss things that their sibling with autism can do well and things their sibling has difficulty doing. As part of this discussion, have group members identify their goals for improving their interactions with their siblings.

3. Instruct group members to divide their paper in half and on one side draw a positive interaction with their sibling and on the other side draw a negative/hard interaction with their sibling. Encourage group members to talk about any feelings of anger, sadness, anxiety, or fear that they might identify in their drawings. Also, have members discuss feelings and issues related to their perceived role in the family.

4. Ask group members to identify or draw three wishes they have regarding their sibling who has autism. Discuss what wishes are realistic and unrealistic, and problem-solve how some of these wishes can be achieved.

5. Teach and reinforce the use of relaxation techniques through song writing and other music activities.

6. Help group members develop a plan for the groups during which they will engage with their sibling who has autism.

7. Review videotaped footage from the sibling interaction groups. Encourage group members to give each other feedback regarding their play interactions, including things that went well and areas that need improvement.

8. Brainstorm with group members about the role their parents might play in assisting them to strengthen their relationship with their sibling who has autism.

9. Have each group member put together a journal in which they can record their thoughts, feelings, and ideas outside of the groups to bring back and share at each support group meeting.

THEMES

A number of themes have emerged throughout these sibling support group sessions regarding group members' understanding of autism, the impact it has on the family, and their feelings about their sibling who has autism. Additionally, other themes have been observed toward the conclusion of the group series. These include siblings' increased realization that there are activities in which they can participate with their sibling who has autism that are mutually enjoyable and an increased understanding of intervention strategies that can help make their interactions more successful. The following group member comments and drawings provide examples of these themes.

UNDERSTANDING OF AUTISM

Siblings often entered the group attempting to understand their siblings with autism; they each came with their own idea about what autism meant. However, their initial understanding of autism seemed based on confusion about some of the behaviors they observed in the family. For example:

- 'My brother knows a lot but just for some reason he doesn't use it.'
- 'He can't really understand. It makes you wild, you get real mad.'
- 'When he hurts others, he doesn't mean it.'
- 'Their brain doesn't develop like others'.'
- 'It's how God made him.'

IMPACT ON THE FAMILY

Siblings used support group times to share their feelings related to the chaos that was caused by their sibling who has autism. They also discussed perceptions of their family roles that have evolved out of their siblings' high-risk behaviors. For example, an 11-year-old boy described an incident in which his brother with autism decided to spend time playing in the toilet and how this impacted his mother. In reference to this picture, he said, '[Brother] in toilet, note mom is mad' (see Figure 9.1).

This same group member talked and drew about feeling as if his role in the family was like a 'sheepdog', because he had to herd his brother back home if he ran out of the house and down the street. In addition he said he always had

Figure 9.1 Playing in the toilet

Figure 9.2 Sheepdog

to keep his eye on his brother to make sure he does not get into trouble (see Figure 9.2).

FEELINGS ABOUT SIBLINGS WITH AUTISM

The siblings spoke about how angry and frustrated they felt and how hard it was to express these feelings in their families. This can be a common coping reaction that results from family members' attempts to maintain a level of normal family functioning 'within an abnormal situation' (e.g. having a child with autism in the family) (Riley and Malchiodi 1994, p.141). Additionally, sibling worries may be overlooked and these feelings 'may reveal themselves in displaced or maladaptive patterns' (Riley and Malchiodi 1994, p.142). One 11-year-old boy talked about holding his anger in and letting it out once a year. He talked about and depicted the 'chaos' that results when his brother enters his room and takes things without permission. He also described how angry he gets when his brother with autism causes problems in the family (see Figure 9.3).

This same group member also drew a powerful picture further describing how furious he becomes with his brother's behavior. This sibling said that when he is no longer able to control his anger, he releases this feeling by holding his fist

Figure 9.3 Chaos

up, throwing things, and yelling. He identified feeling badly when he released his anger in this manner because this results in frightening his brother with autism (see Figure 9.4).

Finally, siblings entered the group with a limited repertoire of coping strategies. For example, several siblings reported going to their rooms and lying down on their beds or physically trying to manage their brothers with

Figure 9.4 Anger

autism. Throughout the group, more adaptive coping strategies were discussed. These strategies included learning that it is okay to be angry, finding appropriate outlets to express their anger, and identifying warning signs to signal when they need to use these coping strategies. For example, one group member said he learned that 'every time he [brother with autism] has a tantrum, he yells…I know to get away.'

MUTUALLY ENJOYABLE ACTIVITIES

At the onset of the groups, siblings tended to have a limited repertoire of activities in which they engaged with their brothers. These activities included such things as playing physical games, counting money, and drawing.

Specifically, one brother said, 'He doesn't like to play very much with me right now.'

Towards the conclusion of the group, after siblings experienced successful interactions with their brothers, siblings expressed more positive feelings about playing with their brothers. The siblings were often pleasantly surprised that despite the frustration they experienced trying to teach their brothers to play, they had fun interacting with them as well. The following comments were made by siblings toward the conclusion of the Sib to Sib groups.

- 'If you cooperate, it's a lot easier.'
- 'My brother isn't so bad after all.'
- 'Being with [my brother] isn't as hard as it looks and [my brother] can share.'

Sibling interaction time

STRUCTURE

During the sibling interaction time groups, behavior intervention strategies are modeled and explained 'in the moment'. Following this, siblings attempt these strategies with support from group leaders. These behavior interaction strategies include prompting, modeling/demonstration, shaping, errorless learning, and positive reinforcement. (See Chapter 5 for definitions of these and other behavioral techniques.) Siblings are also taught to understand the importance of using different sensory-social experiences, such as using music, bubbles, and physical games to help their sibling with autism to attend, engage, and better regulate their behavior. The siblings engage with each of their siblings who have autism for approximately 20 minutes in play activities at the table or on the floor. Following this, there is a brief sensory break time when children are allowed to freely explore the room and engage in gross motor sensory activities (e.g. throwing balls or spinning in chairs). During the last 20 minutes of the group, the children engage in a large group activity or switch and work with each other's siblings with autism, either in a more structured play set or with the sensory activities. This allows siblings a chance to practice behavioral intervention skills while learning about working with other children who have autism. This time also gives the siblings who have autism an opportunity to generalize play skills with children other than their own siblings. In the final group sessions, siblings are asked to bring a toy or game from home to play in the group with their sibling who has autism. The purpose of this activity is to encourage play skill generalization into the home environment.

ACTIVITIES

The siblings initially engage in activities specifically designed to meet the developmental abilities and interests of the sibling with autism. As the child with autism develops mastery, these activities are later expanded and generalized to new toys and games. The activities typically include turn-taking games, imitation games, language and educational play, along with cooperative and pretend play. (See Table 9.1 for a detailed description of these activities.) It is helpful to keep in mind while reviewing Table 9.1, that children with autism need to have developed foundation skills in the areas of attending, nonverbal communication, imitation, and cognition in order to engage in these activities. (See Chapter 5 for more information regarding teaching foundation skills.) However, if children with autism in the group have not yet developed these foundation skills, sibling interaction activities can begin by teaching these skills before moving on to more complex play. For example, siblings can begin to teach their sibling with autism one-step block or toy imitation prior to moving on to more creative or complex imitative play. In summary, because children with autism come to these groups with diverse skills, it is essential to develop initial interactions around familiar toys and activities before moving forward with new play activities in order to ensure their level of confidence. This avoids potentially frustrating the child with autism by not introducing a new environment, new expectations, and new toys all at the same time.

Table 9.1 Sibling group: play progression table

Types of play and techniques *These are listed in a suggested developmental teaching order. Starting places depend on the child's skill level.*	Suggested materials
Turn-taking games • Siblings give and take objects, taking a turn with the toy. Prompts include 'My (or child's name) turn, your (or child's name) turn' with open-handed gesture.	• Cause-and-effect toys including musical toys/instruments or sensory toys, like bubbles. • Puzzles • Matching games
Imitation games • *Basic block or toy/music play imitation*: siblings provide duplicate sets of blocks or toys and prompt their sibling to imitate their one- to two-step toy play actions or block designs. Verbal prompts include 'My blocks, your blocks' as siblings set up the materials, then 'Do this' or 'Make this' after siblings provide demonstration. Verbal prompts can later be generalized to phrases such as, 'Do what I do' or 'Make yours like mine'. • *Turn-taking design imitation (e.g. with blocks)*: siblings take turns picking from a block pile to build identical structures or a common structure. • *Watcher and builder game*: siblings take turns being the 'watcher' and 'builder' of constructions. The 'watcher' is responsible for observing the building process and then is expected to imitate the 'builder's' structure. • **Architect and builder game*: siblings take turns being the 'architect' and 'builder' of constructions. The 'architect' tells the 'builder' how to build a structure (Gustein, 2000).	• Multicolored wooden blocks • Duplicate sets of toys • Lego (large and small) • Play dough • Magnetic shapes and board • Musical equipment (e.g. maracas, drum, guitar)
Language and educational play • Receptive and expressive language skills can be taught within the context of a naturally rewarding task. For example, siblings provide prompts like, 'Find the letter A'. The sibling with autism can then put the letter in the puzzle, which can be naturally rewarding.	• Puzzles (e.g. animals, shapes, colors, numbers, letters, and common objects) • Blocks, Lego, and dominoes • Musical equipment (e.g. keyboards to teach playing letter-coded music) • Simple dramatic play sequences can be used for educational purposes, such as generalizing money-counting skills.

Cooperative and pretend play • *Pretend play:* meaningful structures (e.g. houses, roads, furniture, and towers) can be first built together and then used in simple pretend play sequences. The sibling might say while demonstrating, 'Drive the car over the bridge'. Simple dramatic play sequences can include playing store to buy and sell real or pretend food items. • *Cooperative:* siblings can make simple recipes together, such as making play dough or cookies for snack. Music and art sensory materials can be used to create songs or make a mural together.	• Blocks and toy people, animals, and cars • Cooking materials • Music and art sensory materials

There are many techniques and interventions derived from behaviorism and developmental theories that children can use to effectively elicit play interactions from their sibling who has autism. The following are a list of some of these techniques and interventions.

1. Children can maintain their siblings' attention to play and learning tasks by using a variety of natural (special interest sensory toys and materials) and artificial (favored foods) positive reinforcements. (See Chapter 5 for suggested attending interaction toys and activities.)

2. Children can introduce 'new words in the context of an absorbing activity' with their sibling who has autism (Greenspan and Wieder 1998, p.200). The introduction of words can include feeling words and object words to increase language understanding within a meaningful context. Group members can label their actions as well as the actions of their siblings with autism to increase their siblings' understanding of language within the context of play. They can narrate play with short phrases to increase their siblings' understanding of the play and meaning of words. Children can also pair words with gestures in order to clarify communicative intent within the play.

3. Children can teach their siblings the basic concept of imitation through the use of behavioral techniques like modeling, prompting, errorless learning, and positive reinforcement. (See Chapter 5 for an explanation of these and other behavioral techniques.) Once imitation is learned, this concept can be expanded to teach the sibling to imitate a range of pretend play as well as other skills both in and out of the play environment (Greenspan and Wieder 1998).

4. Children can address the repetitive nature of their siblings' play by building upon their play scripts, rather than eliminating them (Greenspan and Wieder 1998). New play components can slowly be added to their play scripts to expand their creative use of toys and materials. This can be more effective than demanding children with autism to change the direction of their play immediately. For example, when children with autism are forced to change their play completely rather than having others build upon their pre-existing play schemas, too much flexibility is expected too quickly and negative behaviors may result. Children with autism may be repetitious in their play because there is comfort in the familiar. By building upon the familiar, the siblings with autism are able to start in a place that feels comfortable; therefore feelings of anxiety will be lower.

5. Children can introduce challenge and problem-solving into the context of play so as to increase siblings' interactions, flexibility, problem-solving skills, and creativity into a comfortable setting (Greenspan and Wieder 1998). For example, one child increased the interest of a turn-taking activity by spontaneously introducing a problem with the toy (i.e. the child pretended to have the toy get stuck and asked his sibling with autism to help him 'Fix it'). This created a more meaningful interaction that moved this pair beyond the increasing monotony of a simple turn-taking game.

6. Children can experience a higher level of success in their play interactions if they are taught to monitor and 'read' their own affect and arousal levels as well as those in their siblings with autism. Sensory activities can be used to create a comfortable interactive environment so that children receive sensory input to assist in modulating any feelings of overstimulation resulting from the demands of the interactive group experience.

THEMES

Initially, siblings identified a lack of confidence in being able to engage their sibling with autism. For example, one sibling stated, 'I haven't gotten hardly any education on autistic kids. I have no idea how to help them.' However, as siblings began to experience confidence in their ability to engage with their siblings who have autism, they took more initiative in developing new play ideas with the materials available. Siblings' increased confidence was reflected in their statements made during the sibling support meetings.

- 'When they're starting to get upset, you *never* give them what they want [at that time] because if you do they'll realize...all I have to do is get upset and then I get what I want. It's better to ignore them [until they are calmed down].'

- 'What you have to do is teach him now while you still can before he gets too big to teach him.'

Siblings also began to recognize the important roles they play in the lives of their siblings with autism. One of the most poignant examples of this was when one child observed (on videotape) his sibling with autism losing interest in completing a complex block imitation task when he walked away for a moment. When the brother returned, the sibling with autism markedly changed his attention and quickly completed his block design. The sibling's response to observing this interaction on videotape was to comment on being surprised about how much his brother does pay attention to him.

Final multifamily group

Multifamily group formats have been used with other populations (e.g. individuals with chronic illness) to encourage 'identification with others', foster hope, decrease isolation and stress, and generate discussions of coping strategies (Wamboldt and Levin 1995, p.153). With this in mind, the final multifamily group meeting was included as part of the Sib to Sib group series to provide an opportunity for families to review together the videotaped footage of their children's interactions. During this meeting, families are encouraged to ask questions of one another and problem-solve ways siblings can continue to cope and have positive interactions at home. Finally, this meeting offers a time for the children to share their feelings about the group, information they received, the difficulties and successes they may have had with their sibling with autism, and to let their parents know what supports they might need from them at home.

Conclusion

Sibling research has moved toward finding innovative, natural techniques to work with children who have autism. Given the success of peer intervention strategies with children who have autism and the importance of support for siblings, the authors designed a clinical model incorporating both sibling support and interactive interventions.

It is important for professionals and parents to acknowledge the unique roles siblings have within the family when there is a child with autism. One child captured this concept well by saying, 'It's very hard to train my brother. Basically, it's just a hard job.' The Sib to Sib group provides a forum for children to recognize these difficulties, receive support, and learn the means to have successful, mutual interactions with their siblings with autism. Finally, this group fosters children's recognition of their potentially positive role as lifelong teachers and friends.

Question of child: If you had a magic wand, what wish would you make about your brother?

Response: I'd wish for a million dollars to buy toys and see how my brother expresses himself through the toys.

APPENDIX 9.1

Books For Siblings

Bodenheimer, C. (1979) *Everybody is a Person: A Book for Brothers and Sisters of Autistic Kids.* Syracuse, NY: Jowanio – The Learning Place.

Denison, K. and Weinberger, T. (1996) *I Wish I Could Fly Like a Bird.* New York: Wildwood Creative Enterprises.

Dr Seuss (1950) *Jerald McBoing Boing.* New York: Random House.

Edwards, B.E. and Armitage, D. (1999) *My Brother Sammy.* Brookfield, CT: Millbrook.

Gold, P. (1975) *Please Don't Say Hello.* New York: Human Services.

Gutstein, S.E. (2000) *Autism/Aspergers: Solving the Relationship Puzzle – A New Developmental Program that Opens the Door to Lifelong Social and Emotional Growth.* Arlington, TX: Future Horizons.

Katz, I. and Borowitz, F. (1993) *Joey and Sam: A Heartwarming Storybook about Autism, a Family, and a Brother's Love.* West Hills, CA: Real Life Storybooks.

Lears, L. (1998) *Ian's Walk.* Morton Grove, IL: Albert Whitman.

Messner, A.W. (1999) *Captain Tommy.* Arlington, TX: Future Horizons.

Meyer, D.J. (ed) (1997) *View from our Shoes.* Bethesda, MD: Woodbine House.

Minneapolis Children's Medical Center, Exceptional Children with Communication and Interaction Disorders (1989) *Having a Brother like David.* Minneapolis, MN: Minneapolis Children's Medical Center.

Parker, R. (1974) *He is your Brother.* Nashville, TN: Thomas Nelson.

Rosenberg, M.S. (2000) *Everything You Need to Know When a Brother or Sister is Autistic.* New York: Rosen.

Rosenberg, M.S. (2001) *Coping When a Brother or Sister is Autistic.* New York: Rosen.

Spence, E. (1977) *The Devil Hole.* New York: Lothrop, Lee and Shepard, Division of William Morrow.

Sullivan, C. (2001) *I Love my Brother.* Stratham, NH: Phat Art 4 Pub.

Thompson, M. (1996) *Andy and his Yellow Frisbee.* Bethesda, MD: Woodbine House.

References

Bågenholm, A. and Gillberg, C. (1991) 'Psychosocial effects on siblings of children with autism and mental retardation: a population-based study.' *Journal of Mental Deficiency Research 35*, 291–307.

Bank, S.P. and Kahn, M.D. (1982) *The Sibling Bond.* New York: Basic Books.

Celiberti, D.A. and Harris, S.L. (1993) 'Behavioral intervention for siblings of children with autism: a focus on skills to enhance play.' *Behavior Therapy 24*, 573–599.

DeMyer, M.K. (1979) *Parents and Children in Autism.* New York: Wiley.

Downing, J.E. and Eichinger, J. (1996) 'The important role of peers in the inclusion process.' In J.E. Downing (ed) *Including Students with Severe and Multiple Disabilities in Typical Classrooms: Practical Strategies for Teachers.* Baltimore, MD: Paul H. Brookes.

Dyson, L. and Fewell, R.R. (1989) 'The self-concept of siblings of handicapped children: a comparison.' *Journal of Early Intervention 13*, 3, 230–238.

El-Ghoroury, N.H. and Romanczyk, R.G. (1999) 'Play interactions of family members towards children with autism.' *Journal of Autism and Developmental Disorders 29*, 3, 249–257.

Glasberg, B. (1999) 'A review of the research on siblings and autism.' *Advocate: The Newsletter of the Autism Society of America 32*, 6, 24–25, 31.

Gold, N. (1993) 'Depression and social adjustment in siblings of boys with autism.' *Journal of Autism and Developmental Disorders 23*, 1, 147–163.

Goldstein, H. and Wickstrom, S. (1986) 'Peer intervention effects on communicative interaction among handicapped and nonhandicapped preschoolers.' *Journal of Applied Behavior Analysis 19*, 209–214.

Greenspan, S.I. and Wieder, S. (1998) *The Child with Special Needs: Encouraging Intellectual and Emotional Growth.* Reading, MA: Addison-Wesley.

Gutstein, S.E. (2000) *Autism/Aspergers: Solving the Relationship Puzzle – A New Developmental Program that Opens the Door to Lifelong Social and Emotional Growth.* Arlington, TX: Future Horizons.

Handlan, S. and Bloom, L.A. (1993) 'The effect of educational curricula and modeling/coaching on the interactions of kindergarten children with their peers with autism.' *Focus on Autistic Behavior 8*, 2, 1–11.

Harris, S.L. (1994) *Siblings of Children with Autism: A Guide for Families.* Bethesda, MD: Woodbine House.

Kohler, F.W. and Strain, P.S. (1990) 'Peer-assisted interventions: early promises, notable achievements, and future aspirations.' *Clinical Psychology Review 10*, 441–445.

McHale, S.M., Sloan, J. and Simeonsson, R.J. (1986) 'Sibling relationships of children with autistic, mentally retarded, and nonhandicapped brothers and sisters.' *Journal of Autism and Developmental Disorders 16*, 4, 399–413.

Mates, T.E. (1990) 'Siblings of autistic children: their adjustment and performance at home and in school.' *Journal of Autism and Developmental Disorders 20*, 4, 545–553.

Meyer, D.J. and Vadasy, P.F. (1994) *Sibshops: Workshops for Siblings of Children with Special Needs.* Baltimore, MD: Paul H. Brookes.

Odom, S.L. and Strain, P.S. (1984) 'Peer-mediated approaches to promoting children's social interaction: a review.' *American Journal of Orthopsychiatry 54*, 544–557.

Riley, S. and Malchiodi, C. (1994) *Integrative Approaches to Family Art Therapy.* Chicago: Magnolia Street.

Rodrigue, J.R., Geffken, G.R. and Morgan, S.B. (1993) 'Perceived competence and behavioral adjustment of siblings of children with autism.' *Journal of Autism and Developmental Disorders 23*, 4, 665–673.

Roeyers, H. and Mycke, K. (1995) 'Siblings of a child with autism, with mental retardation and with a normal development.' *Child: Care, Health and Development 21*, 5, 305–319.

Schreibman, L., O'Neill, R.E. and Koegel, R.L. (1983) 'Behavioral training for siblings of autistic children.' *Journal of Applied Behavioral Analysis 16*, 2, 129–138.

Strain, P.S. (1985) 'Programmatic research on peers as intervention agents for socially isolated classmates.' *The Pointer 20*, 22–29.

Wamboldt, M.Z. and Levin, L. (1995) 'Utility of multifamily psychoeducational groups for medically ill children and adolescents.' *Family Systems Medicine: The Journal of Collaborative Family Health Care 13*, 2, 151–161.

CHAPTER 10

Programming Social Experiences for Adolescents with Autism

Lee M. Marcus and Barbara Bianco

Your imagination can do anything,
You can fly through the air,
Be millions of times faster than the
Speed of light
Swifter than wind
But stronger than gravity
My imagination is wider than I can explain

(Daniel, Teen Group member)

In this chapter we describe a social group for adolescents with autism, based on the principles and practices of the TEACCH program in North Carolina. As TEACCH has evolved since its inception in the early 1970s (Schopler 1997), along with its continued emphasis on individualized assessment and treatment for persons with autism and their families, the program has developed a variety of group formats to help with social development and support (Mesibov 1984). With the increase in the number of higher functioning adolescents with autism being served in the 1990s, we organized and implemented a teen group, particularly for those individuals who have limited social experiences outside of school. We provide a framework for the development of the group as well as details about its goals and activities. Prior to discussing the group, we will briefly review the literature on social behavior and interventions in autism and the role of groups in the TEACCH program.

Social behaviors and autism

Impairment in social reciprocity, or the failure to develop normal give-and-take relationships, is a core deficit in autism. Many researchers and clinicians would argue that social problems represent the most significant challenge for persons with autism and are likely to continue in some form throughout the lifespan, regardless of the person's level of functioning. Social difficulties include both the cognitive and affective side of relating to people and understanding rules and conventions. Individuals with autism struggle with understanding, perceiving, and sharing feelings, as well as knowing about social customs. What comes naturally to typically developing individuals is an almost painful learning process for people with autism. Even when the learning occurs, it does not come easily. As one of our teens told his mother, 'There are so many rules'.

In the infant and toddler years, signs of autism in the social area include poor imitation, abnormal eye contact, ignoring or being unresponsive to others, little interest in social games, bland affective expression, and a preference for being alone (Stone 1997). Also noted as atypical social development are poor orienting to own name-calling, aversion to social touch, and failure to point and show. Parents have reported concerns about their child being in his or her own world, being too 'independent', tuning out, and showing lack of interest in other children. These early indicators of unusual social development tend to persist throughout the life of the person, although social interest and desire for friendships and other meaningful relationships can occur.

As described by Wing and Gould (1979), several patterns of social impairment can emerge, not just the classic Kanner withdrawal and isolation. For example, many persons with high functioning autism may fit the 'active, but odd' subtype. This pattern describes someone who makes efforts to approach and interact, but clumsily, without sensitivity to others' perspectives or feelings, being intrusive or disinhibited, or, at times, brash or rude. Another subtype is the person who is passive, but willing to participate at the initiation of others; social difficulties may be less obvious, but are characterized by the absence of social overtures or the ability to sustain an interaction beyond a superficial level.

Social intervention strategies and autism

Given the centrality of the social impairments in autism, it is not surprising that these have been the focal point of interventions. Historically, the approaches to addressing social problems have ranged from psychoanalytical (e.g. Bettelheim 1967), with its emphasis on addressing underlying emotional issues, to behavioral, with its emphasis on step-by-step teaching of specific skills (e.g. Koegel and Frea 1993). The various approaches often reflect conceptual frameworks for what is considered the fundamental basis for social development problems. For example, in the mid-1990s research highlighted the presence of theory of mind weaknesses in children with autism, related to the ability to understand another's perspective, empathy and other socially relevant behaviors (Baron-Cohen and Swettenham 1997; see also Chapter 2). Subsequently, some pilot efforts have been made to teach theory of mind strategies and measure the effectiveness on social skills in a natural context (Ozonoff and Miller 1995).

The inclusion movement, which has had its proponents and skeptics (Mesibov 1990; Stainback and Stainback 1992), can be seen as an intervention approach targeting social skills through natural interactions between children with autism and typical peers. Although the research literature does not yet support the advantages of inclusion over other educational frameworks, there are components of integrated environments that have been studied and shown to have some positive effects on the social development of children with autism (e.g. Krantz and McClannahan 1993). The use of peers as role models, tutors, and buddies is one approach; social skills groups and training within public school settings is another, including the use of 'reverse mainstreaming', in which the typical peer spends planned time in the classroom of the child with autism (Wooten and Mesibov 1986). Whatever the specific technique, there is consensus among researchers and clinicians that the program must be carefully organized, peers must be trained and supported, and social goals and objectives individualized.

The TEACCH perspective on developing social skills links individual play and leisure skills to interaction skills, whether in one-to-one, small or large group setting. Although recognizing the importance of ultimately having individuals with autism successfully function in a social environment with others, the program also acknowledges the relevance of basic skills in learning how to play with toys and use playground equipment and other materials in appropriate ways. Without these fundamental skills, learning to do activities with others becomes virtually impossible. Generalization is taught by the process of learning a leisure skill in a direct teaching setting, and then practicing it in an independent area, before using it in a more natural context such as a free play area. Subsequently, this skill can be generalized in a social activity with another child and possibly later in a group setting. Not every child requires such a step-by-step approach, but this framework for understanding and developing social and leisure skills can be very useful.

Social groups

Working with children, adolescents, and adults in group settings has been an established treatment approach in mental health. Typically, such groups have focused on the interpersonal, communication, or other life problems of its participants and the format is primarily verbal. The degree of structure or directedness of the group might vary from leader to leader, but the basic assumption has been that group process can foster social development not achieved solely through individual therapy. In children's groups, the emphasis might be more activity-oriented and behavioral than primarily conversational.

Despite the fundamental social impairment in autism, little has been written about working with individuals who have autism in social groups (Howlin and Yates 1999; Mesibov 1984; Williams 1989). Historically, this may be due to the emphasis on direct individual work or the difficulty of organizing and running social groups. However, as one of its services to persons with autism and their families, TEACCH has developed social groups across the age spectrum. The first formal group was developed for adults (Mesibov 1984) and has functioned without interruption since the early 1980s. After several years of the adult group serving as the prototype, groups for teens and then elementary-age children were established.

At the preschool level, in its model classrooms, TEACCH provides a range of group social activities (Marcus, Schopler and Lord 2000). Successfully running a classroom group requires, in addition to meaningful activities and appropriate structure, awareness of individual differences among students. One basic strategy often utilized is that of a 'layered group', which means that the child should be expected to stay in the group for activities that are appropriate for his or her developmental level and language. By moving children in and out over the duration of the group session, the teacher does not feel pressured to have everyone participate in every activity. As a result, when done properly, the classroom group experience can be valuable for each student regardless of level of social development.

Before describing in detail our experience with adolescents and social groups, we briefly review the basic principles and practices of the TEACCH group approach, also touching upon variations across the different age groups.

Assessment considerations

A fundamental starting point for working with individuals who have autism in the TEACCH program is individualized assessment (Schopler *et al.* 1990). The importance of assessment extends to the development of a group. Questions to be answered include: what are the person's interests? What prior group experiences, successes or lack of successes has he or she had? What are the individual's skills, strengths, and needs? What are the priorities and concerns of the parents and what are their goals? Are there behavioral issues that might compromise the participation of the prospective group member? This information can be gathered from various sources (parents, teachers, the person with autism) through brief questionnaires and observations.

Intervention considerations

A primary principle in the TEACCH approach to intervention is structured teaching (Schopler, Mesibov and Hearsey 1995). The components of structured teaching (e.g. physical structure, schedules, work systems, visual structure, and routines) apply nicely to the group setting. Structure helps clarify expectations, gives predictability and meaning to events, and provides a framework that facilitates learning and participation in activities. Other considerations include:

- composing the group (e.g. age, level of ability, needs of the individuals)
- including typical peers and how their role is defined
- incorporating the interests of different group members into activities and structure
- determining to what extent the group will be focusing on social skills or serve more as a 'social club'
- individualizing goals for each participant within the group context
- identifying the setting or settings where the group will take place (e.g. community locations, school, clinic).

Basic group goals, methods, and variations

GOALS

Across the different age groups, there are common goals. These include:

- providing a positive social experience so that participants 'have fun'
- increasing participants' understanding of social situations, the social environment, conventions, and expectations
- improving social behaviors and skills
- facilitating and developing play, recreation, and leisure skills.

METHODS

Some general considerations that we have found helpful include:

- becoming familiar with group members before they join the group
- having the staff or group leaders involved in all the activities
- finding ways to encourage members' feelings of belonging to the group, including members' interests in planning activities
- providing a consistent meeting place.

VARIATIONS

To accommodate the variations across the age spectrum, the following adjustments are made:

- there is a decreased emphasis on direct teaching of skills/behaviors with increased age of participants
- older children are expected to be more independent (e.g. the ratio of staff to participant is lower)
- older children take more responsibility for planning activities
- there are more community-based activities in the adolescent and adult group than with the elementary age groups.

The Chapel Hill TEACCH Center Teen Group

Having reviewed the basic principles and methods underlying the TEACCH social group program, in the rest of the chapter we describe how these concepts have been applied to the Chapel Hill TEACCH Center Teen Group.

The Teen Group began in the late 1980s in response to the increased number of adolescents with autism who were lacking positive social experiences. These adolescents were not involved in social outlets, even though they were in mainstream school settings and were at or near normal levels of intellectual functioning. As with the existing adult groups (Mesibov 1984), the adolescents recruited for the group fell into the higher functioning range, partly because these individuals were not receiving school-based, autism-specific services and partly because they had expressed a strong desire to have the kind of social opportunities our group would provide.

Purposes and goals

The initial purpose for forming the Teen Group was for the members to have a group they could belong to and have opportunities to engage in fun activities with peers. Initially, coming together and having a positive social experience was the main goal. The intent was to develop a structured model for a social group that taught adolescents how to interact appropriately with peers and learn skills that they could use in a variety of contexts including school and the community.

Over time, other goals unfolded which were shaped, either directly or indirectly, by the teens themselves. The teens demonstrated that they also wanted to feel competent with a variety of things including being a friend, playing games, expressing their creativity, and participating in the community around them. They also wanted to learn these skills in a social setting with a group that was accepting of individual differences, but also had some sense of commonality. This is perhaps because basic social skills training is not emphasized in the group, the focus is on belonging to a group and enjoying one another. In reflecting on how this group has worked, the order of appearance and importance of the key elements has been: the teens, the activities, having fun, using strategies that work with people who have autism, and learning skills. Although social skills are not directly taught with the Teen Group, incidental teaching occurs throughout group activities. Skills addressed in natural contexts include initiating interaction, having conversations, communicating emotions and opinions, and broadening individual leisure interests.

Through the years, the goals of the group have remained remarkably the same. The teens in the group continue to demonstrate that they still just want to have fun and feel they belong. Staffs' and parents' assumptions about the teens' preferences are often incorrect and listening to what the group wants has been essential to its success. The group has become a place where friendships can actually develop. A sense of 'groupness' occurs through shared experiences and understanding others, while meeting on a regular basis. The group has become a stable social outlet the teens can count on in their lives.

Structure and format

The TEACCH Teen Group has grown considerably since the early days. There are approximately 20 members who are on the mailing list, with up to 15 teens who attend regularly. It is this core of individuals who attend consistently that make up the backbone of the group. These are the individuals who remember the names of their friends' family members, pets, where they went for vacation, the airline they flew on, and the types of cars they drive. The same staff members are consistently present for each event with the only variation being university students for additional support.

The format and structure used with the Teen Group is consistent with the TEACCH approach that works well for people who have autism. Information is provided in a predictable way and there are routines for accepting change and chance opportunities. Guidelines are provided for behavioral expectations and social interactions and clear directions for completing an activity. The group is organized around a structure that usually involves some form of schedule to follow. The general group structure involves an opening routine, the activity itself, and a closing routine. 'Structured teaching' strategies include visual or written directions when more structure is required so that the members can be relatively independent of the group facilitators. These 'structural' features of the group remain the same even if the activities change and the group attendance varies.

SCHEDULES

Providing group and individual schedules is an essential part of the structure of group activities. The schedules present a visual sequence of what will happen during a group event or activity, thus helping to reduce anxiety and uncertainty about actions, places, and people involved in the activities. Additionally, schedules prevent confusion and give a touchstone to return to each step of the way during a group event.

The group schedule is written on a flip chart and additional copies are printed out for individuals to refer to when needed. Modifications (e.g. addition of a few pictures or breaking the schedule down into smaller parts) are made to individuals' schedules so they can follow along and make any transitions as independently as possible. Each item or step on the schedule can be checked off or crossed out to indicate being 'finished'. See Appendix 10.1 for a sample group schedule.

ROUTINES

The extent of the group structure depends on the activity. For example, when the group meets at the Chapel Hill TEACCH Center, activities usually begin with an 'update' that includes introducing new members and taking turns sharing 'news'. Placing the topics on a flip chart so that members can see what information to share provides specific prompts to teens if needed. This also helps members to plan what they are expected to say. A group facilitator or experienced member provides a model by going first. The following is an example of group introductions and member updates. Of note, sample visual cues are provided to help members share experiences.

Introductions
- Name ('Hi, I'm _____.')
- Age ('I'm _____ years old.')
- Where you live ('I live in _____.')
- Where you go to school ('I go to _____.')
- State two or three things you like to do in your free time ('I like to ___.')

Updates
- Tell us about somewhere you have gone or something you have done since the group last met, for example: going on vacation, seeing a movie, going out to dinner, having a friend or relative visit you, or something funny that happened to you.

For most of the activities, the large group is divided into smaller groups to facilitate social interaction and general group management. Matching teens according to common interests and neighborhood schools provides greater opportunity for them to build friendships and mutual support beyond the group setting. Some activities include members doing interviews to learn more about each other and to foster connections within the group. Additional connections are made between the parents of the group members who often carpool or get together on their own while their sons and daughters are with their friends in the group.

VISUAL/WRITTEN DIRECTIONS

When out in the community, some activities require more structure than others. There are many activities which members enjoy doing that are naturally structured (e.g. bowling, miniature golf). For these activities, schedules are used as needed or paper and pencil are available for staff to present specific written information or behavioral reminders to avoid having to repeat verbal directions. There are other activities that require more structure. For example, a scavenger hunt in a herb garden or on the university campus requires a written plan of what to look for, how much to look for, when the hunt will be over, and what will come next. Group members are provided with a 'to do' list for activities that are more open-ended or complex. Structuring the activities in this way takes into consideration those skill and functioning areas that are particularly challenging for group members. For example, the structure provides a basis for interaction between the teens as well as having the added bonus of working on skills like language, reading, and negotiating community settings. Without the structure, members would be less independent because they would be struggling to organize themselves socially. An example of written directions for a scavenger hunt is shown in Appendix 10.2.

The structure, routines, and familiarity with each other have encouraged spontaneous interactions among group members. When this happens, group leaders try not to interrupt the natural flow of members' conversations, joking or sharing of an experience or memory just for the sake of using a strategy. The strategies and approaches provide support and enhancement and do not become more important than the impromptu easy exchange between friends who are familiar with each other.

GUIDELINES

Although routines, schedules, and visual directions are key elements to a smooth-running group, there is also the issue of behavior management and coping with any stress that may occur. Typically, the group is not a place where many behavioral problems arise, perhaps because it is a low stress situation. This factor provides an opportunity to work on increasing positive social behavior and teaching coping strategies in a benign setting. With this in mind, group written behavior guidelines are added to the schedule; for example, remembering to give a compliment, staying with the group, and letting someone know when you need to take a break or if there is too much noise.

The consistent use of guidelines within the context of group activities has helped the members generalize some of their social skills in other contexts. There have been several instances when the group has been at noisy bowling alleys or restaurants and group members have been able to communicate the need for a 'quiet break'. Group leaders then establish a place in that environment where the teen member can take a breather from the action, with staff supervision. Following this, the teen member can return to the activity successfully. The result of such a simple strategy is that group members learn an alternative coping mechanism and how to use this in a variety of settings. They experience success with self-control without reverting to inappropriate behavior to effect a change or find a release from the stress.

Some group activities have included identifying certain social situations and appropriate behaviors. Often, the group will 'play act' these situations in meetings at the center in preparation for an event out in the community. The development of the guidelines has been effective in assessing the teens' understanding of social concepts (e.g. compliments), thus creating real-life situations to practice such skills. Some guidelines are already printed on schedules, but additional space is provided for customizing specific suggestions for individual members. The following is an example of some reminder guidelines that might appear on a schedule.

Reminder guidelines

- Stay with the group.
- Tell group leaders or staff if you need a break.
- Asking for help is OK!
- Give someone a compliment today!
- Have fun!

Addressing these complex social behavior issues through games and fun activities and applying them in contexts out in the community enhance maximum generalization of skills.

CURRICULUM AREAS

In addition to helping the group have fun together, there are also several specific skill areas that are addressed within the context of group activities. These areas relate to the core deficits of people with autism, and include:

- increasing social interaction through shared enjoyment of a common activity
- practicing skills needed to socialize (e.g. turn-taking, sharing, learning social cues)
- enhancing language concepts needed to be part of a group and the community at large
- increasing use and understanding of communication (i.e. verbal and nonverbal communication)
- building common memories through the use of familiar and new experiences with the group to provide topics for conversations and sharing of positive feelings
- widening exposure of group members to new recreational skills and possible hobbies based on individual and group interests
- increasing self-esteem
- developing creative expression
- practicing community skills
- involving family members
- increasing independence
- practicing coping strategies and internal control in social situations.

When planning group activities, individual members' strengths, needs, and interests are considered in combination with the entire group's needs and interests. For example, one teen may be an expert in geography, another in film history, and yet another in sea life or music from the 1950s. Group leaders try to find common ground among individuals' special interests and develop new activities based on familiar interests. Approaching deficit areas through the individual's strengths and interests has been essential to building positive social experiences, boosting self-esteem, and reinforcing skills. Often those members who have more knowledge or experience with a particular activity are asked to help lead the event (e.g. nature hike, preparing food, demonstrating a game, introducing new people or welcoming visitors). This also supports the development of leadership skills.

INCLUSION OF PEERS

Peer volunteers from local middle schools, high schools, and universities come to the group through several ways: either they are genuinely interested and have heard that we do some exciting things or they need to fulfill community service requirements for school, church, or clubs.

Volunteers are provided with a brief orientation that involves both written information and discussion about autism and what they can expect to experience in the program. Group strategies are reviewed and they are asked to watch and follow the staffs' approach. These peer mentors usually meet with us before the beginning of each group event to review what will happen and what specific support they can provide. Several friendships between mentors and group members have grown beyond the group experiences into respective school communities. Some of the group members have had lunch dates and involvement in school activities because they knew a peer mentor who spent time with the group.

Teachers, parents, and therapists have also been trained to develop social groups in their neighborhoods and schools. These groups have been successful in that they can meet even more frequently and the members are in a position to see each other at school and in the community. This leads to greater natural 'inclusion' with peers and helps peers who do not have autism develop a deeper understanding of people with autism and the possibilities of their making contributions to their world.

Teen group activities: a closer look

Recurring activities (building a calendar of regular activities)

The TEACCH Teen Group usually meets twice a month for approximately two hours each session. There is also an overnight camping trip that takes place every year. About two-thirds of the activities take place in the community with the remainder in the Chapel Hill TEACCH Center. There are certain events that members look forward to and expect. These events are actually topics of conversation within the group (e.g. 'Are we going bowling this September?' 'Do you remember the time we went canoeing at the lake and I fell in?' 'Will we have our Holiday Pizza Party?'). These familiar events anchor the annual calendar and are the constant features of accumulated group memories. These and other events constitute the fabric of the group's patchwork of 'folklore' or common history that gives the group cohesion. Although the group discussion may perseverate on certain topics like the weather or the size of chocolate chip cookies at a restaurant, group activities build a foundation of experiences to talk about and remember, similar to all groups of friends.

The calendar in Table 10.1 reflects events that are familiar activities that group members look forward to each year. These events, such as dinner out with friends, playing games at the TEACCH Center, or going to the local planetarium, are recurring activities that happen periodically throughout the year. We also visit local museums and botanical gardens, play miniature golf, go bowling, and go boating on a regular basis.

Table 10.1 Sample calendar of teen group events

Dates	Event	Times and location
12/13/00	Holiday Pizza Party, bring a simple gift to exchange (e.g. calendar, small photo album, treats, magazines, joke book).	5:30–7:00 Pizza Hut on Estes Drive in Chapel Hill; please RSVP and call for directions if needed.
1/11/01	Work on Poetry Project	4:30–6:00 at Chapel Hill TEACCH Center
1/25/01	Finish work on Poetry Project	4:30–6:00 at Chapel Hill TEACCH Center
1/26/01	Poetry Party Join us for music, poetry and refreshments. Members and parents are asked to bring refreshments or treats for the party; please call Monica or Barbara to RSVP and find out what you can bring.	7:30–9:00 at the Colony Hills Club House in Durham; directions will be mailed to you closer to the time of the party as a reminder.
2/1/01	Dinner out with Friends! Join us for conversation, checkers, chess and browsing the book, music and video collections at one of our favorite spots in town.	5:00–6:30 Skylight Exchange, Rosemary Street, Chapel Hill; RSVP and call for directions; bring approximately $10.
2/15/00	Bring your favorite card, board game, etc. to play with friends!	4:30–6:00 at the Chapel Hill TEACCH Center

3/1/01	Community Service Project: Cookie/Brownie and Craft sale to raise money for group home playground equipment	4:30–7:00 at Camp Royall. We will have pizza for dinner then bake cookies, brownies and make crafts for our fundraiser.
3/15/01	Dinner with the Stars!	5:30–7:30 Dinner at Pepper's Pizza on Franklin Street, Chapel Hill, followed by a stroll down to the Morehead Planetarium for a show! Bring approximately $15 for dinner and the show.

The community service activities are an example of a one-time event that occurs in our calendar. These activities are usually motivated by a request from the community, an interest of some of the group members or even a special skill of a staff member or invited guest. For example, the calendar in Table 10.1 displays a community service project of making baked goods and craft items to sell to raise money; other community service projects have included making meals for the local Ronald McDonald House and trail maintenance at local parks.

Examples of other activities include creating and publishing a newsletter, creating T-shirts, and making a talent video.

Long-term projects

Long-term projects involve activities that are relatively new for group members and require a process of exposure, teaching, and application leading to a final activity that combines all of the preceding elements. This process is divided into carefully planned modules to teach new skills and build on existing skills. For example, photography, art, and poetry modules include the following components:

1. Introduction to art, photography, and poetry: visiting local art museums, a university photography department, and a local library where poetry books can be checked out and favorite poems read.

2. Creating art, photography, and poetry: materials are provided such as for art, a variety of media (paints, pastels, clay, stencils, etc.); for photography, disposable cameras, 35mm cameras, color and black and white film; and for poetry, paper, pencils, a computer, and sufficient staff to take dictation as needed.

3. Continuation of process and completion of projects.

4. Preparation for presentation, which may include practicing how to present, putting together exhibits and show programs, set-up of space for the event, and making refreshments.

5. Presentation of the group's creations at an exhibit or social gathering.

The final presentations can involve displaying poetry, art, or photography, talent shows, videos, or newsletters. They give the group members a chance to highlight their individual skills and interests. Figure 10.1 is a scene from a photography exhibit reception with two of the teen group members.

Figure 10.1 Scene from photography exhibit reception with two of the Teen Group members

Additionally, the following are examples of poems written by two Teen Group members.

A Brightly Colored Shell

Walking along the shoreline
I see partly dug
A brightly colored shell
Pink with golden highlights
And shaped like a snail.
At this moment I stop
To pick it up out of the sand
And cup it lovingly
In my hands.

(Andrea, December 2000)

Elevators

I like to ride up and down on elevators.
I like to ride them because sometimes
They have two sides and sometimes they have glass.
When I ride in the elevators it makes me feel like
I'm being pulled up into the air.
Sometimes when I'm riding down in an elevator,
It makes me feel like I'm being pulled down.
My favorite elevator has two sides and overlapping doors.
It makes a sound that goes 'Bong, Bong'.
People can ride up and down on elevators and feel OK.

(Derek, January 2000)

Figure 10.2 is a picture taken at a photography exhibit and poetry reading reception. These receptions provide an opportunity for the teens to display their works, socialize with their families and friends, and attain a sense of accomplishment. The consistent format across the different modules (gather information, work on a specific project, showcase at an exhibit/reception) is an important feature incorporating elements of structure (e.g. routines and schedules).

Figure 10.2 Teen Group members at poetry reading and reception

Parent, family, and community involvement

As previously mentioned, the outcome of many of our long-term projects has been to present what we have done in a format that can be enjoyed by family and friends and can involve members of the community (e.g. music or church groups). For example, a pizza party was held in appreciation of a project completed by a local Eagle Scouts troop. Our teens and the Scouts met, dined together, and played some games. Figure 10.3 shows them seated together for a game of hangman.

Conclusion

In this chapter, we reviewed the role of social groups in the TEACCH program, focusing on the Chapel Hill TEACCH Center Teen Group. The longevity of the group, the loyalty of the families, group members, and staff, and the large number of teens served over the years are evidence of the importance of the program in the lives of our clients. Many continue on with the TEACCH adult groups, making a smooth transition. In combination with the essential services provided by public education, the group helps its members achieve successes in social behavior. In conclusion, we offer some

Figure 10.3 Teen Group party with Eagle Scouts with Scout leader in background

guidelines for professionals, parents or others interested in running this type of program.

1. Be flexible.

2. Do reconnaissance work to prepare for the activity or event. Consider noise levels, crowds, waiting; can community setting accommodate groups, are there group rates, how much additional support staff will you need? Assess the need for segmenting or sequencing the activity; is it open-ended and does it need visual cues regarding what to do, how much, when finished and what comes next? How long will this activity take?

3. Try new things in addition to the old favorites; do not be afraid to attempt something that seems out of your comfort range.

4. Remember to look through the lens of autism to see what structure or strategies need to be applied to make the experience successful and fun for all.

5. Do things that you would enjoy or are interested in, so that getting together with the group is something you genuinely want to do.

6. Communicate with parents and teachers about their ideas and suggestions for the group.

7. Do not forget to ask the members what they would like to do, within reason. We have had some suggestions that sounded like fun to one person, but were not of interest to other group members (e.g. visiting favorite bus stops).

APPENDIX 10.1

Sample Group Schedule

Teen Group meeting (date)
Activity: Games and refreshments

Schedule

1. *Introductions and update:* visual cues are posted on flip chart, but sometimes are written on the schedule itself for some individuals (see examples below).

2. *Get into game groups:* depending on the size of the group, there can be several small groups of three or four teens or the larger group can be split into groups of five or six teens.

3. *Select a game:* a choice of perhaps four games are presented, including board games or activities like charades or hangman. Members vote to select games that all enjoy. New games are introduced in smaller groups and then later added to the large group selection.

4. *Play game:* games are modified and visual instructions and demonstrations are provided as needed. Activities are adapted to the variable skill levels of the group members so that the activity remains motivating and stimulating for all.

5. *Refreshments* (e.g. ice cream sodas or sundaes): staff may provide the ingredients needed and the visual support required for preparation, but the goal is for members to be as independent as possible for set-up and clean up. Also included in this time period is joke telling, or members select conversation topics.

6. *Wrap-up and goodbyes:* sometimes this includes parting comments or what each person liked best about the activities, reporting to the group what game their subgroup played, and checking the calendar to see what the next event will be.

APPENDIX 10.2

Scavenger Hunt in the Herb Garden

- Elect a recorder for the group or complete the scavenger hunt sheet in pairs.
- Answer the following 'hunt' questions. Have fun!

1. This herb makes a lovely tea that can help you sleep; unscramble the word and you'll have the answer!

    H L M O I C A E M

2. We've heard that 'time is golden'. Find a 'thyme' that can be described by another precious metal.

3. Complete the sentence with the name of this soft, furry plant. 'Mother sheep's baa baa baa is music to baby _____.'

4. Money does not grow on trees, but find the salad vegetable that dangles from a tree in the garden!

5. The name of this herb will answer the riddle: a body of water where no lies are spoken.

6. You don't have a watch; find something in the garden that can help you tell time.

7. How many different sculptures of animals can you find in the garden?

8. Complete the sentence with the name of this herb: 'If time flies when you are having fun, if you're bored, it's _____ _____.'

9. The name of this plant suggests it is the fastest plant in the garden.

10. Which two plant names suggest opposite movements?

11. What eight-legged creature spun a gate in the garden?

12. What name of a season would describe the blue dog sculpture in the herb garden?

13. Fill in the name of this herb to finish the sentence: 'We follow Eastern Standard Time, sheep follow _____ _____.'

14. The name of this herb will complete the compliment that Lord Byron gave to wife Mary: 'Your cheeks are the color of a red _____ _____.'

References

Baron-Cohen, S. and Swettenham, J. (1997) 'Theory of mind: its relationship to executive function and central coherence.' In D.J. Cohen and F.R. Volkmar (eds) *Handbook of Autism and Pervasive Developmental Disorders*, 2nd edn. New York: Wiley.

Bettelheim, B. (1967) *The Empty Fortress: Infantile Autism and the Birth of the Self.* New York: Free Press.

Howlin, P. and Yates, P. (1999) 'The potential effectiveness of social skills groups for adults with autism.' *Autism 3*, 299–307.

Koegel, R.L. and Frea, W.D. (1993) 'Treatment of social behavior in autism through the modification of pivotal social skills.' *Journal of Applied Behavioral Analysis 26*, 369–377.

Krantz, P. and McClannahan, L.E. (1993) 'Teaching children with autism to initiate to peers: effects of script fading procedure.' *Journal of Applied Behavioral Analysis 26*, 121–132.

Marcus, L.M., Schopler, E. and Lord, C. (2000) 'TEACCH services for preschool children.' In J.S. Handleman and S.L. Harris (eds) *Preschool Education Programs for Children with Autism*, 2nd edn. Austin, TX: PRO-ED.

Mesibov, G.B. (1984) 'Social skills training with verbal autistic adolescents and adults: a program model.' *Journal of Autism and Developmental Disorders 14*, 395–404.

Mesibov, G.B. (1990) 'Normalization and its relevance today.' *Journal of Autism and Developmental Disorders 20*, 379–390.

Ozonoff, S. and Miller, J.N. (1995) 'Teaching theory of mind: a new approach to social skills training for individuals with autism.' *Journal of Autism and Developmental Disorders 25*, 415–433.

Schopler, E. (1997) 'Implementation of TEACCH philosophy.' In D.J. Cohen and F.R. Volkmar (eds) *Handbook of Autism and Pervasive Developmental Disorders*, 2nd edn. New York: Wiley.

Schopler, E., Mesibov, G.B. and Hearsey, K. (1995) 'Structured teaching in the TEACCH system.' In E. Schopler and G.B. Mesibov (eds) *Learning and Cognition in Autism*. New York: Plenum.

Schopler, E., Reichler, R.J., Bashford, A., Lansing, M. and Marcus, L.M. (1990) *Individualized Assessment and Treatment for Autistic and Developmentally Disabled Children: Volume I – Psychoeducational Profile Revised (PEP-R)*. Austin, TX: PRO-ED.

Stainback, S. and Stainback, W. (1992) 'Schools as inclusive communities.' In S. Stainback and W. Stainback (eds) *Controversial Issues Facing Special Education*. Boston, MA: Allyn and Bacon.

Stone, W.L. (1997) 'Autism in infancy and early childhood.' In D.J. Cohen and F.R. Volkmar (eds) *Handbook of Autism and Pervasive Developmental Disorders*, 2nd edn. New York: Wiley.

Williams, T.I. (1989) 'A social skills group for autistic children.' *Journal of Autism and Developmental Disorders 19*, 143–156.

Wing, L. and Gould, J. (1979) 'Severe impairments of social interaction and associated abnormalities.' *Journal of Autism and Developmental Disorders 9*, 11–29.

Wooten, M. and Mesibov, G.B. (1986) 'Social skills training for elementary autistic children with normal peers.' In E. Schopler and G.B. Mesibov (eds) *Social Behavior in Autism*. New York: Plenum.

CHAPTER 11

What Families Wish Service Providers Knew

April Block and Rev. Jo Clare Hartsig

> *...professionals, people who are paid to have something to do with the decision-making process for children with autism, but do not personally have a child with autism...range from those who functionally support us in thoughtful ways to those who are just in the way.* (Lehman 2001, p.6)

While professional service providers may have wonderful information, strategies, and techniques for working with children who have autism, there is also great wisdom in listening to the families of these children – who are most experienced in knowing what has worked with their child, and are the most invested in helping their child. However, in their sometimes desperate efforts to find answers, families of children with autism are known to go to extreme lengths to do what they believe will help their child. Some families have even moved across the United States for promised cures (*Macon Telegraph* August 10 1997, p.8B), or at least to another city with more promising services. Families who have young children with autism can present unique challenges to professional practitioners who are committed to providing the most helpful and appropriate kinds of supports.

The organization of this chapter follows the chronological path that families experience (family life stages) when they have a child with autism and provides suggestions for professionals to best assist families through these stages. The intent of this chapter is to offer some perspectives from the real experts who will have the most profound impact on the life of persons with autism – their families.

Just as an autism diagnosis is a 'spectrum' disorder (which refers to the multiple causes of autism and its many different manifestations), a parent, sibling, or other family member may react to the diagnosis with a full spectrum of emotions and coping strategies. Starting at the time of initial diagnosis, the child with autism and his or her family will probably interact with dozens of professionals (e.g. physicians, psychologists, speech and occupational therapists, teachers, paraprofessionals, special education administrators, insurance bureaucrats, recreation therapists and coaches, legislators, family service coordinators, nutritionists, law enforcement personnel, social workers, and any number of alternative medicine practitioners). There are variations in the levels of support needed by families as they journey on the spectrum. The points of diagnosis, school transitions, puberty, job training and placement, post-high school education, and choosing residential options are times that are usually more intense and times when families rely more on outside support. The longer that parents and family members are involved in this process, the more thorough their knowledge and expertise become. The kind of support families need from professionals by the time their child has grown to be an adult changes remarkably from the beginning of the spectrum journey. At the young adult stage, families usually have become the experts in autism, and the role of professionals may be to provide information on appropriate community options. So we begin the journey with the first step – diagnosis.

Diagnosis

The following is an example of one parent's experience during the diagnostic process.

> 'What exactly are your hopes and goals for your son?' The local 'autism expert' asked me this question after playing with my 3-year-old for about ten minutes. The past month had been a whirlwind of fighting with our insurance company, getting a very blunt diagnosis of 'autism spectrum disorder', and scrambling to figure out how to find and pay for early intervention services. Had my hopes and dreams taken any of *this* into account? I thought about many different answers and then said, with utterly sincere conviction, 'Well, when he is 17, I want him to take his SATs [Scholastic Achievement Tests] with all his classmates and then, when he is 18, I want him to enroll at Princeton.' Another day I might have answered, 'It would be great if we could figure out a way to stop him from wandering at night.' (J.C. Hartsig, personal communication, May 2001)

Autism usually becomes apparent during the first three years of a child's life. Often, an unremarkable birth and delightfully typical early months are suddenly interrupted by odd habits, a loss of language, withdrawal, and spectacular mood meltdowns (see Chapter 1 for further diagnostic information). First-time parents are especially vulnerable to being late in realizing that their child's perceived 'uniqueness' is really a cause for seeking out developmental screening. When the need for a diagnostic referral comes to a professional's attention, the scenario emerges for the professional to begin supporting parents through what is predictably a life-changing experience for them.

Specific suggestions for professionals who refer a child for diagnosis or are part of the actual diagnostic process

UNDERSTAND THE FAMILY'S INITIAL EXPERIENCES

Every parent can recall precisely the moment when his or her child was given an autism diagnosis. Because that experience is so vivid, service providers should ask about that moment. Ask as well what led the family to seek an evaluation, how a particular provider was chosen for diagnosis, when it occurred to the family that their child was not typical, and what was helpful or not helpful about the process or the actions of individuals involved. These kinds of questions can provide some good clues about how to work with a particular family.

PICK YOUR MOMENT

Conversations are often much easier without a toddler present to distract the parent or demolish the office. Providing separate space and staff to entertain youngsters (including siblings) while the parents talk over the results of an evaluation can be enormously helpful to the parents' ability to listen. Whenever possible, have a face-to-face feedback session and do not hide behind charts and notes. If the parents' language is not your own, engage a translator.

BE VISUAL

Handing parents a basic autism symptom checklist to review helps them participate in the diagnostic process. This may motivate parents to take an active role in seeking a more thorough evaluation.

GIVE THE FAMILY A SHORT LIST OR PACKET OF RESOURCES

Make sure your information is current and accurate. One family described their interaction with a pediatric psychologist who told them their child had autism while leafing through the yellow pages to see about resources. Families deserve and need better. Appendix 11.1 contains an example of what a good resource list might include.

In addition to the information on the resource form, consider providing also a brochure (or even a packet) from a local chapter of the Autism Society of America (ASA). The ASA website, www.autism-society.org, is also a good source for materials. The local ASA chapter can provide practitioners with the names and phone numbers of other parents with children who have autism, preferably families who have recently gone through the process of accessing resources. Provide parents with a list of the closest place for a thorough pediatric diagnosis or for a second opinion and the name and telephone number of a professional to contact. Because intake contact for services is usually the next step after initial diagnosis, supply the name and number of the relevant early childhood services agencies mandated by law to provide support to families of children with disabilities. These agencies are usually affiliated with school districts (in the United States, ask for Child Find services), health departments, county government, or umbrella agencies like Easter Seals.

DO FOLLOW-UP

A phone call to check with the family after the diagnosis is made in order to help the family begin to negotiate 'the system' will help them feel a little less lost. Busy professionals or those who do not feel skilled in doing this should find someone who will do it, and do it well.

AVOID GUESSING AT THE FUTURE, EVEN THOUGH PARENTS WILL WANT DEFINITE ANSWERS

Parents may want to know about younger siblings. They may also want to know about their child 20 years from now. Professionals should answer the questions they can. While being encouraging, professionals should try to focus on the current situation. All toddlers are moving targets on any developmental scale, so it is risky to predict future outcomes. Stephen Shore (2001), in his book *Beyond the Wall: Personal Experiences with Autism and Asperger Syndrome*, places himself in the autism spectrum, using a chart to illustrate where he began at age 3 and where he sees himself 35 years later. It is best practice not to predict the future of the child, neither dooming the child's future nor giving parents false expectations.

SUPPORT PARENTS' NEED TO EXPRESS THEIR CONCERNS ABOUT SIGNIFICANT
BEHAVIORS, WITHOUT NECESSARILY RELATING THE BEHAVIORS TO THE CHILD'S
AUTISM

We have seen how some children's very real symptoms of pain (e.g. hearing problems, gut or ear infections with consequent screaming, or screaming for unknown reasons) have been dismissed, attributed only to their autism. Then, several years after the initial diagnosis, when another significant cause is discovered for earlier behaviors, parents may be furious at professionals and themselves for ignoring the child's only means of communication.

APPROACH EACH FAMILY AS UNIQUE, WITHOUT PRECONCEIVED IDEAS OF HOW
THE FAMILY MIGHT BE EXPECTED TO FEEL OR ACT DURING THIS INITIAL
DIAGNOSIS PERIOD

Gilkerson and Stott (2000) observed that in the recent past, society's attitudes toward persons with disabilities have been predominately negative. Therefore, a disability may be characterized as a hopeless tragedy to the family. The process of individualizing treatment for each family calls for a re-examination of our expectations of family reactions along with the actual reactions unique to each family. Two common assumptions that may bear re-evaluating relate to 'grief cycles' of families and the stress that families must be under with the autism diagnosis.

Since the late 1960s, some professional literature has compared possible parental emotional responses, upon diagnosis of their child's disability, to stages of dealing with the death of loved ones (Kubler-Ross 1969; Moses 1983; Olshansky 1962). The same literature set forth theories that those parental reactions were part of a 'grief cycle', described as fairly predictable, sequential responses occurring in stages which include shock, denial, anger, depression, and guilt, culminating in acceptance. However, as Turnbull and Turnbull (2001) point out, proponents of those theories have based those beliefs largely on clinical case studies from the 1960s and 1970s, which focused on grief stages experienced primarily by mothers. In practice, the 'grief cycle' concept may be too simplistic and stereotypical for understanding *every* family with a child who has a disability. At the same time, it is also important to recognize the potential for emotional, physical, financial or marital hardships that might be experienced by parents of a child with autism. Many parents have claimed to experience and re-experience shock, denial, pain, and sadness. As one father said, 'It hurts, and it comes in waves' (Gilkerson and Stott 2000, p.457).

Another common belief that may need to be re-examined, in terms of how service delivery occurs, is that each family is under tremendous stress. A body of literature about stress in the family (Hodapp, Dykens and Masino 1997; Koegel *et al.* 1992; Randall and Parker 1999; Sanders and Morgan 1997) as well as anecdotal observations by families support the belief that families of children with autism have unique stresses and experiences. An initial professional response might be to implement programs to reduce stress for the family, but well-meaning efforts are not necessarily effective. Zaldo (1996) conducted research designed to decrease stress, and focused on three sources presumed to reduce stress for parents of a child with autism: factual information about autism, knowledge about stress and stress management, and social support and advocacy skills. Parents who received these stress-relief interventions had a slight, but not statistically significant, increase in factual information about autism, but no reduction in overall stress was reported. One mother frankly observed that money on programs could be more effectively funneled directly to families, who would probably do a pretty good job in using it to reduce their day-to-day stresses.

Turnbull and Turnbull (1996) observed that too often it is assumed that children without disabilities are easy to raise whereas children with disabilities inevitably are a burden, biasing research on children and families toward stress. However, families of children with disabilities often affirm that, even with the difficulties of parenting their child, the child is a source of great joy, love, blessing, satisfaction, learning life lessons, and of becoming better people through increasing patience and understanding the dignity of all individuals (Turnbull *et al.* 1986). Professionals need to try for balance and perspective, acknowledging the reality of conditions that occur when a child in the family has autism, simultaneously making allowance for full development (and unique responses) of the family and individuals within the family (Zola 1993).

HELP FAMILIES SORT THROUGH THE TREATMENT MAZE

Parents particularly need to be encouraged and empowered during this critical initial diagnosis and informational period. The child's family is the child's best, and sometimes only, advocate for life. To become informed advocates, most parents begin intense information-gathering efforts at this stage. Contradictory, competing, and controversial information and approaches may inundate and overwhelm parents, leaving them feeling undermined and powerless. Parents must somehow negotiate through the maze of information. One parent described their family's trek:

I have found the task of trying to understand…autism to be rather like going into an uncut forest; there is no clear path, just lots of 'big trees' of information. You are not exactly sure where and when you will come out, or in what condition. When I first started [to gather information] I was so overwhelmed by the vast amount of information that I nearly quit. (Frazier 2001, p.10)

Professionals can assist families at these information-overload periods by being empathic and providing a perspective on available information.

Further suggestions for professionals

In order to help families sort through the myriad of information on autism, the following are suggestions for professionals adapted from Nickel (1996).

1. Be as knowledgeable as possible about standard and non-standard approaches. Invest a few hours surfing the websites related to autism. Keep updated and aware of treatment trends, existing and emerging research, and new resources that might not be seen in any professional journal, as this may be the same information families have access to. Many families have created their own websites, which are fascinating sources of perspective. (See also suggested websites in Appendix 11.2.)

2. Ensure that families have at least awareness of available standard services.

3. Provide frank and tactful sharing of your concerns about treatments, and label your concerns as individual biases.

4. Readily refer families to other professionals as needed.

5. Discuss the 'red flags' of promises of 'cures' or 'one treatment fits all' without undermining the family's hopeful optimism and willingness to try a treatment that *might* help their child.

6. Explain the potential problem of placebo effects, and why controlled research trials are important.

7. Discuss non-traditional and controversial treatments as part of any planning and whenever asked. Be sure that openness to discussion is not taken as endorsement. Frici-Patti (1994) suggests that an open discussion of controversial therapies should lead to re-examination of what is meant by success or failure in treatment. One parent said

that what works wonders for one individual may have absolutely no effect on another, defining successful treatment as what improved the quality of the child's or family's life, even if that was in small but significant ways (Frazier 2001). The fact is, the parent is the ultimate advocate for the child and has the ultimate responsibility for weighing of treatments and decision-making.

Basics about childhood disability legislation

After the initial diagnosis, parents usually begin to become familiar with legislation that will affect services the child will receive from the time of diagnosis through his or her school years. It is essential for professionals to be aware of relevant legislation and how that legislation is applied in their area. In the United States, a body of disabilities- and prevention-related early intervention Federal legislation exists, primarily embodied in the Individuals with Disabilities Education Act (IDEA). (See www.wrightslaw.com for relevant legislation outside the United States.)

The 1997 amendments of the IDEA, Part C provisions, apply to children from birth to 3 years old. Under Part C, an infant or toddler is first identified when the child's condition meets the state's definition of a disability. Often a pediatrician makes the initial diagnosis, but to enter the services under Part C, the child must have a free, multidisciplinary evaluation, followed by the development of an individualized family service plan (IFSP), which can include a variety of services.

Family experiences under Part C provisions are widely varied. In some states families are satisfied with services received under Part C, while families in other states experience great discouragement when they find that their state is one that is very delayed in establishing structures and systems for delivery of the services. For instance, because Part C has limited funding, implementing an IFSP becomes cost prohibitive for many families. Currently, applied behavioral analysis (ABA) type home programs can cost a family the equivalent of another mortgage payment.

Service delivery provisions under Part C variously support or not current family preferences for treatment of their child with autism. For instance, there is a requirement for services to be delivered in 'natural environments', defined as everyday settings where the child's peers are typically engaged, with interventions to be based in the child and family's everyday routines. Families sometimes find that the inclusion- and routines-based emphasis in Part C, runs counter to some autism treatment programs that require many hours a week of one-on-one training.

Part B (for children age 3 through school age) of IDEA is implemented in the United States primarily through the public school systems. Part B emphasizes inclusion of children with disabilities within the same settings as children their own age who do not have disabilities, and regardless of disability a 'free and appropriate public education' (FAPE) as determined through development and implementation of an individualized education plan (IEP).

The rights of children with disabilities under Part B are law. Parents and many professionals, however, are painfully aware that the law is universally under-funded in the United States. Variations from school district to school district are huge. For example, a child may qualify in one state for two half-days of preschool in an inclusive setting with occupational therapy and speech therapy offered within that context. When the family moves to another state, the child may be eligible to receive in-home ABA for some 40 hours a week, occupational therapy and speech therapy, and even some respite funding for the parents. It is not surprising to learn that families relocate to get better, or at least more, services for their children.

School years (age 3 to age 18)

Preschool years

For most parents, age 3 may be the first time their child becomes involved in formal activities outside their own home. For families who have a typically developing preschooler, it can be a traumatic time. Families who have a child with autism not only face separation issues from their vulnerable child, but also enter the world of special education provisions.

The following is a list of suggestions for professionals to consider when assisting families in negotiating through the preschool years.

BECOME AWARE OF THE IEP PROCESS

The family's first experience with the IEP process and document is probably when their child turns 3 years old and enters formal services. The IEP will become the most important document connecting the family, the child, and the school. Professionals can be more helpful to families if they become familiar with the IEP process. To make the IEP process go more smoothly, we suggest that the professional obtain some of the excellent available publications, access helpful websites with suggestions for creating good IEPs (e.g. www.wrightslaw.com), and find out from special education school district personnel what family advocacy groups specialize in assisting families through the IEP process. It is important to remember that the child's needs may not be met by what is offered within the school district's programs. The law provides that the district must finance sending the child to another program that will meet his or her needs even if the program is in another school district. This is usually a point of great discussion, if not dissension. Families, and professionals who support them, must remember to pick their battles. A 'due process' hearing costs a lot of time and money.

ASSIST PARENTS IN SORTING THROUGH THEIR PRESCHOOL PROGRAM OPTIONS

Since the 1970s, most intervention programs have included parents as co-therapists, as parents are considered essential in any intervention program with their children (Dawson and Osterling 1997). There are many possible preschool programs, with very different philosophical backgrounds and approaches. It may be helpful to encourage families to visit several programs to compare resources available to their child.

WHENEVER POSSIBLE, HELP THE FAMILY OBTAIN A COMPUTER WITH INTERNET ACCESS

If there are family support funds, encourage the family to buy a personal computer. After the diagnosis, it is always hard for families to spend money on what may be termed 'non-essentials'. Every expense translates into therapies or interventions that the money could buy. A family might weigh the purchase of a new computer against weekly occupational therapy sessions in the summertime. These are hard choices. However, the benefits of a computer in the home can be immense to families, a few of which are listed below.

1. Not only are there some great computer programs designed for teaching children on the autism spectrum, but also people with autism often develop a proficiency working on computers. (See Appendix 11.2 for website list.) Going to the library or a classroom to use a computer sounds realistic, but given the hectic schedules of many families, it makes sense to have a computer to access at home.

2. It can be used as a primary connection to family support organizations, a critical source for emotional support. Although family support groups often have face-to-face meetings, email has replaced many support groups since harried parents can attend

online, and not just when they can get a babysitter. The internet also makes families more global: they can get immediate information about what other parents are experiencing with different programs.

3.   Chat rooms can offer some support, but can also be very time-consuming. List serves or various subscription services can provide other connections with others affected by autism. Families need to remember that not all sites give reliable information. Anyone can set up a website and link it to autism resources.

SUPPORT THE FAMILY IN THEIR ATTEMPTS TO NORMALIZE THEIR DAY-TO-DAY LIFE

For example, one family shared how they 'normalized' their child's bedroom, while still addressing concerns about their son's banging his head and wandering at night instead of sleeping. These parents upholstered around the walls, using large sheets of 2-inch soft polyfoam, covering the foam in a soothing but juvenile pattern. Mattresses put on the floor minimized fall injuries and were beds for mother and father taking turns monitoring his night wandering. The bedroom looks appropriate for any young child.

HELP FAMILIES RECOGNIZE AND SUPPORT THEIR CHILD'S STRENGTHS

Too much therapy-driven focus can diminish the potential enjoyment of what strengths any child has naturally. Children with autism are, first, children, each with their own gifts, and each can benefit from doing many of the typical things other children do. Parents enjoy opportunities to see their children involved in typical child activities, and experience natural parental pride in their child and their own abilities to parent well.

Painting case example: Eli

One mother encouraged her child with autism, Eli, to paint, as Eli seemed to enjoy this activity. Interestingly, this child's painting demonstrates a developmental progression in his motor skills that has been encouraging to this parent. For instance, when Eli was a preschooler, he had difficulty crossing midline, and his paintings reflected a right-sided dominance (see Figure 11.1).

Figure 11.1 Eli's early painting

Through the years, he received tremendous amounts of intervention for fine and gross motor skills and also vision therapy. As his physical skills improved, his ability to use the whole canvas also increased, as shown in Figure 11.2, which Eli painted at age 9.

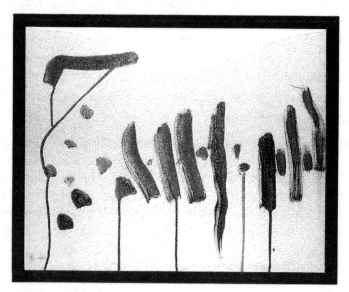

Figure 11.2 Eli's later painting

Eli's art not only provided a positive creative outlet, but also brought him recognition from others. His mother characterizes his style as that of a minimalist; it is modern art – which makes one think of something or feel something. His parents, friends, teachers, therapists, and neighbors all feel emotion and communication from him through his paintings. (B. Lehman, personal communication, May 2001)

BECOME ENGAGED PERSONALLY IN SOME REAL-LIFE SENSITIVITY TRAINING

One therapist said to a parent of a preschool child with autism, 'I think it's a parenting problem.' To which the parent replied, 'I have a great idea. I've arranged to bring my child to your home for a week. I'll come back, I promise. Then we can judge you and see how you've done with him.' The therapist declined. Developing an understanding empathy does not translate to sympathy. Family members' daily lives might be difficult, but they do not want sympathy. Instead, as one parent expressed (B. Lehman, personal communication, May 2001), they want *respect* for what they experience, what they know from experiences, what they know about their child at each stage, for the uniqueness of their family, what they feel, what they need or are concerned about, and who they are becoming through this experience.

Elementary years

The transition from preschool programs to regular elementary school programs is frequently difficult for parents. Personnel in preschool programs often come from a different educational culture than personnel who serve in early grades. Families sometimes observe that services shift from being family-friendly and family-centered to being school-centered. In public schools, the classes are likely to be large and the teachers are busy. Sometimes public school personnel express resentment that government and administrative funding does not follow the child who needs special supports in the classroom. A child who needs extra attention may be seen as decreasing the teacher's ability to educate the rest of the children. Special needs legislation remains an underfunded mandate. Parents may experience IEP meetings as unfriendly and feel reduced to going to IEP meetings to beg for services that do not exist or that the school district insists are unaffordable. Parents may relate too well to the dialogue in Figure 11.3.

Figure 11.3 School stage parent cartoon   *Nathan Koch 2001*

The following is a list of suggestions for professionals to consider when assisting families in negotiating through the elementary school years.

BE AWARE OF THE POTENTIAL STRESS ON FAMILIES AND CHILDREN CAUSED BY MOVING FROM A KNOWN PRESCHOOL SYSTEM OF SERVICES TO A NEW ELEMENTARY SCHOOL SYSTEM

Give parents names to contact of other parents who have a child with autism in the same school district who can give them the 'real story' about how that school system works.

SUPPORT FAMILIES IN BECOMING ACTIVE IN THE CHILD'S SCHOOL, BEYOND THE IEP

Some possibilities include:

1. Support parents' involvement on school district committees. They have a unique perspective to contribute. Usually the school district has a special education committee or committees specific to elementary, middle, and high school, where parents can meet allies and get to know some of the people who will be making decisions about their child.

2. Suggest that parents inquire about 'bully-proofing' programs for the school. Children with exceptional needs can become victims of bullying behavior. Parents can provide materials for the child's classroom to help the other children better understand some of the child's behaviors and need for extra support.

CONTINUE TO ADVOCATE FOR RESPITE SERVICES TO FAMILIES

Sometimes different agencies can help with the cost, but parents are also concerned about finding an appropriate person to provide care for their child. As their child grows, demands for the 24-hour, 7 days a week attention needed during preschool years probably will not diminish. To adjust to the extreme demands of their preschooler, family members may have had less time and energy for their own individual growth (e.g. marital relationship, other children, personal time, and friends). For a school-age child with autism, there may be no relief from attention needed, and the time to develop other important relationships within the family might not come without targeted support. For the sake of the health of the family unit, respite may be needed now as much as before.

Adolescence and transition to adulthood

Besides having teenage-typical concerns about hormones and physical changes, parents may at this time become increasingly aware of more long-term implications of their child's disability, including long-time dependence on them. Adolescence is a critical time for parents to prepare for another major transition – 'emancipation'. Because some states do not put adult services into the entitlement category with adequate funding, parents may be shocked that there may be long waiting lists for services when their child reaches the age of majority. Professionals may want to remind them as early as when the child is 12 years old to inquire into adult services available in their state, and find out when to sign up their child for supports needed at the end of high school.

All parental rights under special education law end when the child reaches the age of majority (usually between ages 18 and 21) or earlier if the child is emancipated. Parents are propelled out of a public school system and into an adult services system. Familiar parental rights under IDEA – consent for evaluation, decisions about services and placement, and due process – will no longer be applicable to parents, unless they have earlier pursued guardianship of their child. School systems are required to notify parents of this transfer of rights from the parent to the child a year (minimally – usually done at 16 years old) before the child reaches the age of majority, and the IEP must include a transition plan for the transfer of services and rights. It is not unusual, however, that the school system and the adult services system do not plan together for the transition.

Suggestions for professionals

The following is a list of suggestions for professionals to consider when assisting families in negotiating through the transition from adolescence to adulthood.

BE AWARE OF HOW DIFFICULT THIS PERIOD IS FOR PARENTS

Parents who have a child with autism are being asked to give over the care of their child from a familiar IDEA-influenced public school system to another unknown system for emancipated adults, but now without parental control or even input. Emancipation may be as hard, or even harder than other challenges the parents have faced.

BECOME KNOWLEDGEABLE ABOUT ANTICIPATED CHANGES IN THE NEW SYSTEM AND SHARE THE INFORMATION WITH PARENTS WHEN APPROPRIATE

The following lists some changes that can be disconcerting for families.

1. Young adults will have an individual plan (IP: different states use different plan terms) instead of an IEP. The emancipated child will have due process rights but his or her parents will not.

2. Placements may be made without the luxury of matching the needs of the young adult with the placement. A young adult might need a quiet and orderly living place with no more than two other people, or a low-key working environment, with concrete tasks and minimal distractions. However, with the lack of suitable residences for persons receiving adult services, finding any availability may be the final determinant, even if that is an incompatible placement.

3. Parents can expect to be left 'out of the loop'. Parents will not have the right to be told everything about their child's life. In fact, some young adults at 21 years old may tell their service coordinator not to tell their parents about something, and the service coordinator is bound by privacy laws not to divulge the information.

4. Medicaid coverage changes. Services that may have been covered for an under-aged child may not be covered in a residential program or host home.

5. Whereas previous IEP designations may have required using a certain communication system, in adult services, staff may not have adequate exposure to certain technology or interventions.

6. The behavioral learning model sometimes changes significantly from the school system to the adult services system. While consequating for inappropriate behaviors is more commonly used in public schools, a model of positive behavioral support tends to be preferred in adult services. For young adults, that means exposure to major rules changes about their behavior, and they must learn new, or relearn old, behavior patterns, a distinct difficulty for many persons with autism.

Conclusion

This chapter focused on the individualized nature of family reactions, preferences, and needs, as they create family lives together with a child with autism. As family issues, needs, and emphases change with child maturation, the best role for professionals will also change. Treatment options and programs change throughout the life of the child, with new approaches or scientific discoveries modifying known treatments or programs. However, the overarching professional principle relevant to all family life stages is to tailor supports respectfully, based on the family and child's uniqueness.

APPENDIX 11.1

Autism Resource List

Current as of_____

Received from: Name_____ Phone #_____

1. Support/resource group contacts

    Local ARC (Association of Retarded Citizens) –Advocacy group:

    Name_____ Phone # _____

    Local Chapter of Autism Society of America (ASA):

    Name_____ Phone # _____

2. Public school resources

    Birth–3 years old Developmental Screening Unit (Part C of IDEA):

    Name_____ Phone # _____

    3–5 years old Developmental Screening Unit (Part B of IDEA – may be same as above):

    Name_____ Phone # _____

    Director of Special Education (family's local school district):

    Name_____ Phone # _____

3. Medical professionals (as needed)

    Pediatrician:
    Name_____ Phone # _____

    Psychologist:
    Name_____ Phone # _____

    Dentist:
    Name_____ Phone # _____

    Dietician/nutritionist:
    Name_____ Phone # _____

4. Other medical resources

Your medical insurance company:

Name_____ Phone # _____

Medicaid contact:
Name_____ Phone # _____

Medicaid waivers contact:
Name_____ Phone # _____

5. Treatment/educational supports (as needed)

Psychologist:
Name_____ Phone # _____

Social worker:
Name_____ Phone # _____

Other mental health professional:
Name_____ Phone # _____

Occupational therapist with sensory integration background:
Name_____ Phone # _____

Speech/language therapist:
Name_____ Phone # _____

6. Other parents who have a child with autism

Parent of preschooler:
Name_____ Phone # _____

Parent of elementary/middle school child with autism:
Name_____ Phone # _____

Parent of teenager/young adult with autism:
Name_____ Phone # _____

7. Websites for more treatment information and treatment tools

_____

_____

_____

8   Other
Name_____ Phone # _____

APPENDIX 11.2

Recommended Websites

The following are some good basic entry sites for learning more about local, national, and global autism resources. All the various therapies also have sites and can be found by links or by searches under specific topics.

1. **www.asp.org/advocacy/releases/mayautism.htm**
   This site contains the policy statement by the American Academy of Pediatrics on the early diagnosis of autism.

2. **www.autism-society.org**
   Autism Society of America, Bethesda, MD. This is a multidimensional site with some good definitions for the uninitiated. Also an excellent map feature helps locate autism services in a particular state. Links are provided to all local ASA society chapters.

3. **www.autism.com/ari/**
   Autism Research Institute (ARI), San Diego, CA. This site offers information about biological issues and corrective therapies (diets, vitamins, secretin etc.). ARI has led the discussion in North America regarding the safety of vaccines, particularly about MMR immunizations. Good resource list and more links.

4. **www.devdelay.org**
   Developmental Delay Resources, Bethesda, MD. Publishes a directory of parents and professionals with specific expertise and experience listed by state, and an excellent newsletter *New Developments*.

5. **www.do2learn.com**
   An NIH grant-funded site for child education of autism and learning disabilities. Has free pictures for visual communication strategies to download.

6. **www.edmark.com**
   preK–12 Educational software on range of subjects, including children with disabilities. Also has accessibility software and hardware.

7. **www.infantswim.com**
    Site for infant swimming research, focusing on survival swimming skills. Found helpful for children fascinated by water, but lacking safety skills.

8. **www.familyvillage.wisc.edu/edu/lib_autism**
    Autism link in this website. Good lists and other links.

9. **www.FEAT@feat.org**
    Families for Early Autism Treatment, Sacramento, CA. Offers a free, daily newsletter that covers a wide range of topics including legislative updates, new scientific studies, autism in the media, and new directions in intervention.

10. **www.kinderstart.com**
    Large search engine for information about parenting, child development, health, education, learning activities, etc. pertaining to children under the age of 7. Good links to broad range of topics.

11. **www.laureatelearning.com**
    Reading comprehension programs for children, particularly for children with disabilities.

12. **www.medigenesis.com**
    A large database that can be utilized by patients with chronic conditions. By accessing data from others with similar symptoms, treatment plans can be specifically targeted. The database has symptom, treatment, and outcome data from thousands of people with autism. This can be a very helpful resource for spectrum disorders as treatment/intervention results can be compared with patients in a similar place on the spectrum. A reasonable subscription fee is necessary to access this confidential database.

13. **www.pacer.org**
    The Pacer Center, Minneapolis, MN. A good site for tips on helping a family negotiate early intervention, school, and transition to the community issues. Also good site for creating handouts for teachers and other professionals and for links.

14. **www.peakparent.org**
    PEAK, Colorado Springs, CO. Another advocacy site designed to empower families. Good tips for all 'ages and stages'.

15. **www.solvingthepuzzle.com**

    Site for regional autism group that has permission to host a segment created by Nickelodeon cable channel. The five-minute news story on autism is kid-friendly, a good resource for school-age peers of a child with autism.

16. **www.taaliance.org**

    Parent organization for training and advocacy groups throughout the United States. Good site for locating resources close to home.

17. **www.wrightslaw.com**

    The Special Ed Advocate site provides good special education information for understanding IDEA legislation, the IEP process, and legal rights for families and students with disabilities. Online library for case law and newsletters. Subscription to Special Ed Advocate newsletter available online. More links and lists of resources. Mailing address: The Special Education Advocate, PO Box 1008, Deltaville, VA 23043, USA, (804) 257 0857.

APPENDIX 11.3

Recommended Books Professionals
Should Have on the Shelf

'Tried and true' recommendations by parents

Attwood, T. (1998) *Asperger's Syndrome: A Guide for Parents and Professionals.* London: Jessica Kingsley. Comprehensive treatment of a specific part of the autism spectrum. Excellent resource to explain or introduce a fairly new diagnosis.

Gill, B. (1997) *Changed by a Child: Companion Notes for Parents of a Child with a Disability.* New York: Doubleday. Similar in style to a daily meditation book, perfect for the busy and stressed. Delivers a wonderful overview of how families struggle with and celebrate their differences. Great resource to use in a parent group.

Grandin, T. (1996) *Thinking in Pictures.* New York: Random House. Insight into the realm of 'visual thinking' written by a world-renowned speaker, writer, advocate for people with autism and authority on the design and implementation of products used in the livestock industry. This author also has a diagnosis of autism.

Greenspan, S. and Wieder, S. (1998) *The Child with Special Needs.* Reading, MA: Perseus. A great 'how-to' book with concrete suggestions for maximizing impact of daily activities on enhancing child's development.

Kranowitz, C.S. (1998) *The Out of Sync Child.* New York: Skylight Press. Thorough, understandable explanations of sensory integration dysfunction. Pointers for recognizing and addressing sensory problems, one of the baffling aspects of some forms of autism.

Other suggested reading

American Academy of Pediatrics (Committee on Children with Disabilities) (2001) 'Technical report: the pediatrician's role in the diagnosis and management of autistic spectrum disorder in children.' *Pediatrics 107*, 5, May 2001, p. e85.

Middence, K. and O'Neill, M. (1999) 'The experience of parents in the diagnosis of autism: a pilot study.' *Autism 3*, 3, 273–285.

References

Dawson, G. and Osterling, J. (1997) 'Early intervention in autism: effectiveness and common elements of current approaches.' In M.J. Guralnick (ed) *The Effectiveness of Early Intervention: Second Generation Research.* Baltimore, MD: Paul H. Brookes.

Frazier, J. (2001) 'My experience with "alternative" treatments for autism.' *Quarterly, Autism Society of America, Colorado Chapter 7*, 2, 10.

Frici-Patti, S. (1994) 'Commitment to theory.' *American Journal of Speech and Language Pathology* *3*, 2, 30–34.

Gilkerson, L. and Stott, F. (2000) 'Parent–child relationships in early intervention with infants and toddlers with disabilities and their families.' In C. Zeanah (ed) *Handbook of Infant Mental Health*. New York: Guilford.

Hodapp, R., Dykens, E. and Masino. L (1997) 'Families of children with Prader-Willi Syndrome: stress support and relations to child characteristics.' *Journal of Autism and Developmental Disorders 27, 1, 11*–24.

Individuals with Disabilities Education Act (IDEA), United States Public Law 105–17, 20 usc 1400 *et seq*. Full text available at www.ideapractices.org

Koegel, R., Schreibman, L., Loos, L., Dirlich-Welhelm, H., Dunlap, G., Robbins, F. and Plienis, A. (1992) 'Consistent stress profiles in mothers of children with autism.' *Journal of Autism and Developmental Disorders 22*, 20, 201–216.

Kubler-Ross, E. (1969) *On Death and Dying*. New York: Macmillan.

Lehman, B. (2001) 'Word to the wise.' *Quarterly, Autism Society of America, Colorado Chapter 7*, 2, 6–7.

Macon Telegraph (1997) 'Make believe world helps autistic boy come alive.' *Macon Telegraph* August 10, 8B.

Moses, K.I. (1983) 'The impact of initial diagnosis: mobilizing family resources.' In J.A. Mulick and S.M. Pueschel (eds) *Parent–Professional Partnerships in Developmental Disability Services*. Cambridge, MA: Ware.

Nickel, R. (1996) 'Controversial therapies for young children with developmental disabilities.' *Infants and Young Children 8*, 4, 29–40.

Olshansky, S. (1962) 'Chronic sorrow: a response to having a mentally defective child.' *Social Casework 43*, 190–193.

Randall, P and Parker, J. (1999) *Supporting the Families of Children with Autism*. Chichester, England: John Wiley.

Sanders, J. and Morgan, S. (1997) 'Family stress and adjustment as perceived by parents of children with autism or Down syndrome: implications for intervention.' *Child and Family Behavior Therapy 19*, 4, 15–32.

Shore, S. (2001) *Beyond the Wall: Personal Experiences with Autism and Asperger Syndrome*. Shawnee Mission, KS: Autism Asperger Publishing.

Turnbull, A.P., Blue-Banning, M., Behr, S. and Kerns, G. (1986) 'Family research and intervention: a value and ethical examination.' In P.R. Dokecki and R.M. Zaner (eds) *Ethics of Dealing with Persons with Severe Handicaps: Toward a Research Agenda*. Baltimore, MD: Paul H. Brookes.

Turnbull, A.P. and Turnbull, H.R. (1996) *Families, Professionals, and Exceptionality: A Special Partnership*, 3rd edn. Upper Saddle River, NJ: Merrill Prentice Hall.

Turnbull, A.P. and Turnbull III, H.R. (2001) *Families, Professionals, and Exceptionality: Collaborating for Empowerment*, 4th edn. Upper Saddle River, NJ: Merrill Prentice Hall.

Zaldo, C. (1996) 'A family systems model of service delivery for parents of children with autism: promoting adaptation to family stress.' Unpublished dissertation, Rutgers, State University of New Jersey.

Zola, I.K. (1993) 'Self, identity, and the naming question: reflections on the language of disability.' *Social Science and Medicine 36*, 2, 167–173.

The Contributors

Barbara Bianco, B.S., Ed., is a Psychoeducational Therapist at the Chapel Hill TEACCH Center and has been involved in the assessment and teaching of children, adolescents and adults with autism for twenty years. She has provided consultation and training in autism for parents and professionals in the United States, Ireland, and Israel. She has developed and directed social groups for teenagers with autism at the Timothy School and Chapel Hill TEACCH Center.

April W. Block, Ph.D., is Early Childhood Special Education Program Coordinator on faculty at the University of Northern Colorado. Her Ph.D. is in Early Childhood Special Education. She has over 30 years of early childhood/early childhood special education professional experience at community, state, and federal project levels. Her experience includes providing direct services in early intervention, coordinating infant/toddler services at the state level, and managing nation-wide Head Start consulting projects.

Teresa D. Bunsen, Ph.D., is an Associate Professor at the University of Alaska in special education. Dr. Bunsen is also an international autism consultant and has published numerous articles and given presentations in the field of autism. Dr. Bunsen conducts research in the areas of children/youth with autism, focusing on family, friendship and classroom support networks. She is currently examining intervention methods in the United States and Russia.

E. Cheryl Fletcher, MA, CCC, is a licensed speech pathologist in private practice in Camarillo, California, who has presented at local and national meetings on autism spectrum disorders. She has an extensive private practice focusing on assessing and treating young children with autism spectrum disorders. Ms. Fletcher creates and supervises in-home programs utilizing an eclectic approach with an emphasis on a social communication approach.

Robin Gabriels, Psy.D., is a licensed clinical psychologist and affiliate faculty at the University of Colorado Health Sciences Center, Department of Pediatrics, with over 18 years of experience assessing and treating a variety of child, adolescent, and adult populations. Dr Gabriels has published articles and book chapters in the fields of autism, asthma and art therapy and has lectured and conducted workshops on autism both nationally and internanionally. Dr Gabriels divides her time between an autism-specialty private practice and conducting autism research.

Edward Goldson, M.D., pediatrician at The Children's Hospital in Denver, Colorado, since 1976, works with a variety of children with developmental difficulties, chronic illnesses, and special needs. Dr. Goldson is also a Professor of Pediatrics at the University of Colorado Health Sciences Center. He has published articles and book chapters in the field of developmental pediatrics, provided pediatric consultation for several developmental evaluation programs sponsored by the Colorado Department of Health, and served for six years on the Governor's Interagency Coordinating Council for the implementation of the Individuals with Disabilities Act (IDEA).

Rev.Jo Clare Hartsig is a parent-advocate for families affected by disabilities. She has served over 15 years in community-based ministries with poor and marginalized people. She is a columnist for Fellowship magazine and has been published as a regular feature in the Denver Post and in several essay collections. Jo Clare lives in Minnetonka, Minnesota with her husband and two sons, one of which is diagnosed with Asperger syndrome.

Dina E. Hill, Ph.D., is a licensed clinical psychologist and Assistant Professor at the Center for Neuropsychological Services, University of New Mexico. She completed a research post-doctoral fellowship at the University of Utah's Center for Advanced Medical Technology where she was involved in a neuroimaging study of children with autism. The focus of her research has been on the cognitive and neuro-anatomical correlates of neurodevelopmental disorders, including ADHD and autism.

Lauren H. Kerstein, LCSW, is a licensed clinical social worker in private practice specializing in working with children, adolescents, and adults with autism spectrum disorders and their families. She is also an Early Childhood Education consultant with the Colorado Agency for Jewish Education and consults in two preschools. Ms. Kerstein completed a post-masters fellowship at the University of Colorado Health Sciences Center, JFK Partners, with children, adolescents, adults with autism spectrum disorders and their families.

Piyadasa Kodituwakku, Ph.D., is a clinical neuropsychologist at the Center on Alcoholism, Substance Abuse, and Addictions (CASAA), University of New Mexico. The focus of his research has been on executive control functioning in children with neurodevelopmental disorders, specifically with autism and fetal alcohol syndrome. He is currently involved in a number of national and international research projects on fetal alcohol syndrome funded by the National Institute of Health.

Jill Laschober, MS, OTR, has been an occupational therapist with the Cherry Creek School District in Colorado for over 11 years. She currently works as a member of the district's Autism Team providing consultation and training to colleagues throughout the district. Ms. Laschober is certified to administer the Sensory Integration and Praxis Test and has experience evaluating and treating children with sensory integration concerns. She also has had extensive training and experience in implementing TEACCH-based interventions with children with autism in the public school system.

Lee Marcus, Ph.D., is the Clinical Director of the Chapel Hill TEACCH Center, and Professor in the Department of Psychiatry, University of North Carolina School of Medicine. Dr. Marcus has been involved in the diagnosis, assessment, and treatment of individuals with autism, parent counseling, and training of professionals. He has written on a wide range of topics in autism, has conducted workshops and training in North Carolina, and other states and countries.

Tracy Murnan Stackhouse, OTR, is currently the Head of Occupational Therapy and Research Associate at the M.I.N.D. Institute at the University of California, Davis Medical Center, and completing her Ph.D. in Developmental Psychology/Developmental Cognitive Neuroscience at the University of Denver. She has worked in pediatric occupational therapy for over 15 years as a Sensory Integration Clinical Specialist as well as conducting fragile X treatment and research at The Children's Hospital in Denver, Colorado. Her research interests include the role of praxis and sensory-motor processes in the developmental difference found in autism, fragile X syndrome and related neurodevelopmental disabilities.

Adriana Schuler, Ph.D., is a professor of Special Education at San Francisco State University and has written extensively on the speech, language, and communication features associated with autism spectrum disorders. She has also researched the underlying differences in learning and thinking as well as the impact of peer-supported play. Recently, she served as the guest editor of a special issue of the International Autism Journal examining the efficacy of early intervention. Currently, she is investigating the school experiences of adults with Asperger Syndrome as they relate to their perceived quality of life.

Nancy Seccombe Graham, OTR, is an occupational therapist with over 22 years of experience in pediatrics. She currently works with the Cherry Creek School District in Colorado as a member of the district's Autism Team providing consultation and training to colleagues throughout the district. She completed a 12-month residency in Advanced Leadership in Occupational Therapy with the autism clinic at JFK Partners, University of Colorado Health Sciences Center, and participated in the development of the Transdisciplinary Play Based Assessment when she was an adjunct faculty member at the University of Denver.

Cory Shulman, Ph.D., is a lecturer at the Hebrew University in Jerusalem in the Schools of Education and Social Work. Her clinical work in the field of autism for the past 25 years has included diagnosing young children in the Child and Family Developmental Clinics located throughout Israel, and establishing educational and service programs for individuals with autism and their families. Dr Shulman has published articles and book chapters, and edited books in the field of autism. Her research and intervention interests include involving families in communication and social skill development of individuals with autism.

Subject Index

academic achievement 47, 51
  strengths and weaknesses in autism 48, 49
  tests of 49
active gaze 133, 134, 138–141
adaptive functioning 48, 54
  strengths and weaknesses in autism 50
Ad Hoc Task Force on Definition of the Medical Home 83
adulthood 75, 181, 269, 270
adult services 16, 19, 269
adolescents 16, 19, 269
  teen groups 231–54
advocate 262, 269, 276
aggression 28, 113, 130, 139, 140, 163, 211
American Academy of Pediatrics 69, 74, 83, 84, 274
American Occupational Therapy Association (AOTA) 155, 175
American Psychiatric Association (APA) 16, 19, 20, 26, 31, 34, 42, 64, 69, 72, 84, 106, 107, 108, 110, 111, 121, 180, 201
American Psychological Association (APA) 111
amygdala 61, 62
Applied Behavioral Analysis (ABA) 96, 180, 181, 262, 263
  see also behavioral intervention strategies
art therapy 116
arithmetic 49, 51
assessment
  autism specific screening 28
  autism specific diagnostic tools 29–32
  testing considerations 32–4, 47, 49, 50
  see also neuropsychological assessment
attention 48, 49, 52, 57, 61, 95, 98, 105, 120
  attending 99, 100, 101, 106

joint 58, 102, 103
  strengths and weaknesses in autism 49
  tests of 49
Attention Deficit/Hyperactivity Disorder (ADHD) 57, 80, 162
Auditory Brainstem Response (ABR) examination 79 *see also* hearing
auditory defensiveness 161
  processing 142, 143
Autism Behavior Checklist (ABC) 30
Autism Diagnostic Interview-Revised (ADI-R) 31
Autism Diagnostic Observation Schedule-Generic (ADOS-G) 31
Autism Screening Questionnaire (ASQ) 28
Autism Society 35, 258, 272, 274
Autism Spectrum Disorders (ASD) 19, 180
autobiographical memory 53
autopsy 59–61, 63

behaviors, autism diagnostic impairments
  repetitive behaviors and restricted interests 16, 26–8, 56, 59, 69, 103, 105, 165, 180
behavior intervention 37
  data collection 186, 190
  early intervention 92, 93, 114, 181, 258
  strategies
    backward chaining 95, 117
    Discrete-Trial-Teaching (DTT) 96, 149, 220, 223
    errorless learning 117, 118, 220, 223
    functional analysis 113, 115, 118
    generalization 105, 116, 118, 143, 193–5, 199, 214, 221, 233, 241
    modeling 48, 97, 104, 108, 110, 119, 180, 190, 211, 220, 223

operant teaching techniques *see* behavior learning theory
  prompting 101, 106–10, 119, 180, 181, 211, 212, 220, 223
  reinforcement, positive 34, 48, 96, 104, 106–09, 117–19, 180, 181, 185, 199, 211, 212, 220, 223
  shaping 107–10, 119, 212, 220
behavior learning theory 16, 92, 95
  classical conditioning 95
  operant conditioning 17, 50, 95, 96, 100, 103,104, 106–10
behaviorism 95, 96, 223
Boardmaker© 182
brain
  behavior 47, 59, 158
  development 69
  functions 18, 47, 70
  impairments, autism specific 59–63 74, 94
  neuroimaging 47, 59, 63
  regions 59–63, 77

central coherence 55,57,59
cerebellum 59
  histological findings 61
  MRI findings 60, 61, 70
  cognitive correlates 61
Checklist for Autism in Toddlers (CHAT) 28, 29
Child Find 258
Childhood Autism Rating Scale (CARS) 31
child-centered programming 181, 191
cognition 76, 167
  deficits *see* brain impairments, autism specific
  development 104
  intervention 96, 98, 103–05, 221
cognitive social learning theory 96
Committee on Children with Disabilities 82, 83, 84, 277
communication 102, 103, 127–53
  expressive language 32, 162, 188, 222
  function 141
  gestures 53, 58, 77, 102, 103, 107, 129–34,

139–43, 146, 147, 223
impairments, autism specific 16, 26–8, 55, 69, 70, 73, 180
  interview 138–40
  intervention 64, 93, 96, 98, 102, 107, 112, 116, 141–52, 182, 221, 234, 242
  language 129
  non-verbal 27, 53
  partners 131, 150
  receptive language 32, 104, 162
  social 149
  speech language pathologists 137
  supports 33, 48, 187, 188, 271, 274 *see also* picture exchange communication system; TEACCH
  vocalizations 53, 103, 108, 120, 132–4, 168
  see also echolalia
  comprehension 50, 133, 141–4, 149, 151, 152
  impairments, autism specific 27, 51
  reading 49, 136, 188, 275
Computerized Axial Tomography (CAT/CT Scans) 74
controversial treatments
  secretin 78, 79, 82, 274
  vitamins 274
  see also diet
congenital rubella 17, 79
coordinator
  service 270
  treatment 40, 111–15
core characteristics of autism
  social impairment 55–9, 233
  communication impairment 16, 26–8, 55, 69, 70, 73, 180
  repetitive behaviors and restricted interests 16, 26–8, 56,59, 103, 105, 165,180
cued recall 53

decoding skills 51, 136
delayed echolalia *see* echolalia
Denver model 99
depression 113, 209, 259
development 26, 29, 31, 36–9, 160, 165, 166
  adaptive 158
  cognitive 16, 97, 104, 109
  language 16, 102, 103, 116, 130, 131, 141, 147, 161, 163
  motor 103, 116, 156, 167

Author Index

285